DESIGNING
Interactive
Documents

with Adobe™ Acrobat™ Pro

John Deep
Peter Holfelder

John Wiley & Sons, Inc.

New York • Chichester • Brisbane • Toronto • Singapore

Copyright ©1996 John Wiley & Sons, Inc.
Published by John Wiley & Sons, Inc.

Portions reprinted with permission of Adobe™ Systems Inc.

ISBN 0471-12789-2

Printed in the United States of America
10 9 8 7 6 5 4 3 2 1

ABOUT THE

Authors

John Deep is President of *ReadMe.com*, an interactive media firm specializing in electronic publishing and document management.

He has developed several multimedia titles for national distribution, including *The GeekSpeak Top 10*, and over the last three years has developed and produced more than 20 print/electronic titles for several major publishers. He is a graduate of Harvard University.

Peter Holfelder, a principal in *ReadMe.com*, is a writer, software developer, and Internet consultant. At *ReadMe.com* he develops Acrobat applications for a variety of clients, including commercial publishers, health-care providers and professional societies. He is a graduate of Rensselaer Polytechnic Institute.

Other ReadMe.com books published by *John Wiley & Sons* include *Developing Interactive Web Applications with Perl*. Visit *ReadMe.com*'s web-site at: http://www.readme.com; or send e-mail to: acrobat@readme.com.

CONTENTS

Overview

▌ BROWSING Interactive Documents

The Free Acrobat Reader 2.1

▌▌ CREATING Interactive Documents

Creating PDF with PDFWriter

III ENHANCING Interactive Documents

Enhancing PDF with Acrobat Exchange

IV PUBLISHING Interactive Documents

The Easiest Way To Publish On The World-Wide Web

V ADVANCED Interactive Documents

Advanced Topics in Acrobat

TABLE OF

Contents

Introduction xxvii

I

BROWSING Interactive Documents
The Free Acrobat Reader 2.1

CHAPTER
1

Interface 3
Becoming Familiar with Acrobat

CASE STUDY   *Developing Floor Plans and Seating Maps*
for Adobe Facilities   34

CHAPTER
4
Features 35
Thumbnails, Links, Bookmarks, Notes, Articles

CASE STUDY   *On-line Instructions for
Adobe's Demo Room   48*

CHAPTER
5
Printing 49
Creating and Customizing Printed Output

CASE STUDY   *Acrobat Keeps the Field Sales Offices Connected
and Up-to-Date   57*

CHAPTER
6
Clipboard 59
Sharing Information Between Applications

CREATING Interactive Documents
Creating PDF with PDFWriter

▌▌▌

ENHANCING Interactive Documents
Enhancing PDF with Acrobat Exchange

CASE STUDY   *Saving Money Managers*
                 Time and Money   125

CHAPTER
11

Thumbnails 129
Using Small-scale Document Views

CASE STUDY   *Improving Customer Relationships by Making*
                 Clients an Integral Part of the Creative Process   137

CASE STUDY   *Easy Access to a World of Information*   193

IV

PUBLISHING Interactive Documents

The Easiest Way To Publish On The World-Wide Web

CHAPTER
16
The Web 199

An Introduction to the World Wide Web

CONTENTS

CHAPTER

20

The Publisher

Serving PDF Documents on the Web

CHAPTER

21

Cool Sites

Web Sites With Cool PDF

V

ADVANCED Interactive Documents
Advanced Topics in Acrobat

CHAPTER

23

Catalog 303

Creating Indexes with Adobe Catalog

CHAPTER

24

Distiller 341
Converting PostScript to PDF

Introduction

The interactive document—what is it? Trying to answer that question in this book, titled *Designing Interactive Documents*, presents a certain challenge, since the interactive document is not part of ordinary experience. Unlike a pair of pants, a table and chair, or a breadbox, there is no visual image that springs to mind, no familiar example of an interactive document that can be pointed to.

There are, however, many ordinary things we call documents: books, newspapers, memoranda, and many more. And certainly, we interact with all of these—when we browse through a library or a filing catalog where the documents are stored, pick up a particular document and open it, and then begin to turn its pages.

Indeed, the interactive document can also be described through these familiar activities. It can be created, stored, browsed, opened, read or searched—just as an ordinary document can.

The difference is this: the interactive document is defined by our interaction with it. Stored electronically and having no physical existence beyond the magnetic alignment of particles, the interactive document is what we make of it.

Each time we open the interactive document, rendering it on the screen, there is a sense in which *we make it*. The paths that we take through it, the pages we turn to, define the interactive document for only that moment. For the interactive document, as for a work of art, each experience of it is unique.

Finally, there is a sense in which the interactive document must exist, because it is necessary. In the evolution of information we have reached the point at which our very accomplishments—the sheer amounts of information that we create, which burgeon exponentially—would surely bury us, under slowly advancing glaciers made of paper. The interactive document offers a ready solution for storing, retrieving, and coping with the staggering volumes of our Information Age.

Interactive CD-ROM. *Designing Interactive Documents: with Adobe Acrobat Pro* attempts to be what it describes. Following its own directions, the book uses the many features of Adobe Acrobat—including movie-links, Web-links, and full-text search—to make itself into an interactive document. This document is included on the enclosed CD-ROM and is also maintained at readme.com at: http://www.readme.com/acrobat.

Organization. *Designing Interactive Documents: with Adobe Acrobat Pro* is organized into five parts. The first four parts each describe a familiar way of interacting with documents—browsing, creating, enhancing, and publishing. The fifth part covers advanced topics in Adobe Acrobat. Each part also introduces a different product in the Adobe Acrobat Pro Suite.

Activity	Acrobat product
Part 1—Browsing	Adobe Acrobat Reader 2.1
Part 2—Creating	Adobe Acrobat PDFWriter
Part 3—Enhancing	Adobe Acrobat Exchange
Part 4—Publishing	Adobe Acrobat Web-Link
Part 5—Advanced	Adobe Acrobat Search, Catalog, and Distiller

Case Studies. Many Case Studies are also presented. These show real-world examples of people interacting with Adobe Acrobat documents, both at work and at leisure. The Case Studies are taken from two sources:

1. An audit done by the accounting firm of KPMG analyzing the application of Acrobat within Adobe Systems.
2. Interviews conducted with people at other companies or institutions who are using Adobe Acrobat.

The Case Studies are listed in the following table.

Case Study	Source	Page
A Finger on the Company Pulse	KPMG—Executive Staff	13
On-line Access to Human Resources Documents and Forms	KPMG—Human Resources	26
Developing Floor Plans and Seating Maps for Adobe Facilities	KPMG—Finance	34
On-line Instructions for Adobe's Demo Room	KPMG—Customer Support	48
Acrobat Keeps the Field Sales Offices Connected and Up-to-Date	KPMG—Sales	57
Presentations Inside and Outside Adobe	KPMG—Marketing	69
Reduced Federal Express Shipments	KPMG—Finance	82
Adobe's Shrinking Copier and Paper Costs	KPMG—Finance	96
Distributing the Engineering Project Status Report	KPMG—Engineering	107
Saving Money Managers Time and Money	First Call Corporation, a Thomson Financial Services company	125
Improving Customer Relationships by Making Clients an Integral Part of the Creative Process	Buck & Pulleyn Advertising Agency	137
Intel Embraces More Cost-Effective, Efficient Electronic Communications	Intel	155
Reducing Higher Education Costs	Virginia Polytechnic Institute and State University (Virginia Tech)	167
Adding Functionality to Sales Information System and Reducing Product Development Time	The Siebel Sales Information System	183
Easy Access to a World of Information	The Wharton Information Network	193

BROWSING
Interactive
Documents

The Free Acrobat
Reader 2.1

1

Interface

Becoming Familiar with Acrobat

The interface of a program is the part of the program that you interact with. While programs typically do much of their work "behind the scenes," invisible to you, they must receive instructions from you to do their work, and they must display their results to you. This is the job of the interface.

The interfaces of Acrobat Reader and Exchange are designed to make viewing simple and intuitive, so you can quickly identify and use the important information in a document. The two programs share many interface elements, such as document windows, toolbars, status bars, and navigation tools; it is easy to learn one of the programs if you have experience using the other. The two programs also share menu commands; every command in the Reader menu is available in Exchange.

In this chapter, you will learn how to:

- Distinguish Application windows from Document windows

- Distinguish different parts of a window

- Open Document windows

- Manage windows

- Customize your display of windows

- Find Acrobat Help.

The Application Window

The application window is what you see when you start Reader or Exchange; it is often thought of as *the program*. The Acrobat Reader and Exchange application windows are made up of:

- The title bar, which contains the application name, Acrobat, and the standard platform-specific controls (in Windows, a control menu button, a minimize and maximize button)

- The menu bar, which contains pull-down menus

- The toolbar, which contains toolbar buttons

- The client area. Documents you open will be displayed in this area.

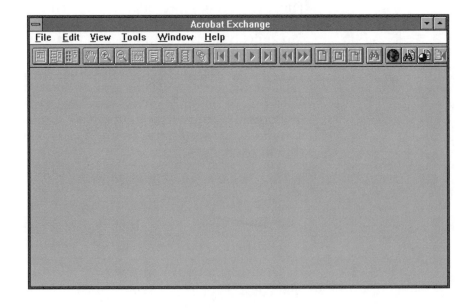

Document Windows

When you display a PDF document in Reader or Exchange, the document appears in a document window in the application window's client area. You can display up to ten documents at a time in separate document windows. You can move document windows around in the application window's client area, maximize them, so they take up the entire client area, or minimize them, so they appear at the bottom of the client area as an icon. Document windows are made up of:

- The title bar, which contains a Control menu button, a minimize button, and a maximize button

- The status bar, which contains a page button, a zoom button, and the size of the active page

- A horizontal scroll bar and a vertical scroll bar, for browsing through a document

- The overview area, where bookmarks and thumbnails are displayed. The overview area has its own vertical scroll bar.

Opening a Document Window

To open a Document window:

1. Select the **File | Open** command. The Open dialog box will appear.
2. Use the controls of the Open dialog box to select the file that you want to open.
3. Press the **OK** button. If you decide you do not want to open a file, press the **Cancel** button.

Or

- Select a file name from the list of recently viewed files that Acrobat keeps at the bottom of the File menu.

To select a different drive:

1. Click on the **Drives:** drop-down list box. A list of the available drives will appear.
2. Double click on the drive name. The dialog box will then display the directory tree of the new drive in the **Directories:** list box and a list of the files in the new default directory in the **Files:** list box.

To move up and down the directory tree:

- Double click on the directory names in the **Directories:** list box

To select a file:

- Double click on its name in the **Files:** list box

Or

- Click on its name and press the **OK** button

Or

- Enter the name of the file in the **File Name:** edit box and press **Enter**.

You can ask the dialog box to list files that have the .pdf extension only, or to list files with any extension. Acrobat Exchange displays files with the .pdf exten-

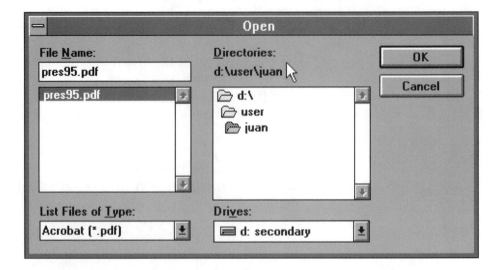

sion by default. To switch between displaying files with the .pdf extension and displaying all files:

1. Click on the **List Files of Type:** drop-down list box.
2. Double click on the file specification.

Acrobat will not allow you to open two copies of a PDF document. If you attempt to open a PDF file that is already open, Acrobat will make that document the current document.

When you have ten documents opened, Acrobat disables the **File | Open** command. If you attempt to open a file by another means, such as a link, a bookmark, or the Help menu, Acrobat will display an error message.

If the file you specify in the **Open** dialog box is password-protected, Acrobat will display the Password dialog box which prompts you to enter the password. To enter the password:

1. Type the password in the **Password:** edit box.
2. Press the **OK** button. If you decide you don't want to open the PDF document, press the **Cancel** button.

Minimizing Document Windows

To minimize a document window:

- Click on the document window's **Minimize** button

Or

1. Click on the document window's **Control menu** button. The Control menu will appear.
2. Select the **Minimize** command from the Control menu.

Maximizing Document Windows

To maximize a document window:

- Click on the document window's **Maximize** button

Or

1. Click on the document window's **Control menu** button. The Control menu will appear.
2. Select the **Maximize** command from the Control menu.

Or

- Double click on the document window's title bar.

When you maximize a document window, its title bar disappears, and the text in the title bar is added to the text in the application window's title bar.

Restoring the Document Window

When you restore a document window, you display the entire window, but the window does not fill the application window's client area. To restore a document window:

- Click on the document window's **Maximize** button

Or

1. Click on the document window's **Control menu** button. The Control menu will appear.
2. Select the **Restore** command from the Control menu.

Or

- Double click on the document window's title bar.

The Active Document Window

Only one document window is active at a time. The active window is the target of Reader and Exchange commands. For instance, if you select the **Zoom | Actual Size** command when several document windows are open, only the document in the active window will have its magnification changed. To make a document window the active window:

- Click anywhere on the window

Or

- Select the window from the list in the **Window** menu.

Managing Document Windows

When you open several document windows in Reader and Exchange, it can be difficult to find and display the one you want to see. Reader and Exchange can display the document windows in several different ways, making it easy to find and view the document that interests you.

Cascading Windows

Cascaded windows are displayed in a sort of "stack" so that no window is completely obscured and each window's title bar and buttons are visible.

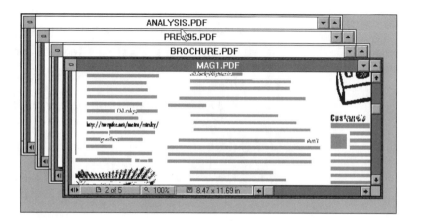

To cascade document windows:

- Select the **Window | Cascade** command.

Tiled Windows

Windows that are tiled are, as the name implies, placed in the client area as tiles are placed on a floor. Tiled windows do not overlap each other; each window is displayed in its own portion of the application window's client area. To tile windows:

- Select the **Tile Horizontally** or the **Tile Vertically** command from the Window menu.

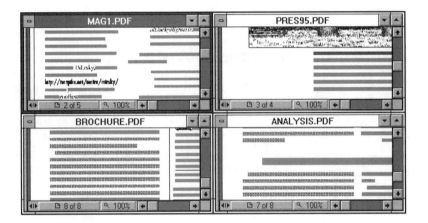

Closing a Window

To close a document, make the document you want to close the current document, then:

- Click on the **File | Close** command

Or

- Double click on the system menu of the document

Or

- Press the **<Alt >** *and* **<->** keys simultaneously, then the **<c>** key

Or

- Press the **<Ctrl >** and **<F4>** keys simultaneously.

To close a minimized file:

- Click on the file's icon, then select the **Close** command from the pop-up window that appears.

To close every open file:

- Select the **Window | Close All** command.

Closing All Windows

To close every document window:

- Select the **Window | Close All** command.

The Toolbar

The toolbar is a gray rectangle located directly below the menu bar. The toolbar contains buttons that allow you to execute the most common Reader and Exchange commands with one click.

To execute a command that is associated with a toolbar button, click on the button once.

Sometimes you may want to remove the toolbar from the application window, or hide it, to provide more room in the client area for you to display documents. To hide the toolbar, select the **Window | Hide** toolbar command. To display the toolbar again, select the **Window | Show** toolbar command. Reader and Exchange keeps track of whether the toolbar is hidden or visible when you close them. When you restart Reader and Exchange, they will restore the application window to the state it was in when you closed it; if the toolbar was hidden, it remains hidden, and if the toolbar was visible, it remains visible.

On-line Help

If you are not sure how to do something while using Reader or Exchange, you can display on-line help. To display on-line help:

- Select the **Help | Acrobat Reader Help** or the **Help | Acrobat Exchange Help** command

Or

- Press the **<F1>** key.

Acrobat's on-line help is (naturally) in PDF format; Reader and Exchange open their PDF help file when you select the appropriate **Help** menu command. Unfortunately, Acrobat's help is not context-sensitive. The help document is always opened to the first page, and you must move to the command you want using hyperlinks or a text find operation.

If you are using any plug-in modules with Reader or Exchange, PDF help files for the plug-in modules will be available from the Help menu also, provided they have been installed correctly.

Case Study

Adobe has a large number of internal documents in PDF format, which are available on their network. These documents, though they were created using many applications, can be browsed with one interface.

Results

From the KPMG Audit:

Chairman of the Board and Chief Executive Officer John Warnock was found to be an enthusiastic user of Acrobat products, both for his own activities and to better understand the workings of the Adobe organization.

Executive Staff

A Finger on the Company Pulse

A critical activity for senior management, especially those in general management positions, is to understand the various functional activities that are being performed throughout the organization. John Warnock browses the growing database of over 7,000 Portable Document Format documents on the Adobe companywide servers to better understand what is being done and how activities are progressing. Without Acrobat software, the only sources of information for senior executives are written reports, briefings and presentations that often give a condensed view of activities. Such presentations often don't give a feel for the breadth and variety of the successful activities within an organization.

The major benefit to senior management from Acrobat software is increased availability and visibility to current information on Adobe's activities. They see the same documents that functional managers are using to manage their activities. With Acrobat applications, there is also no need to know or care which platform or software was used to create the document. The annotation feature of Acrobat software can also be used to quickly review documents and immediately send them to the author. Bookmark and linking features in Acrobat applications also make it much easier to navigate a PDF document than a printed copy.

CHAPTER

2

Navigating

Learning How to Move Around a Document

PART 1

Browsing
  Interface
  Navigating
  Zoom
  Features
  Printing
  Clipboard
  Preferences
Creating
  PDFWriter
  PDF Files
Enhancing
  Pages
  Thumbnails
  Bookmarks
  Notes
  Links
  Articles
Web Publishing
  Introduction
  Getting On
  Reader
  Author
  Publisher
  Cool Sites
Advanced
  Search
  Catalog
  Distiller

To be effective, a document viewing program must do three things: display any part of the document on demand; allow you to search for words and phrases in the document text; and keep track of what parts of the document you have viewed in what is known as a *history list,* so you can return to them easily.

Acrobat meets these demands with a file format and navigation tools that are designed for efficient document viewing. The PDF format is "page based;" within a PDF file, each page of a document is stored separately. It's as if a PDF file had "page numbers" that allowed you to find a page directly, rather than counting pages until you found the right one. This allows Reader and Exchange to find and display a page quickly, no matter where it is located in a document.

Reader and Exchange feature a variety of navigation tools. Many of them are located on the toolbar, where they can be activated with a single mouse click. Both programs keep track of each document view they display, letting you move forward and backward through previous document views by clicking on toolbar buttons. They also allow you to search the document's text, with options for case-sensitive or whole-word searches to make searching more efficient.

In this chapter, you will learn how to use the navigation tools in order to:

- Move relative to the current page
- Move to specific pages in a document
- Browse through articles
- "Find" specific occurrences of text.

Moving Around the Current Page

If either the width or the height of the current page is greater than what is displayed in the document window, you can use the **Hand** tool or the document scroll bars to move around the current page.

To use the **Hand** tool to move around the current page:

1. Click on the toolbar's **Hand** tool button, or select the **Tools | Hand** command. The mouse cursor will turn into an open hand.

2. Click on the page. The mouse cursor will turn into a closed hand.
3. Drag the mouse in the direction you want to move the page. As you drag the mouse, the page view will change. If the document's thumbnails are visible, the page view box on the current page's thumbnail will move as you move the mouse.
4. Release the mouse button when you are satisfied with the page view.

To use the scroll bars to move around the current page:

- Click on the scroll bar button that points in the direction that you want the page to move

PART

Browsing
   Interface
   Navigating
   Zoom
   Features
   Printing
   Clipboard
   Preferences
Creating
   PDFWriter
   PDF Files
Enhancing
   Pages
   Thumbnails
   Bookmarks
   Notes
   Links
   Articles
Web Publishing
   Introduction
   Getting On
   Reader
   Author
   Publisher
   Cool Sites
Advanced
   Search
   Catalog
   Distiller

Or

- Click on the scroll bar, on the side of the scroll bar thumb to which you want the page to move

Or

- Drag the scroll bar thumb in the direction that you want the page to move. When you drag the vertical scroll bar's thumb, a box with the page number that corresponds to the scroll bar thumb's current position appears. If you want to remain on the current page, make sure that you do not move the vertical scroll bar so much that the page number changes.

If the height of the page is greater than what is displayed in the document window, you can use the **<Page Up>** and **<Page Down>** keys to move up and down within the page.

Moving to Specific Pages

Acrobat has controls and commands that allow you to move directly to the first page of a document, to the last page of a document, or to any page in the document.

Moving to the First Page

To move to the first page of a document:

- Click on the toolbar's **First Page** tool button

Or

- Select the **View | First Page** command

Or

- Press **<Ctrl> < Home>** simultaneously.

Moving to the Last Page

To move to the last page of a document:

- Click on the toolbar's **Last Page** button

Or

- Select the **View | Last Page** command

Or

- Press **<Ctrl> <End>** simultaneously.

Moving to Other Pages

To move to a specific page within a document:

- Select the **View | Go To Page** command. When you select this command, Acrobat displays the Go To Page dialog box. Enter the page number that you want to move to in the Page: edit box and press the **OK** button. If you decide you don't want to move to another page, press the **Cancel** button.

- Drag the vertical scroll bar's thumb. When you click on the thumb, a box with the current page number will appear next to the scroll bar. As you move the scroll bar's thumb, the page number will change to the page number that corresponds to the thumb's current position. When the page number of the page that you want to view is displayed in the box, release the mouse button; Acrobat will display the page.

- Click on the page's thumbnail.

Page Numbering

Acrobat gives a number to each physical page in a document, including tables of contents, indexes, cover sheets, or other pages that may not normally be numbered in a printed document. Acrobat does not have any knowledge of page numbers you may have placed in your document. If you have generated page numbers for your document, and there are pages within the document that are not numbered, the physical page numbers will be different than the page numbers that are printed in your document. If you are designing documents to be read with Acrobat, number each physical page of your document to make sure that the printed page numbers are the same as the physical page numbers.

Moving Relative to the Current Page

Moving to the Previous Page

To move to the previous page:

- Click on the toolbar's **Previous Page** tool button

Or

- Select the **View | Previous Page** command

Or

- Press the **<Left arrow>** key

Or

- Press the **<Up arrow>** key

Or

- Press the **<Shift>** and the **<Tab>** keys simultaneously

Or, when the page view is set to **Fit Page**,

- Press the **<Page Up>** key.

Moving to the Next Page

To move to the preceding page:

- Click on the toolbar's **Next Page** tool button

Or

- Select the **View | Next Page** command

Or

- Press the **<Right arrow>** key

Or

- Press the **<Down arrow>** key

Or

- Press the **<Tab>** key

Or, when the page view is set to **Fit Page**,

- Press the **<Page Down>** key.

Moving to Different Page Views:
Go Forward and Go Back

Acrobat keeps a running list of up to 64 of the page views you selected, and lets you move forward and backward to the different page views in the list. The list includes bookmarks and hyperlinks (within and across PDF documents), other navigation tools, magnification tools, files that are opened with file menu commands, and documents that are displayed with Window menu commands. If you move to a point in the list and then change the page view using another tool, the rest of the list is discarded and the new page view is added to the end.

To move forward in the page view list:

- Click on the toolbar's **Go Forward** button

Or

- Select the **View | Go Forward** command.

To move backward in the page view list:

- Click on the toolbar's **Go Back** button

Or

- Select the **View | Go Back** command.

Browsing Through Articles

When you pass the hand tool over a section of a document that is marked as an article, Acrobat draws a down arrow in the open hand mouse cursor. To browse through the article, click on it. Subsequent clicks of the mouse cursor move you to the next section of the article's text until you reach the end of the article.

When you reach the end of the article, Acrobat will beep to let you know it cannot scroll any further, and then return to the page view that was in effect before you started viewing the article.

Finding Text

Acrobat has the ability to perform full-text searches on any PDF document. To search the text in a PDF document for a phrase, word, or word fragment:

1. Select the **Tools | Find** command or press the **Find** toolbar button.

   Acrobat will display the Find dialog box.
2. Enter the text you want to search for in the **Find What** edit box.
3. Set the Find options.
4. Press the **Find** button. If you decide you do not want to search the text, press the **Cancel** button.

Acrobat will search through all of the text of the active document for the text you entered. As Acrobat searches, it displays the number of the page it is searching on the page button of the active document's document window.

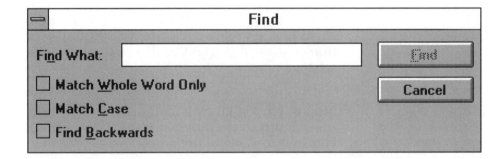

If Acrobat finds the text you specified in the document, it will display the page containing the text and highlight the text. If the text you specified is not found in the document, Acrobat will display a dialog box to tell you that it could not find the text, and return to the page that was active when you started the search.

If you start a search from the middle of a document (rather than from the first or last page), Acrobat will display a dialog box when it reaches the end of the document, asking you if you want to continue the search from the beginning of the document. If you do not want to continue the search, press the **No** button; if you want to search the remainder of the document, press the **Yes** button, and Acrobat will search from the beginning of the text to the point where you started the search. If you search backwards through a document, Acrobat will ask you if you want to continue the search when you reach the beginning (see the *Find options* subsection of this section for more information on search directions).

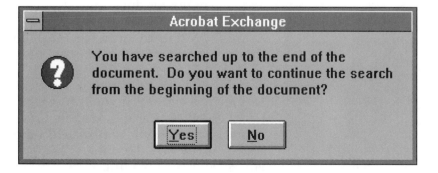

Find Options

Acrobat's Find feature has several options to make your searches more specific, and thus faster and easier. You can search for whole words only, make case-sensitive searches, and specify the search direction with these options.

Searching for Whole Words Only

Normally, Acrobat will report a match whenever it finds the text you were looking for, no matter if it's embedded. For instance, if you search for the word *cross*, Acrobat will report a match if it finds *cross*, but also if it finds *double-cross*, *cross-hatch*, *crossing*, or *across*. You can tell Acrobat that you want to search for whole words only by setting the **Match Whole Words Only** option. When you set this option, Acrobat will report a match only if the text you specify is surrounded by white space or punctuation. If you search for the word *cross* with the **Match Whole Words Only** option set, Acrobat will report a match if it finds *cross*, *double-cross*, or *cross-hatch*, but not if it finds *crossing* or *across*.

To search for whole words only:

• Click on the **Match Whole Words Only** check box.

When you set the **Match Whole Words Only** option, it remains set for subsequent searches, until you clear it by clicking on the **Match Whole Words Only** check box again.

Specifying Case-sensitive Searches

Normally, Acrobat searches are not case-sensitive; they will not take lowercase and uppercase into account. For instance, if you search for the word *next*, Acrobat will report a match if it finds *next*, *NEXT,* or *NeXT*. You can tell Acrobat to perform case-sensitive searches by setting the **Match Case** option. When you set this option, Acrobat will report a match only if text in the PDF document matches exactly the text you specified, including case. If you search for the word *next* with the **Match Case** option set, Acrobat

PART 1

Browsing
Interface
Navigating
Zoom
Features
Printing
Clipboard
Preferences
Creating
PDFWriter
PDF Files
Enhancing
Pages
Thumbnails
Bookmarks
Notes
Links
Articles
Web Publishing
Introduction
Getting On
Reader
Author
Publisher
Cool Sites
Advanced
Search
Catalog
Distiller

will report a match if it finds *next*, but not if it finds *NEXT* or *NeXT*.

To specify a case-sensitive search:

- Click on the **Match Case** check box.

When you set the **Match Case** option, it remains set for subsequent searches until you clear it by clicking on the **Match Case** check box again.

Specifying the Search Direction

Normally, Acrobat searches forward from the active page to the end of the document. If you think that the text you are searching for occurs before the active page, you can tell Acrobat to search backward to the beginning of the document by setting the **Find Backwards** option.

To search backwards:

- Click on the **Find Backwards** check box.

When you set the **Find Backwards** option, it remains set for subsequent searches until you clear it by clicking on the **Find Backwards** check box again.

Repeating a Search

Acrobat will stop searching for text as soon as it finds an occurrence of it in your document. If you want to search for another occurrence of the text, you can repeat the search from the point in the text where the first search left off. To repeat a search:

- Select the **Edit | Find Again** command.

Case Study

Adobe keeps employee forms and procedures on-line. Navigating through these documents and filling out forms is faster and easier using the navigation tools.

From the KPMG Audit:
Adobe Human Resources (HR) is a major creator and user of standard forms and reports. The individuals we interviewed, Marnie and Megan, are enthusiastic proponents of Acrobat software, although they confessed to initial fear and skepticism.

Human Resources

On-line Access to Human Resources Documents and Forms

A characteristic of any HR group is the creation and management of numerous forms and proce-dures. In the case of Adobe, the major HR docu-ments which are frequently updated are listed in the table below.

Document	Frequency	# Pages
Job posting	Weekly	20
Requisition/offers list	Weekly	5
Month-end report	Monthly	4
Headcount report	Monthly	4
Organization chart	Bi-monthly	32

All of these documents, along with other HR forms, the Adobe Employee Benefits Handbook, and other employee assistance documents, are now converted to PDF and placed on the Adobe server for employee use. Prior to Acrobat software, HR staff maintained an inventory of forms and reports and had to distribute them throughout Adobe. HR also developed a benefits open enroll-ment system which uses PDF documents to lead the employee through the benefit selection pro-cess interactively and collects each individual's benefits choices.

While there are cost benefits owing to Acrobat software from reduced printed paperwork in HR, the major benefit is that HR staff no longer has to respond to routine requests for forms and reports, allowing them to concentrate on more value-added activities. Adobe's open enrollment system allows benefit selections to be verified and cap-tured at the time they are selected, eliminating the effort and potential for errors when HR had to re-key benefit selections for nearly 1,000 employees. All of these Acrobat applications have improved internal customer satisfaction.

Customizing Your View of Acrobat

Because of the wide variety of video hardware and document types that exist, the ability to "zoom in" on a particular section of a document is important. Documents that are clear when displayed on one computer may be illegible on another, unless the viewing program has the flexiblity to vary the magnification. This is a central challenge for Acrobat since it is designed for viewing documents of any type on a wide variety of platforms.

Acrobat meets this challenge through a group of magnification (zoom) tools in Read and Exchange. Some of the zoom tools are based on preset zoom levels. They allow you to display the entire page, or certain parts of a page, with one command. For instance, the **Fit Width** tool automatically calculates the zoom percentage at which the page view takes up the entire width of the document window.

Other zoom tools display the document at preset magnification percentages that vary between 12.5% to 800% of actual size. Still other zoom tools allow you to enter the magnification percentage, rather than using a preset value. The zoom tools that are graphical in nature allow you to select the area of the page that will fill the document window. These customizing zoom tools allow you to select a magnification that suits your purpose.

The zoom tools are accessible through the toolbar, the **View** menu, and the zoom button on the document window's status bar.

In this chapter, you will learn how to:

- Enlarge or shrink views of the current document
- Change how the page appears in the document window.

The Zoom Tools

Acrobat has two zoom tools on its button bar, **Zoom In** and **Zoom Out**. The **Zoom In** tool can be used either to double the magnification or to magnify the page view by a custom amount. The **Zoom Out** tool can be used either to halve the magnification, or to reduce the page view by a custom amount. When you select these tools, the mouse cursor becomes the icon of the tool you selected.

To double the magnification with the **Zoom In** tool:

1. Click on the **Zoom In** tool in the button bar; the mouse cursor will turn into the **Zoom In** tool icon.

2. Click on the page.

Acrobat will double the magnification and redraw the page, centering the page view around the point where you clicked, if possible.

To adjust the page view to a custom zoom level with the **Zoom In** tool:

1. Click on the **Zoom In** tool in the button bar; the mouse cursor will turn into the **Zoom In** tool icon.
2. Click on one corner of the area that you want to magnify.
3. Drag the **Zoom In** tool to the opposite corner of the area that you want to magnify; Acrobat will display a rectangle as you drag.
4. Release the mouse button.

Acrobat will fill the page view with the contents of the rectangle you selected.

To halve the magnification with the **Zoom Out** tool:

1. Click on the **Zoom Out** tool in the button bar; the mouse cursor will turn into the **Zoom Out** tool icon.

2. Click on the page.

Acrobat will halve the magnification and redraw the page, centering the page view around the point where you clicked, if possible.

To adjust the page view to a custom zoom level with the **Zoom Out** tool:

1. Click on the **Zoom Out** tool in the button bar; the mouse cursor will turn into the **Zoom Out** tool icon.
2. Click on a point in the page.
3. Drag the **Zoom Out** tool to another point in the page; Acrobat will display a rectangle as you drag.
4. Release the mouse button.

Acrobat will reduce the page so that the previous page view fits in the rectangle you described.

The **Zoom In** and **Zoom Out** tools will remain active until you select another tool. If you want to switch temporarily from one of the tools to the other, click on the **<Ctrl>** key (Windows) or the **<Command>** key (Macintosh). The mouse cursor will switch to the other tool's icon. Once you click the mouse, you can release the key; the other tool will be active until you have changed the magnification.

The Magnification Box

The Magnification Box is found in the status bar, at the bottom of each document window. You can use the Magnification Box to set predefined zoom levels or to enter a custom zoom level.

When you click on the Magnification Box, a pop-up menu appears. The pop-up window contains three types of commands, separated by menu bars: **numerical zoom levels**, **view fitting zoom levels**, and the **Other...** command, which allows you to set a custom zoom level.

When you select the **numerical zoom level** command or the **view fitting zoom level** command from the pop-up menu, Acrobat will rescale the page view to the new zoom level.

When you select the **Other...** command, the **Zoom To** dialog box appears. To set a custom zoom level, enter the zoom level in the **Magnification**: edit box, then press the **Enter** button. If you decide to keep the present zoom level, press the **Cancel** button. If you decide to use a predefined numerical zoom level or a view fitting zoom level, click on the **Magnification**: drop-down list arrow, then select the zoom level you want from the list that appears.

Note: The **Zoom To** dialog box also appears when you select the **View | Zoom To...** command.

Actual Size

The **Actual Size** tool and the **View | Actual Size** command set the zoom level to 100%.

When the zoom level is set to 100%, the document is not really displayed at actual size, but at some reasonable approximation of it. For instance, when I measured the width of a 4" page viewed at actual size, it was 3" wide. The Actual Size zoom level remains at 100% as you scroll through pages of different sizes. Unlike the Fit Page, Fit Width, and Fit Visible zoom levels, the Actual Size zoom level is not a sticky option; Acrobat will maintain the zoom level at 100% as you navigate through the document, regardless of how well the page fits into the document window at that zoom level.

Fit Page

The **Fit Page** tool and the **View | Fit Page** command adjust the zoom level so that the entire page you are viewing fits in the document window.

The **Fit Page** zoom level is a sticky option; Acrobat will adjust the zoom level for each page you view so that the entire page fits in the document window. If you make a document window so small that Acrobat cannot fit the page in the window at a magnification of 12.5%, the page will be clipped at the edge of the document window.

Fit Width

The **Fit Width** tool and the **View | Fit Width** command adjust the zoom level so that the width of the page you are viewing fits in the document window.

The Fit Width zoom level is a sticky option; Acrobat will adjust the zoom level for each page you view so that the width of the page fits in the document window. If you make a document window so small that Acrobat cannot fit the width of the page in the window at a magnification of 12.5%, the page will be clipped at the edge of the document window.

Fit Visible

The **Fit Visible** tool and the **View | Fit Visible** command adjust the zoom level so that the text and graphics on the page you are viewing fit in the document window.

The Fit Visible zoom level is a sticky option; Acrobat will adjust the zoom level as you navigate through the document, so that the text and graphics fit in the document window. If you make a document window so small that Acrobat cannot fit the text and graphics on the page into the window at a magnification of 12.5%, the page will be clipped at the edge of the document window.

Full Screen

The **View | Full Screen** command enlarges the document window so that it fills the entire screen area. If you have bookmarks or thumbnails displayed when you select the **View | Full Screen** command, they will disappear, and they will not be redisplayed when you return to "document window mode."

In **Full Screen** mode, you can move forward page by page by pressing keys on the keyboard, or you can let Acrobat move to the next page after a certain period of time. This behavior is defined with the **Edit | Preferences | Full Screen** command. You can also click hyperlinks to navigate through the document. To leave **Full Screen** mode, press the **<Escape>** key.

Zoom To...

When you select the **View | Zoom To** command, the Zoom To dialog box appears. To set a custom zoom level, enter the zoom level in the **Magnification:** edit box, then press the **Enter** button. If you decide to keep the present zoom level, press the **Cancel** button. If you decide to use a predefined numerical zoom level or a view fitting zoom level, click on the **Magnification:** drop-down list arrow, then select the zoom level you want from the list that appears.

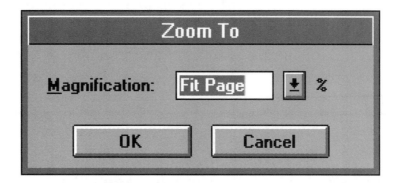

Note: The Zoom To dialog box also appears when you select the **View | Zoom To...** command.

Changing Magnification with Thumbnails

The thumbnail of the current page contains a page-view box that you can resize to change the magnification of the current page.

To change the page magnification with the page-view box:

1. Place the mouse cursor above the page-view box handle at the bottom-right corner of the box; the cursor will change from an arrow to a line with arrows at each end.
2. Resize the page-view box by dragging the handle to a new position.
3. Release the mouse button.

When you release the mouse button, Acrobat will adjust the zoom level to display the portion of the page contained in the box. When you change the magnification with thumbnails, the change is not sticky; Acrobat will maintain the new zoom level as you navigate through the document, regardless of how well the page fits into the document window at that zoom level.

Case Study

Adobe makes its floor plans available in PDF format so that all employees have immediate access to the latest version. Acrobat's zoom tools make it easy to view every detail of the plans, no matter what type of video hardware an employee uses.

From the KPMG Audit:

We spoke to Roxanne about her use of Acrobat products in the Facilities group. Her major Acrobat application is updating Adobe's floor plans and seating maps for the Bay Area facilities.

Finance

Developing Floor Plans and Seating Maps for Adobe Facilities

Roxanne creates current floor plans and seating maps for a total of eleven floors in six Bay Area buildings. Based on requests from her internal customers, she converts each floor plan into PDF, and also creates another document containing all eleven floor plans together. The PDF floor plans and seating maps are then mounted on the Adobe server, where they are immediately available for use. Prior to Acrobat software, Roxanne had to have approximately 1,000 copies of the floor plans made each month and distributed by inter-office mail.

Information availability and timeliness are the major benefits of this application. Acrobat software also allows Roxanne to spend less time keeping the seating maps current, giving her more time to devote to space planning and coordinating an average of 40 employee moves per month. She also uses Acrobat software to create schematics and move instructions, which can be exchanged electronically with employees to facilitate a smooth transition for each employee who must move. Roxanne's use of Acrobat also saves paper and copier use, even further Adobewide cost-cutting measures.

4

Features

Thumbnails, Links, Bookmarks, Notes, Articles

In Chapter 2, we introduced several browsing tools which allow you to move to a specific page in a document efficiently.

In this chapter, we discuss the tools that take advantage of the electronic medium: thumbnails, links, bookmarks, notes, and articles. These features allow you to browse through a document based on attributes other than the page number. Each feature provides you with a way to enhance the view of your document or to "jump" to another page or document located in a separate file.

Thumbnails, which are small-scale graphical views of pages, make it easier to navigate within a document when each page has a distinct layout.

Links are hypertext elements that can perform two types of actions. They are a way to quickly move to related material, whether it is in the active document or another PDF document. Links can also open other applications to display files that are not in PDF format.

Bookmarks are a hierarchical list of links that are displayed in a separate area of the document window.

Notes are remarks added to a document after its creation. Acrobat can automatically locate notes in a document.

Articles are collections of text that are designed to be read sequentially. They thread together related sections of a document regardless of their location. They are typically used for documents that have complex lay-outs or multi-column flows.

In this chapter you will learn how to browse using these elements:

- **Thumbnails**
- **Links**
- **Bookmarks**
- **Notes**
- **Articles.**

Browsing with Thumbnails

To view a document's thumbnails:
- Press the **Thumbnails and Page** toolbar button.

Or

- Select the **View | Thumbnails and Page** command. Acrobat will display the thumbnails on the left side of the active document's document window.

When you display a document's thumbnails, the current page view is marked with a rectangle on the thumbnail representing the current page; this rectangle is called the *page-view box*. A *page number box* appears below each thumbnail; the current page's thumbnail page number box has a grey background, and the others are white.

If thumbnails do not exist for some or all of the pages of a document, they will be displayed as grey boxes. You can navigate and manage pages with these "placeholder" thumbnails as if they were thumbnails with page views.

Thumbnails of pages up to 11" x 11" are sized proportionally. Thumbnails of pages that are larger than 11" x 11" are scaled to the size of a thumbnail of an 11" x 11"

page; Acrobat places an asterisk in the page number box of thumbnails that it scales to a smaller size.

You can use thumbnails to do the same things you can do with Acrobat's navigation and magnification tools: move from page to page, select which portion of a page you view, and change the magnification of a page.

Moving from Page to Page Using Thumbnails

To view another page, click on its thumbnail. Acrobat will display the page, using the current magnification, and will center the page view around the point you clicked, if possible.

Moving Around a Page Using Thumbnails

To move around a page:

1. Place the mouse cursor inside the page-view box; the cursor will change from an arrow to an open hand.
2. Drag it the page-view box to its new location on the page.

You can change the page and the page view simultaneously by clicking on the new page and dragging to create a new page-view box.

Changing the Magnification Using Thumbnails

To change the page magnification:

1. Place the mouse cursor above the page-view box handle at the bottom-right corner of the box; the cursor will change from an arrow to a line with arrows at each end.
2. Resize the page-view box by dragging the handle to a new position.
3. Release the mouse button.

When you release the mouse button, Acrobat will display the portion of the page contained in the box.

Browsing with Bookmarks

To view the bookmarks in a document:
• Press the **Bookmarks and Page** toolbar button

Or

Browsing
   Interface
   Navigating
   Zoom
Features
   Printing
   Clipboard
   Preferences
Creating
   PDFWriter
   PDF Files
Enhancing
   Pages
   Thumbnails
   Bookmarks
   Notes
   Links
   Articles
Web Publishing
   Introduction
   Getting On
   Reader
   Author
   Publisher
   Cool Sites
Advanced
   Search
   Catalog
   Distiller

- Select the **View | Bookmarks and Page** command. Acrobat will display the bookmark list on the left side of the active document's document window.

Bookmark lists can have a hierarchy with up to 20 levels. Each bookmark in the list has a *bookmark name* and a *bookmark page icon*, which are displayed to the left of the bookmark name. *Subordinate* bookmarks are bookmarks that have a lower position in the hierarchy than the current bookmark. Bookmarks with subordinate bookmarks are marked with triangles.

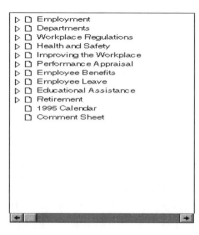

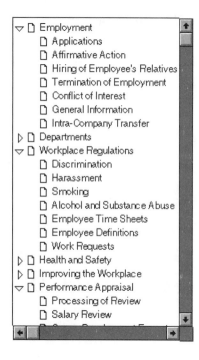

Expanding Subordinate Bookmarks

When subordinate bookmarks are not displayed, they are said to be *contracted*. Bookmarks with contracted subordinate bookmarks are marked with a triangle that points to the right. To expand the bookmarks, click on the triangle. The subordinate bookmarks will be *expanded* (displayed) and the triangle next to the higher-level bookmark will point down.

Contracting Subordinate Bookmarks

When subordinate bookmarks are displayed, they are said to be expanded. Bookmarks with expanded subordinate bookmarks are marked with a triangle that points down. To contract the bookmarks, click on the triangle. The subordinate bookmarks will be *contracted* (hidden) and the triangle next to the higher-level bookmark will point to the right.

Selecting a Bookmark

When you move the mouse cursor over a bookmark name, the cursor changes to the Pointing Finger cursor. To select a bookmark:

- Click on the bookmark name

Or

- Double click on the bookmark page icon.

Acrobat will either move to the location in the document the bookmark refers to or it will open the external file specified by the bookmark.

Browsing with Links

When you move the mouse cursor over a link, the mouse cursor will change from the Hand cursor to the Pointing Finger cursor. To select the link, click once on the link. A link may perform a number of possible actions, depending on how it was set by the person who created it. It may:

- Go to a different view in the same file

Or

- Go to a different file.

Other Types of Links

In Acrobat 2.0, links may have additional capabilities that allow you to:

- Go to a different application

- Play an audio clip

- Play a Quicktime movie or animation

- Go to a different location on the World-Wide Web.

Browsing with Go Back/Go Forward

Whenever you use bookmarks or links to browse, you may wish to retrace your steps—to return to a view where you were previously. With **Go Back** and **Go Forward**, you are given the option to retrace any path you have taken.

Using the Go Back Button

Once you have selected a bookmark or link, the **Go Back** button becomes active. To return to where you were before selecting the link, press the **Go Back** button.

Using the Go Forward Button

Once you have pressed the **Go Back** button, the **Go Forward** button becomes active. To return to where you were before you pressed the **Go Back** button, press the **Go Forward** Button.

Browsing with Notes

Browsing the text in a note is simple; just double click on a note icon, and the note's text window appears.

Note Icons

Note icons are icons on a page of a PDF document that signify the presence of a note. Note icons are either *active* or *inactive*. Only one note in a PDF document may be active at a time. To make a note active, click on its icon; the note will turn from a color to gray.

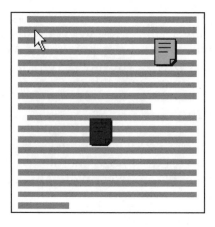

Opening and Closing Note Windows

Double click on the note icon to open the note window.

To close a note window, double click on the window's **Close** button. Acrobat will minimize the note window, and make it a note icon.

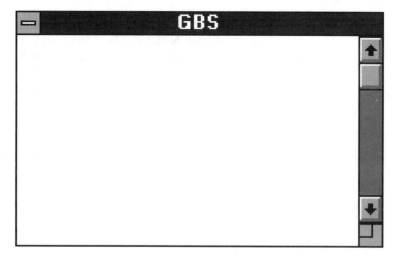

Moving Note Windows

To move a note window, click on the window's title bar and drag the mouse cursor to the new position. As you drag the mouse cursor, Acrobat will display an outline of the window's new position.

Moving Note Icons

To move a note icon, click on the icon and drag it to the new location. As you drag the mouse cursor, Acrobat will display an outline of the icon's new position. You cannot move a note icon to a different document, or from one page in a document to another. If you attempt to move a note in this manner, you may move the note icon outside the view area. If this happens, you can move the note back onto the page by unzooming.

Resizing Note Windows

To resize the window, click the window's resizing handle and drag the mouse cursor. As you drag the mouse cursor, Acrobat will display an outline of the new window size.

Finding the Next Note in a Document

To find the next note in a document, select the **Tools | Find Next Note** command. If the next note in the document is minimized, Acrobat will find the icon and make it active. If the next note in the document is displayed in a window, Acrobat will display the note. If you select the **Find Next Note** command when you are at or beyond the last note in the document, Acrobat will ask you if you want to continue the search from the beginning of the document.

Browsing with Articles

Browsing Through Articles

When you pass the hand tool over a section of a document that is marked as an article, Acrobat draws a down arrow in the open hand mouse cursor. To browse through the article, click on it. Subsequent clicks of the mouse cursor move you to the next section of the article's text until you reach the end of the article.

When you reach the end of the article, Acrobat will beep to let you know it cannot scroll any further, and then return to the page view that was in effect before you started viewing the article.

Selecting an Article to View

To select an article to view:

1. Select the **View | Articles** command. Acrobat will display the Articles dialog box.

2. In the **Title** list box, double click on the title of the article you would like to view, or click on the title and then press the **View** button.

Or

1. Position the hand tool over the article you want to read; Acrobat will draw a down arrow in the open hand mouse cursor when it is positioned over an article.
2. Click on the page.

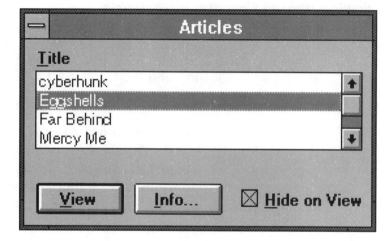

Browsing Through an Article

When you pass the hand tool over a section of a document that is marked as an article, Acrobat draws a down arrow in the open hand mouse cursor. To browse through the article, click on it. Subsequent clicks of the mouse cursor move you to the next section of the article's text until you reach the end of the article.

When you select an article, Acrobat will automatically adjust the zoom level, so that the article text fills as much of the document window as possible. To move to the next section of the article's text, click the mouse cursor; Acrobat will display the next section and briefly display a black triangle to show you where the next section starts. Each time you move to a new section of the article, the previous view is saved in the page-view list; you can use the **Go Forward** and **Go Back** tools and commands to move through the article.

When you reach the end of the article, Acrobat will beep to let you know it cannot scroll any further, and then return to the page view that was in effect before you started viewing the article. If you change the page view using any of the navigation or magnification commands while you are scrolling through an article, Acrobat will stop scrolling through the article. If you want to scroll through the article after selecting another command, use the **Go Back** tool or command to return to the article.

Viewing Information About an Article

If previously entered by the creator of the article, you can display the title of the article, its subject, its author, and the keywords that describe it.

To view information about an article:

1. Select the **View | Articles** command. Acrobat will display the Articles dialog box.
2. In the **Title** list box, click on the title of the article whose information you would like to view, or click on the title and then press the **Info** button.

Acrobat will display the Article Properties dialog box, with the article's information in its edit fields.

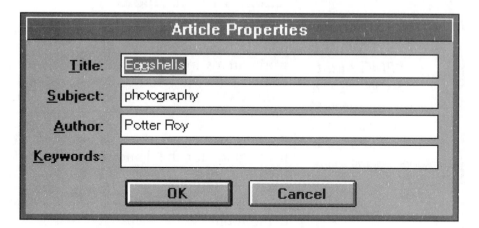

Case Study

Adobe has created a PDF user's guide for their demo room. This guide, which is highly graphical, is used to teach people how to operate various pieces of equipment. Thumbnails are an efficient way to navigate through such documents.

Results

From the KPMG Audit:

Ross developed a novel application of Acrobat software to assist people using Adobe's demo room.

Customer Support

On-line Instructions for Adobe's Demo Room

Adobe's demo room contains several PCs using both DOS and Windows, Macintoshes, and UNIX workstations installed with Adobe's products and demonstrations of Adobe's technologies. The demo room also contains audio/visual and other equipment.

Ross employed Acrobat software to develop a user's guide for the demo room. Since PDF documents are identical across platforms and are independent of the source application, the same user's guide is accessible on every computer in the demo room.

At the top level of the guide is a floor plan showing the location of each piece of equipment in the demo room, as well as the location of light switches and electrical outlets in the room. The user can select an item on the floor plan and see a detailed description of that piece of equipment. The descriptions take the user through the operation of each piece of equipment. The descriptions also incorporate photographs of the equipment in which buttons and switches have been identified and their operations explained.

The demo room guide allows people using the demo room to quickly learn to operate the computers and equipment. The guide itself is also a compelling demonstration of the use of Acrobat technology.

CHAPTER

5

Printing

Creating and Customizing Printed Output

Reader and Exchange take advantage of the printer support found in the Macintosh and Windows environments. This enables Acrobat to print documents on a large number of printers, even those that don't understand PostScript.

Acrobat's font substitution and embedding technology make it possible to print your documents as they appeared when they were created; your computer does not need to have the fonts that were used to create the document.

In this chapter, you will learn how to:

- Specify and setup a printer
- Customize your printout with **Pages Setup** and printer **Options**
- Print to a disk file.

Printing to Paper

Typically, you will want to print PDF files on a local printer that is either connected directly to your computer or that is connected to your local area network.

To print a file to a local printer:

1. Select the **File | Print** command.
2. Select the pages of the document that you want to print.
3. Specify the print quality.
4. Specify the number of copies you want to make by entering the number in the **Copies:** edit box.
5. Specify whether or not multiple copies should be collated. If you want collated copies, click the **Collate Copies** check box. The **Collate Copies** check box will remain checked every time you select the **File | Print** command, until you click on it again to clear it.
6. Specify if oversized pages should be shrunk to fit the paper. If you want to shrink oversized pages, click the **Shrink to Fit** check box. The **Shrink to Fit** check box will remain checked every time you select the **File | Print** command, until you click on it again to clear it.
7. Press the **OK** button. If you decide you don't want to print the document, press the **Cancel** button.

Selecting the Pages to Print

Acrobat can print the entire document, the current page, or a range of consecutive pages of the document. You may use the controls of the **Print Range** frame of the Print dialog box to specify which pages should be printed.

To print the entire document:

- Click on the **All** radio button

To print the current page of the document:

- Click on the **Current page** radio button.

To print a range of consecutive pages:

1. Click on the **Pages** radio button.
2. Enter the beginning and the ending pages in the **From:** and **To:** edit fields.

Specifying the Print Quality

The levels of print quality and the units (or lack of same) used to measure print quality vary from printer to printer. For instance, some printers will give you a choice of resolutions, say 300 dpi and 600 dpi, while others will list quality modes, such as High, Medium, and Low, or Letter and Draft. To specify the print quality:

1. Click on the **Print Quality:** drop-down list box.

2. Click on a quality mode in the list.

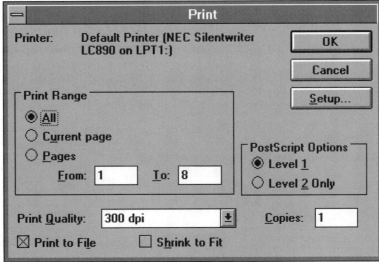

Printing to a File

There may be times when you would rather store the printer commands in a disk file rather than sending them directly to the printer. For instance, you may want to store a printer file on a disk and bring it to a printer at another location. Acrobat conveniently makes this feature available for any printer driver.

To print to a file instead of to a printer:

1. Select the **File | Print** command. Acrobat will display the Print dialog box.
2. Click on the **Print To File** check box on the Print dialog box.
3. Press the **OK** button. Acrobat will display the print status dialog box and the Print To File dialog box.
4. Enter the file name where the printer commands will be stored in the **Output File Name** edit box. If you do not specify the path, the file will be stored in the same directory that the PDF file you are printing is stored in.
5. Press the Print To File dialog box's **OK** button. If you decide you don't want to print the file, press the **Cancel** button.

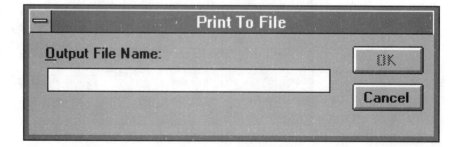

Acrobat will then send the printer commands to the disk file you specified. The Print Status dialog box will still indicate that the output is going to the default port for the printer. Don't worry; it is sending the output to a file.

The **Print To File** check box will remain checked every time you select the **File | Print** command, until you click on it again to clear it.

Selecting and Configuring a Printer

In Windows, when you select the **File | Print** command, Acrobat prepares to print the document to the default printer, using the printer settings in effect when the command was selected. If you would like to use a different printer, or would like to change the printer settings, you can do so, even if you have already selected the **File | Print** command. To select and configure a printer:

- Select the **File | Print** Setup command

Or

- Press the **Setup** button of the Print dialog box, if you have already selected the **File | Print** command.

Selecting a Printer

Acrobat can print using any printer driver that is installed on the computer system you are working on.

To select a printer:

- Click on the **Default Printer** radio button in the Printer frame

Or

1. Click on the **Specific Printer** radio button in the Printer frame.
2. Click on the **Specific Printer** drop-down list box.
3. Click on a printer in the list.

Specifying the Page Orientation

You can choose from two page orientations, Portrait or Landscape. In the Portrait orientation, the bottom of the page is the shorter side of the paper. In the Landscape orientation, the bottom of the page is the longer side of the paper.

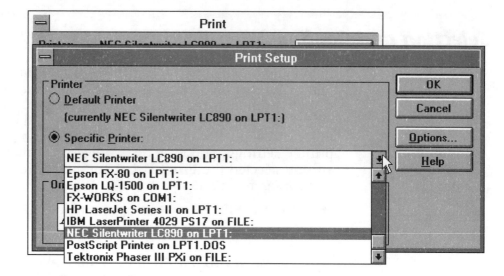

To choose the page orientation:

- Click on the appropriate radio button, **Portrait** or **Landscape**, in the Orientation frame.

Specifying the Paper Size and Source

Many printers support more than one paper size, and the printer's driver can adjust the output to fit the paper sizes the printer supports. Many printers also have several trays from which they load sheets of paper for printing. You can specify the paper size and source in the Print Setup dialog box.

To specify the paper size:

1. Click on the **Size:** drop-down list box in the Paper frame.
2. Click on a paper size in the list.

To specify the paper source:

1. Click on the **Source:** drop-down list box in the Paper frame.
2. Click on a paper source in the list.

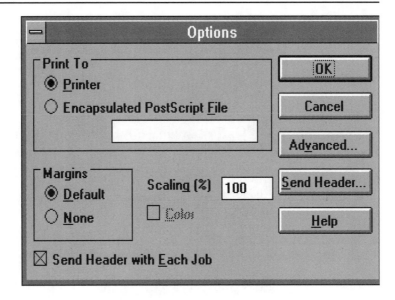

Setting Printer Options

The type of printer options that are available will depend on the printer you have selected.

To set the printer options:

1. Press the **Options** button. The options dialog box for the printer driver you selected will appear.
2. When you have set the printer options in the printer driver's dialog box, close the dialog box to return to the Print Setup dialog box.

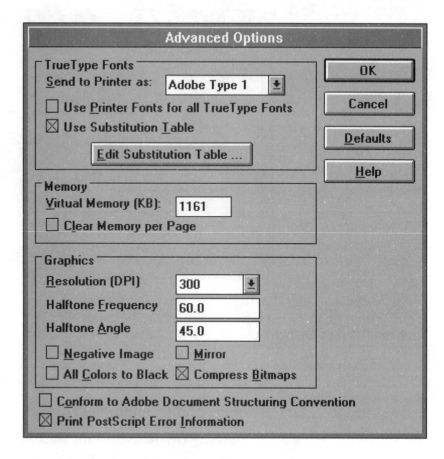

Case Study

Acrobat is able to print documents from DOS, Windows, Macintosh and SUN computers. In this example, Adobe employees use this capability to quickly solve a printing problem.

From the KPMG Audit:

Acrobat software is used extensively by both the field sales force and the inside sales organization. KPMG interviewed Clint, Chris, Judy, and Melody in field sales.

Sales

Acrobat Keeps the Field Sales Offices Connected and Up-to-Date

Adobe's Acrobat field sales organization makes extensive use of its own product. Account status reports are available to headquarters and field sales personnel in PDF. Sales presentations are all developed in PDF, allowing the product to show itself. The sales force can also draw from the presentation database of PDF documents on the Adobe server. Acrobat sales people also perform demonstrations by taking the client's own files, converting them to PDF, and demonstrating Acrobat product features on "live data." Third-party customer files are also demonstrated.

A major benefit of using Acrobat software as a sales tool is the ability to cross platforms without any loss of document quality. This was illustrated by an example where Acrobat software's own features avoided the delay or cancellation of a sales call. A field sales person was about to leave for the airport to make a sales call and needed a printed copy of sales materials for the potential client. He was unable to print out the materials on his laptop PC, and the other laptop PC in the office was unavailable. The problem was resolved by converting the materials into PDF format, and printing them on the secretary's Macintosh.

Another Acrobat benefit to the field sales group is identical access to documents that headquarters' staff enjoys. Such common access allows sales activities to be better coordinated and helps to create a feeling of being "connected."

CHAPTER 6

Clipboard

Sharing Information Between Applications

To use an electronic document fully, you must be able to use the contents of a document in other contexts. Adobe Acrobat has Clipboard commands to help you do this.

The Clipboard is a part of your computer's operating system that allows you to share data between applications. It is a temporary storage space in which you can place data and from which you can retrieve the data later.

To understand the instructions in this chapter, you should familiarize yourself with the following three terms:

- **Cut:** when you cut data from a document, it is removed from the document and placed on the Clipboard.

- **Copy:** when you copy data from a document, it is placed on the Clipboard, and the original data remains in the document.

- **Paste:** when you paste data into a document, you copy the data from the Clipboard into your document, and the data remains on the Clipboard.

You use the Clipboard by cutting or copying information from one place and pasting it into another.

In this chapter you will learn how to:

- Cut information from note text, bookmarks, or other areas to the Clipboard
- Copy information from the document and other areas to the Clipboard
- Paste information from the Clipboard to note text, bookmark labels, and other areas.

Selecting Text

When you select text, you make it available for placement on the Clipboard, for replacement by text currently on the Clipboard, or for deletion. You can select any portion of the text on the current page of a PDF document with the **Select Text** tool,

or you can select all the text on the page at once with the **Select All** command. Acrobat selects text on a word-by-word basis; you cannot select single letters from a PDF document. When you select text, Acrobat highlights it, so you can be sure of what text will be affected.

The Select Text Tool

The **Select Text** tool allows you to select portions of text that are on the current page of a PDF document. You do not use the **Select Text** tool to select text that is in notes or bookmarks; text in these objects can be selected using your system's normal selection methods.

To select a single word:

1. Activate the **Link** tool by selecting the **Tools | Select Text** command or by pressing the **Select Text** toolbar button.
2. Click on the word.

To select a block of text.

1. Activate the Link tool by selecting the **Tools |
   Select Text** command or by pressing the **Select
   Text** toolbar button.
2. Click on the first word of the block of text.
3. Drag the mouse cursor to the last word in the
   block of text. Both words must be on the current
   page.
4. Release the mouse button.

Sometimes, you select a block of text and release the
mouse button, only to realize that you did not select
the entire block of text you wanted to. To select the
text you missed, you must click on or drag over the
text, which would cancel the text selection you just
made. Acrobat helps you avoid this problem by letting you *expand* the block of text you selected, as long
as all the text is on the current page.

To expand a block of selected text:

1. Press the **<Shift>** key.

2. While holding the **<Shift>** key, click on the word
   in the block of text you want to add that is far-
   thest from the block of text you have already
   selected.

3. Release the mouse button and the **<Shift>** key.

By default, the **Select Text** tool selects all the text
from the left to right margin of the page when you
select a block of text. Often, however, you may want
to select text that does not stretch from margin to
margin; many documents, such as newsletters,
spreadsheets, and reports with tables, arrange their
text in a columnar format. Acrobat makes it easy to
select text from documents of this type by allowing
you to select text within a rectangle.

To select text within a rectangle:

1. Activate the **Link** tool by selecting the **Tools |
   Select Text** command or by pressing the **Select
   Text** toolbar button.
2. Press the **<Ctrl>** key.
3. Click on a corner of the rectangle. Acrobat will
   draw a rectangle on the mouse cursor.
4. Drag the mouse to the opposite corner of the rectangle. As you drag the mouse, Acrobat will draw a
   rectangle to show you the text you are selecting.
   Both corners of the rectangle must be on the current page.
5. Release the mouse button.

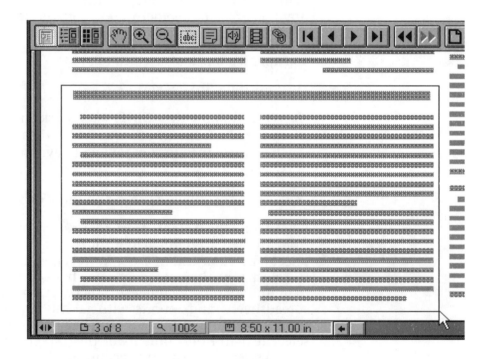

The Select All Command

The **Select All** command allows you to select all the
text on the current page at once. To select the text:

• Select the **Edit | Select All** command.

Or

1. Right click the mouse. It does not matter what tool is active when you do this.
2. Select the **Select All** command from the pop-up menu that appears.

Selecting Text in Bookmarks and Notes

You do not use the **Select Text** tool to select text that is in notes or bookmarks; text in these objects can be selected using your system's normal selection methods. In Windows, you can select text by moving the cursor while the **<Shift>** key is pressed or by dragging the mouse across the text.

Canceling a Selection

Occasionally, you may select text, then realize you did not want to select any text at all. To cancel a selection:

- Click anywhere on the page where no text is displayed, or click outside the page boundaries.

Selecting Graphics

When you select graphics, you make a portion of a page available for placement on the clipboard. You can select any portion of any page in a PDF document as graphics, not just areas of the page that contain embedded graphics. You can also select the area beyond the boundaries of the page as graphics; there will be no graphics in the areas beyond the boundaries, but the graphics image will be larger. You cannot select thumbnails as graphics.

To select graphics:

1. Activate the **Select Graphics** tool by selecting the **Tools | Select Graphics** command. The mouse cursor will turn into a crosshair.
2. Click on one corner of the page area that you would like to select as graphics.

3. Drag the mouse to the opposite corner of the area. As you drag the mouse, Acrobat will draw a rectangle to show you the area you are selecting. The corners of the rectangle do not need be on the current page, but you cannot select graphics across pages.

4. Release the mouse button. Acrobat will display a rectangle to show you the area you selected.

Copying Data to the Clipboard

To copy text or graphics to the Clipboard once you have selected it:

- Select the **Edit | Copy** command

Or

- Press **<Ctrl> + <Ins>**.

You can only select text on the active page with the text tool, which means you cannot select in one step text that spans pages.

To copy text that spans pages:

1. Select the text on the first page.
2. Copy it to the Clipboard.
3. Paste it into the destination.
4. Repeat the process for every page in the block of text that you want to copy.

When you copy graphics to the Clipboard in Windows, the graphics data is stored in Windows Metafile format; on the Macintosh, it is stored in PICT format.

Cutting Text to the Clipboard

The text in a PDF document cannot be removed from the document, so it cannot be cut to the Clipboard; only the text in bookmarks and notes can be cut.

To cut text in a bookmark or note to the Clipboard once you have selected it:

- Select the **Edit | Cut** command.

Or

- Press **<Shift>** + **<Del>**.

Clearing Text

Acrobat uses the **Edit | Clear** command to provide a consistent way of deleting things. In any case where you would use the **<Delete>** key, you can use the **Edit | Clear** command. If you are a Windows user, note that the **Edit | Clear** command does not remove data from the Windows Clipboard. You cannot clear selected text or graphics from a PDF document; you can clear selected text bookmarks and notes with the **Edit | Clear** command, however.

Copying an Entire File to the Clipboard— Using Acrobat with Windows OLE

To copy all of the text in a PDF document to the Windows Clipboard, or to make a PDF file available for OLE embedding or linking:

- Select the **Edit | Copy File to Clipboard** command.

Adobe has added OLE support to the Windows version 2.0 of Exchange. Exchange 2.0 is an OLE server application, which means that other Windows applications that are OLE client applications can embed PDF documents within their own documents or make links to PDF documents in their documents. The file that is embedded or linked with OLE is called the source document in this case, the source document is a PDF document. The file in which the source document is embedded or linked is called the destination document.

When you embed a source document in a destination document, a copy of the source document is placed inside the destination document. Once you have embedded the source document, it becomes part of the destination document, and you can modify the original copy of the source document without the modifications affecting the destination document. When you link a source document to a destination document, the destination document "points to" the location of the source document. If you make changes to a PDF source document (for instance, by creating an updated copy of the PDF document with PDFWriter or Distiller, or by adding notes, links, or bookmarks to the document), the changes can be incorporated into the destination document by updating the link. Links can be updated manually or automatically; see the instructions of the destination document's application for more details. Note that you cannot paste graphics or the text in bookmarks and notes into a destination document using OLE.

PDF source documents can be placed in destination documents as Adobe Acrobat Document Objects, or as text in Rich Text Format (RTF). When you link or embed a PDF document as an Adobe Acrobat Document Object, only the Acrobat icon will appear in the destination document. To view the PDF document, double click on the Acrobat icon; the client application will launch Acrobat and load the PDF document. When you link or embed a PDF document as RTF text, all of the page text of the document is placed in the destination document with as much of the formatting information as possible preserved. Placing the full text of the PDF document in the destination document makes it larger, but allows you to:

- Perform full-text searches of the PDF text using the destination document's application

- Edit the text

- Print the text as an integral part of the destination document

- Use Acrobat to view an embedded OLE document.

Some of Acrobat's File menu options are different when the program is launched from an embedded PDF document in an OLE client application. Since the PDF document Acrobat is displaying is not contained in its own disk file, but is a part of another document's disk file, Acrobat will not save any changes to the PDF document. Instead, Acrobat updates the information in the destination document. To make this difference clear, the **File | Save** command is replaced by the **File | Update** command. Note that no information has been saved to disk when you select the **File | Update** command; if you want to save the updated information to disk, you must return to the OLE client application and save the destination document that contains the embedded PDF file.

For similar reasons, the **File | Save As** command is replaced by the **File | Save Copy As** command when you launch Acrobat from an OLE client application. When you select the **Save Copy As** command, Acrobat displays the Save As dialog box, and you enter the name of the file in the same manner as you would if you had selected the **Save As** command. After the copy is saved, however, the **Save Copy As** command returns you to the embedded document, rather than to the copy.

Lastly, Acrobat replaces the **File | Exit** command with the **File | Exit & Return to Document** command, where document is the name of the destination document. When you select this command, Acrobat terminates, and you return to the OLE client application.

If you have opened other PDF documents besides a document embedded in a destination document, the **Update** and **Save Copy As** commands will appear in the File menu only when the embedded document is the active document. The **Exit & Return to Document** command will appear at all times. If you want to close the embedded document, but want Acrobat to remain running, select the **File | Close** command. The OLE client application will become the active window, but Acrobat will not terminate.

Viewing the Contents of the Clipboard

There are times when you may want to verify what the Clipboard contains before you paste the contents into a document. Acrobat has made this very easy to do by adding a command to its View menu. In Windows, the **Window | Show Clipboard** command will invoke the Windows Clipboard Viewer (Windows) or the Windows Clipbook Viewer (Windows for Workgroups).

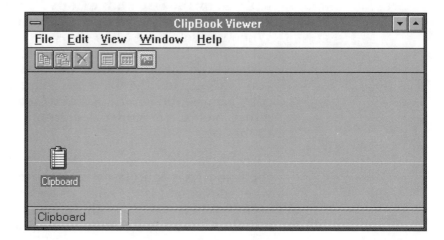

Case Study

The following case study illustrates how employees are able to create an entire presentation in hours by using the Clipboard tools and a database of previous presentations.

PART 1

Browsing
  Interface
  Navigating
  Zoom
  Features
  Printing
  Clipboard
  Preferences
Creating
  PDFWriter
  PDF Files
Enhancing
  Pages
  Thumbnails
  Bookmarks
  Notes
  Links
  Articles
Web Publishing
  Introduction
  Getting On
  Reader
  Author
  Publisher
  Cool Sites
Advanced
  Search
  Catalog
  Distiller

Results

*From the
KPMG Audit:*

*We spoke with Nancy
regarding Acrobat
software's role in
presentations. She
coordinates the
development of 110
presentations per year
throughout Adobe.
Each person we
interviewed used
Acrobat software for
presentations.*

Marketing

Presentations Inside and Outside Adobe

Nancy uses Acrobat software for the presentation review process, no matter the source application. There is also a growing database of presentations in PDF on the server which presenters can draw from to speed up their development. Nancy and the presentation creator often have the identical PDF document open on their computers and make real-time modifications over the phone. Before using Acrobat software, Nancy spent additional time making copies of presentations and delivering them for reviews.

Using Acrobat software for presentations has reduced the turnaround time by up to two days, which is critical since presentations often must be built under tight time constraints. Nancy gave the example of one 20-page presentation that was requested at 3:00 PM on Friday, and was completed thanks to Acrobat software in two hours.

Preferences

Setting Document Options and Viewing Document Info

Because you are able to browse files across many computer systems, information regarding these files becomes very important. Perhaps you want to know the original author of the document, or how recently it was written or modified. As a viewer of a document, maybe you want to customize the display of the document by changing its default magnification or its page size.

In this chapter, you will learn how to:

- Find and revise document information (author, title, subject, date of creation, etc...)

- Find information on the fonts used to create document

- View a document's security information

- Set general preferences of a document.

Document Info

PDF documents contain several pieces of information besides the document itself. These pieces of information can be divided into 4 categories: general information, font information, open information, and security information.

General Info

General information refers to the contents of the document, how it was produced, and when it was produced, including:

- **Title:** The name of the document. The title is different from the document's filename, but you can use a filename as a document's title

- **Subject:** What the document is about

- **Author:** The name of the person or organization that created the document

- **Keywords:** Words that summarize the document's topic or that appear frequently in the document

- **Creator:** The program used to create the document. This can be any application that can create PostScript files, or use PDFWriter to create a

---

General Info

D:\USER\KATE\MAG1.PDF

Title:

Subject:

Author: |

Keywords:

Creator: Acrobat Capture 1.0b

Producer: Acrobat PDFWriter 2.0 for Windows

Created: 6/8/95 10:42:03 AM

Modified: 6/9/95 10:16:37 AM

OK   Cancel

PDF file, such as: a word processor, a spreadsheet, or a presentation graphics program

- **Producer:** The program used to create the PDF version of the document, either PDFWriter or Distiller

- **Created:** The date and time when the PDF file was created

- **Modified:** The date and time when the PDF file was last modified.

To display general information:

- Select the **Document Info | General** command. Acrobat will display the General Info dialog box.

You can edit the **Title, Subject, Author,** and **Keywords** fields with **Reader;** the other fields cannot be modified.

To modify the fields:

1. Click on the field's edit box.
2. Edit the text in the edit box using your system's editing commands.

These four fields can be indexed with Catalog, and you can search for them with Exchange's indexed Search feature.

To close the General Info dialog box:

- Press the **OK** button.

If you have modified any of the fields in the dialog box and you do not want the modifications to be recorded, press the **Cancel** button.

Font Info

The PDF file contains the names of all the fonts that were used to create the document, so Acrobat can search for those fonts on any system used to display the document. You can display a list of the fonts used to create the document and the fonts Acrobat is using to display the document.

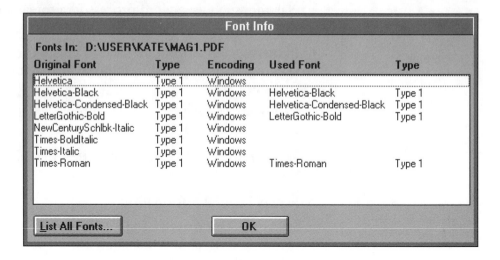

To display font information:

- Select the **Document Info | Fonts** command.

For each font used in the original document, the Font Info displays the following information:

- **Original Font:** The name of the font used to create the document.

- **Type:** The font type, such as Adobe Type 1 or TrueType.

- **Encoding:** The method used to store the Original Font.

- **Used Font:** The local system font used to display the document. If the font used to create the document is available on the local system, the Used Font and Original Font will be the same.

- **Type:** The method used to store the Used Font.

Acrobat only displays those fonts that it has encountered while displaying the document. Other fonts may have been used in parts of the document you have not yet viewed.

To display these fonts in the Font Info dialog box:

- Press the **List All Fonts** button.

When you press this button, Acrobat searches through the document for the names of the fonts that were used to create it. Acrobat displays a status bar in the document window to inform you of its progress in the search. Fonts listed with the **List All Fonts** button that have not yet been displayed will include the Original Font, Type, and Encoding information, but not the Used Font or Type information.

Security Info

Acrobat Reader allows you to view the security settings for a document, including password protection and permission to print.

To display security information for a document:

- Select the **Document Info | Security** command.

You cannot edit security information with the **Document Info | Security** command. These options are set by the creator of the document in Acrobat Exchange.

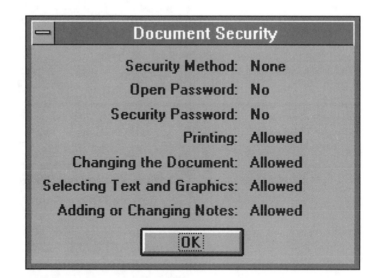

Preferences

With the commands of the **Edit | Preferences** submenu, you can customize how documents are displayed, the properties of notes, how Acrobat works in

Browsing
    Interface
    Navigating
    Zoom
    Features
    Printing
    Clipboard
  Preferences
Creating
    PDFWriter
    PDF Files
Enhancing
    Pages
    Thumbnails
    Bookmarks
    Notes
    Links
    Articles
Web Publishing
    Introduction
    Getting On
    Reader
    Author
    Publisher
    Cool Sites
Advanced
    Search
    Catalog
    Distiller

Full Screen mode, and how Exchange performs indexed searches.

General...

To customize Acrobat's page display and operation options:

1. Select the **Preferences | General** command. The General Preference dialog box will appear.
2. Use the controls of the General Preferences dialog box to set the page display and operation parameters you want.
3. Press the **OK** button. If you decide you don't want to change the options, press the **Cancel** button.

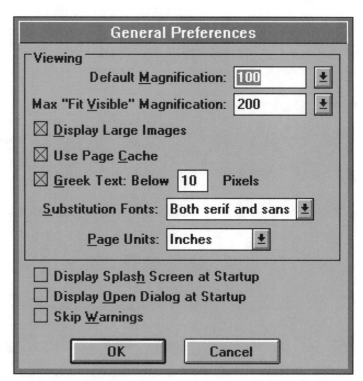

Default Magnification

The default magnification is the magnification at which Acrobat will display a document when it is first opened, if the initial magnification of the document has been set to **Default** (if the initial magnification of the document has been set to another level with

Browsing
Interface
Navigating
Zoom
Features
Printing
Clipboard
Preferences
Creating
PDFWriter
PDF Files
Enhancing
Pages
Thumbnails
Bookmarks
Notes
Links
Articles
Web Publishing
Introduction
Getting On
Reader
Author
Publisher
Cool Sites
Advanced
Search
Catalog
Distiller

the **File | Document Info | Open** command, Acrobat will use that magnification).

To change the default magnification:

1. Click on the **Default Magnification** drop-down list box. A list of magnification levels will appear.
2. Click on the magnification level you want to use as the default magnification level.

Maximum Fit Visible Magnification

The Maximum Fit Visible Magnification is the highest magnification that Acrobat will use to display a page when you select the Fit Visible zoom level. Sometimes, filling the document window with the "printed" area of the page requires a higher magnification than the Maximum Fit Visible Magnification.

If this is the case, Acrobat displays white space around the text and graphics. To change the maximum Fit Visible magnification:

1. Click on the **Maximum Fit Visible Magnification** drop-down list box. A list of magnification levels will appear.
2. Click on the magnification level you want to use as the Maximum Fit Visible Magnification level.

Display Large Images

This option allows you to specify whether large images are displayed or if gray boxes are displayed in their place. Acrobat distinguishes between large and small images based on the number of bytes it takes to store the image, not the size of the image on the page. A small image with fine detail and many colors may take more space to store than a large, simple image, and thus will not be displayed if the **Display Large Images** option is turned off. To change the setting of the **Display Large Images** option:

- Click on the **Display Large Images** check box.

Use Page Cache

When the **Use Page Cache** option is on, Acrobat creates a temporary storage area in memory where it stores page views. This decreases the amount of time it takes to display a new page. You may want to turn this option off if you do not have enough free memory for other tasks. To change the setting of the **Use Page Cache** option:

- Click on the **Use Page Cache** check box.

Greek Text

When the **Greek Text** option is on, Acrobat greeks, or displays as gray lines, all text whose height is below the number of pixels specified in the **Greek Text** edit box. Greeking text speeds up page display, but makes text illegible; you should set the pixel number in the **Greek Text: Below** edit box to a number of pixels below which screen fonts are illegible. To change the setting of the **Greek Text** option:

- Click on the **Greek Text** check box.

To specify the pixel height below which text is greeked,

- Enter a new number in the **Greek Text: Below** edit box.

Substitution Fonts

When Acrobat cannot find a font used to create a document on your computer, it uses built-in serif and sans serif Multiple Master fonts to recreate the look of the font. You can control which of these fonts Acrobat uses with the **Substitution Fonts** option. To change the **Substitution Fonts** option setting:

1. Click on the **Substitution Fonts**: drop-down list box.
2. Click on the substitution font type you want to use: **Serif Only**, **Sans Only**, or **Both Serif and Sans**.

The **Substitution Fonts** option affects the appearance of documents on the screen as well as on the printer. The **Serif Only** option will use a Serif font as a substitute for all fonts that Acrobat cannot find on the local system, even if the original font was a Sans Serif font. The **Sans Only** option will use a Sans Serif font as a substitute, even if the original font was a Serif font. When the **Both Serif and Sans** option is active, Acrobat will determine whether the original

Browsing
  Interface
  Navigating
  Zoom
  Features
  Printing
  Clipboard
Preferences
Creating
  PDFWriter
  PDF Files
Enhancing
  Pages
  Thumbnails
  Bookmarks
  Notes
  Links
  Articles
Web Publishing
  Introduction
  Getting On
  Reader
  Author
  Publisher
  Cool Sites
Advanced
  Search
  Catalog
  Distiller

font was a Serif or Sans Serif font, and use the appropriate Multiple Master font as a substitute for it.

The **Serif Only** and **Sans Only** options are useful if you are having trouble printing PDF documents because of a lack of printer memory. By using only one substitution font, you will reduce the amount of printer memory required. Note that the Sans Serif font requires less memory than the Serif font.

If you have a Windows or a Macintosh system, this option setting will not change until you restart your system.

Page Units

Acrobat can express page dimensions in inches, points, or millimeters. To change the units Acrobat uses to express page dimensions:

1. Click on the **Page Units:** drop-down list box.
2. Click on the page unit you want to use.

Display Splash Screen at Startup

The splash screen is a window that displays the program name and logo, the version number, and copyright and licensing information. When Acrobat is installed, the option to display the splash screen at startup is on. To reduce the time it takes for Acrobat to launch, you can specify that the splash screen not be displayed when you launch Acrobat. To turn the display of the splash screen on and off:

- Click on the **Display Splash Screen at Startup** check box.

Display Open Dialog at Startup

When Acrobat is installed, the option to display the Open dialog box at startup is on, and the Open dialog box is displayed when launching Acrobat, just as if you had selected the **File | Open** command. If you do not want to open a file every time you launch Acrobat (for instance, if you start the program automatically when you start your system), you can tell Acrobat not to display the Open dialog box. To turn the display of the Open dialog box on and off:

- Click on the **Display Open Dialog at Startup** check box.

Skip Warnings

By default, Exchange will ask you for confirmation when you delete pages, notes, bookmarks, or links. If you do not want Acrobat to ask for confirmation, you can switch the messages off. To turn warning messages on and off:

• Click on the **Skip Warnings** check box.

You can customize the default appearance of any notes you create, including the label that appears in the note window's title bar, the default color, and the font and point size of the note text.

For more information on this topic, see page 162.

Full Screen…

You can customize how Acrobat changes pages in **Full Screen** mode by indicating whether the pages are shown in a loop and what the background color of the screen will be.

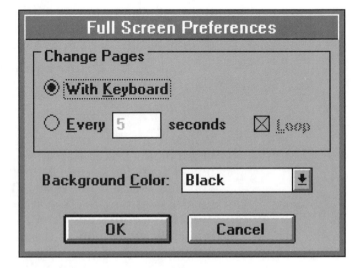

To change the **Full Screen** mode options:

1. Select the **Preferences | Full Screen** command. The Full Screen Preferences dialog box will appear.

2. Use the controls of the Full Screen Preferences dialog box to change the default properties in Full Screen mode.

Specifying How Pages are Changed

In Full Screen mode, the menu bar and toolbar are not accessible, so the navigation commands and tools cannot be used to move from page to page in a document. Instead, you move forward from page to page in a document, using two methods:

• Keyboard Page Changing, where any key press changes a page

• Automatic Page Changing, where Acrobat changes pages at regular intervals.

To specify Keyboard Page Changing:

• Click on the **With Keyboard** radio button.

To specify Automatic Page Changing:

1. Click on the **Every: seconds** radio button.

2. Enter the time interval in the **Every: seconds** edit box.

3. If you want Acrobat to display the pages in a loop, set the Loop option by clicking on the **Loop** check box.

Selecting a Background Color

To select a background color for Full Screen mode:

1. Click on the **Background Color:** drop-down list box. A list of color names will appear.

2. Click on the name of the color you want to use.

Case Study

From the KPMG Audit:
KPMG analyzed outgoing Federal Express shipments at Adobe to see if the widespread availability of Acrobat software was resulting in reduced demand for this service. Renee gave us historical data on shipment volumes and costs.

Finance

Reduced Federal Express Shipments

KPMG compared outgoing Federal Express shipments for the twelve months ending in June 1994 with the prior twelve month period. Since Adobe's workforce was increasing during this period, we normalized the results by determining per employee outgoing Federal Express shipments.

Based on our analysis, outgoing Federal Express shipments per employee were 6% lower in 1993–1994 than in 1992–1993. This equates to an estimate of over 1,100 fewer outgoing Federal Express document shipments. At an average cost of $8.71 per shipment, the annual savings are estimated to be nearly $10,000. See the appendix for details of this cost analysis.

II

CREATING Interactive Documents

Creating PDF with PDFWriter

CHAPTER

8

PDFWriter

Printing to PDF

To be an acceptable substitute for a paper document, an electronic document must be as simple to create as a paper document. Paper documents are created in a wide variety of applications, such as word processors, spreadsheets, presentation graphics programs, and drawing programs. These applications then use printer driver programs to convert the documents to a printer language. Finally the documents are "converted" to paper by sending the printer language commands to a printer.

Acrobat creates electronic documents in the same way, using two programs that create PDF documents, PDF-Writer and Distiller. Distiller, described in Chapter 17, creates PDF files from PostScript language files. PDF-Writer is a printer driver that works with any Macintosh or Windows application that uses the printing facilities of the operating system. It sends PDF format data to a disk file rather than sending printer commands to a printer.

One of Acrobat's major design goals was to preserve the exact look of documents, including their fonts. Acrobat includes two technologies to achieve this:

- **Font substitution**: Acrobat obtains font information from the operating system and stores it in the PDF file. Reader and Exchange use the font information to mimic the font. This is Acrobat's default unless you specify otherwise.

- **Font embedding**: Acrobat stores all the information about the font in the document, so that Reader and Exchange can recreate the font on systems that do not have it installed. You choose the fonts that PDFWriter embeds.

In this chapter, you will learn how to:

- Create PDF files using files from other applications

- Set the page size, resolution, and scaling of a document

- Compress the text and graphics data in a file

- Embed fonts.

More options are discussed in Chapter 8: "PDF Options."

Creating a PDF File with PDFWriter

How you use PDFWriter to create a PDF file is highly dependent on the operating system and the application with which you are using it. In this section, we will give you a brief overview of the process.

To create a PDF file with PDFWriter:

1. Select your application's **Printer Setup** command.
2. Select **Acrobat PDFWriter** as the printer driver.
3. Select your application's **Print** command. PDF-Writer will display the Save PDF File As dialog box.
4. Enter a filename using the controls of the Save PDF File As dialog box.

Setting PDFWriter's Options

PDFWriter's options fall into three categories: page layout and general options, compression options, and font embedding options. These options have a large

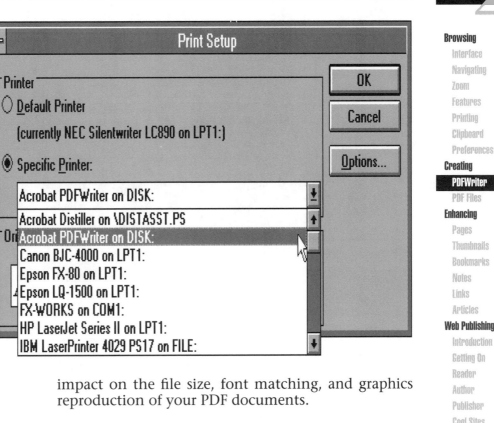

impact on the file size, font matching, and graphics reproduction of your PDF documents.

Setting the Page Size

PDF document pages can be any size from a minimum of 1" x 1" to a maximum of 45" x 45". PDFWriter's page layout options let you define the size of the pages in a PDF document, as well as their orientation (portrait or landscape) and the resolution at which the pages are generated.

To select a standard page size:

1. Click on the **Standard:** radio button.
2. Click on the **Standard:** drop-down list box.
3. Click on one of the page sizes in the drop-down list.

To select a custom page size:

1. Click on the **Custom:** radio button.
2. Click on the **Units:** drop-down list box.

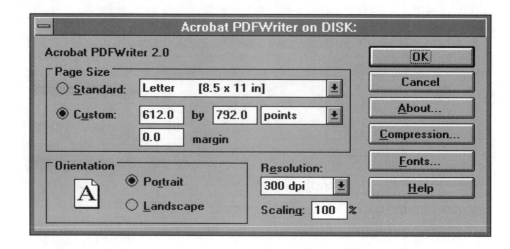

3. Enter the width and height of the page in the **Custom:** edit boxes.
4. Enter the margin width in the **Margin** edit box.

To select a screen orientation:

• Click on the **Portrait** or **Landscape** radio buttons.

Setting the Resolution

In version 2.0, PDFWriter can adjust the resolution at which something is saved/generated/printed. The available resolutions are: screen resolution, 150dpi, 300dpi, and 600dpi. Screen resolution will vary according to your video hardware.

To change the resolution at which a document is printed:

1. Click on the **Resolution:** drop-down list box.
2. Click on one of the resolutions in the drop-down list.

Setting the Scaling

PDFWriter can scale pages from 25 to 400 percent of their original size. This capability can be helpful if you decide you want to scale the sizes of the pages in your document to a larger or smaller size. For instance, if you decide that a document you created with 8.5" x 11" pages should be scaled up to 11" x 17" pages, you can alter the page size used by PDFWriter to 11" x 17", then increase the scaling to 200%. If you do not increase the scaling, you will generate 11" x 17" pages with an 8.5" x 11" text area; by increasing the scaling, you can increase the text area to 11" x 17" as well.

To select a scaling factor:

- Enter the scaling factor (in terms of a percentage) in the **Scaling:** edit box.

Setting Compression Options

PDFWriter's compression options allow you to balance the file size of PDF documents and the accuracy with which images are displayed. The Acrobat PDFWriter Compression Options dialog box also has an option to use ASCII format to store the PDF files, which could open up a whole can of worms. If your documents have bitmapped graphics or other types of images embedded in them, you can use the compression options to achieve substantial reductions in PDF file size compared to uncompressed documents.

The text in PDF files is compressed with the LZW compression scheme. LZW is a lossless compression scheme; when you decompress information that you compressed with LZW, the information is preserved exactly. Document text must be compressed with a lossless algorithm; otherwise, the decompressed text will contain garbage.

I took a file containing text and screenshots in the Windows bitmap format, and generated a PDF file using no compression. I generated a PDF file from the same source file, using compression of text and graphics using the LZW scheme. The uncompressed PDF file was 228217 bytes; with LZW, it was reduced to 42488 bytes, an 80% compression!

While the LZW compression scheme achieves high compression ratios, especially on graphics that have large areas of single colors, such as bitmapped screen shots, it is not suitable for every type of image. In particular, it is not well suited to compressing photographs and images that have a large number of colors in smaller areas; LZW can actually *increase* file size when used on these types of images. You can use the JPEG compression scheme to compress these types of images. JPEG is a *lossy* compression scheme; as it compresses the information, it discards some of it. When you decompress information compressed with JPEG or other lossy compression schemes, detail is lost. In many cases, however, the image has a higher resolution than typical monitor or printer resolutions, and the loss of detail cannot be noticed.

Acrobat gives you five compression options when you use JPEG compression: low, medium-low, medium, medium-high, and high compression. These five options balance compression ratio and the quality of the reconstructed image; the higher the compression, the lower the quality of the reconstructed image. Some examples of a bitmap that has been compressed with each of the five JPEG options can be found in the *Distiller and Images* section of the Distiller chapter.

Compressing Text and Graphics

Acrobat defines line art as (vector) graphics, as opposed to bitmap art, which are images. Unlike bitmaps, vector graphics cannot be compressed with lossy compression schemes. PDFWriter compresses text and line art with the lossless LZW compression scheme. To compress text and graphics:

- Click on the **Compress text and graphics** check box, so that an "x" appears in the box.

Writing PDF Files in ASCII Format

Some transfer methods will mistake certain binary characters in a file for control characters; this can lead to corruption of the file. To avoid this problem, you can direct PDFWriter to write PDF files using only the printable ASCII characters. To write PDF files in ASCII format:

- Click on the **ASCII format** check box, so that an "x" appears in the box.

Compressing Color and Grayscale Images

Unlike Distiller, PDFWriter cannot apply different compression options to color and grayscale images; it applies the same options to both types of images. To compress color and grayscale images:

1. Click on the **Compress using:** drop-down list box in the Color/Grayscale Images frame. A list of compression schemes will appear.
2. Click on the compression scheme you want Acrobat to use to compress color and grayscale images.
3. Click on the **Compress using:** check box, so that an "x" appears in the box.

Compressing Monochrome Images

To compress monochrome images:

1. Click on the **Compress using:** drop-down list box in the "Monochrome Images" frame. A list of compression schemes will appear.
2. Click on the compression scheme you want Acrobat to use to compress color and grayscale images.
3. Click on the **Compress using:** check box, so that an "x" appears in the box.

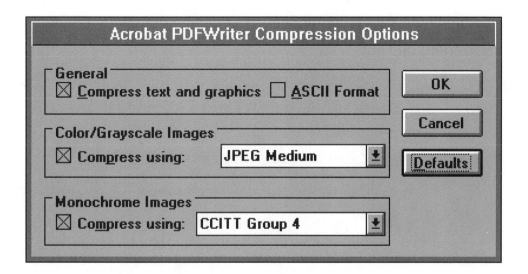

Font Embedding

There may be times when you want to make sure a font is reproduced exactly as it appears on your system. For instance, the substitutions for certain unusual fonts may be unsatisfactory. In these cases, font embedding can be used to make sure the font is exactly recreated. When a font is embedded in a PDF document, all the information about the font is stored in the document, so the font can be recreated on other systems that do not have the font installed. If you do not embed a font in a PDF file, and the font is not available on a system where the document is read, Acrobat will use its font substitution technology to try to recreate the font.

PDFWriter can embed TrueType fonts in a PDF document; Distiller does not have this capability. Unlike Distiller, however, PDFWriter cannot embed Type 1 fonts with the Latin 1 character set in a PDF document; it can only embed "exotic" character sets, such as Cyrillic and Expert. PDFWriter writes a "font descriptor" for ISO Latin Type 1 fonts, which gives the widths of all characters in the font. This means that Exchange and Reader will be forced to use the Adobe Multiple Master fonts as a substitute for PostScript Type 1 fonts if PDFWriter is used to generate the document. With Distiller, you have the option of embedding the Type 1 font, or writing only the font descriptor.

Embedding all Fonts

To embed all the TrueType fonts used in a document:

- Click on the **Embed All Fonts** check box, so that an "x" appears in the box.

Embedding Specific Fonts: The Always Embed List

You use the **Always Embed** list to specify those fonts that you want to embed in PDF documents. If you want to embed fonts in one document only, you can add the font to the **Always Embed** list when you create that document, and then remove it from the list when you create other documents.

Adding Fonts to the Always Embed List

PDFWriter will embed the fonts in the **Always Embed List:** check box. You can only add a font to, or remove a font from the Always Embed List when the **Always Embed List:** check box is checked.

To embed a specific font:

1. Click on the **Always Embed List:** check box, so that an x appears in the box.
2. Highlight the font(s) you want to embed in the **Available Fonts:** list box.
3. Drag the fonts to the **Always Embed List:** list box.

Or

1. Click on the **Always Embed List:** check box, so that an x appears in the box.
2. Highlight the font(s) you want to embed in the **Available Fonts:** list box.

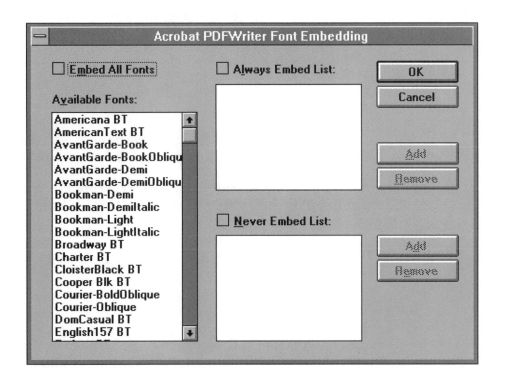

3. Press the **Add** button which is located next to the **Always Embed List:** list box.

Removing Fonts from the Always Embed List

To remove a font from the **Always Embed List:**

1. Click on the **Always Embed List:** check box, so that an x appears in the box.
2. Highlight the font(s) that you want to remove from the **Always Embed List:** list box.
3. Drag the font(s) to the **Available Fonts:** list box.

Or

1. Click on the **Always Embed List:** check box, so that an x appears in the box.
2. Highlight the font(s) that you want to remove from the **Always Embed List:** list box.
3. Press the **Remove** button which is located next to the **Always Embed List:** list box.

Excluding Fonts from Embedding: The Never Embed List

You exclude fonts from embedding by placing them in the **Never Embed** list and checking the **Never Embed List:** check box. Fonts in the **Never Embed** list will not be embedded, even if the **Embed All Fonts** option is on.

Adding Fonts to the Never Embed List

PDFWriter will exclude the fonts in the **Never Embed** list from embedding when the **Never Embed List:** check box is checked. You can only add a font to, or remove a font from the **Never Embed** list when the **Never Embed List:** check box is checked.

To never embed a specific font:

1. Click on the **Never Embed List:** check box, so that an x appears in the box.
2. Highlight the font(s) you want to embed in the **Available Fonts:** list box.
3. Drag the fonts to the **Never Embed List:** list box.

Or

1. Click on the **Never Embed List:** check box, so that an x appears in the box.
2. Highlight the font(s) you want to embed in the **Available Fonts:** list box.
3. Press the **Add** button which is located next to the **Never Embed List:** list box.

Removing Fonts from the Never Embed List

To remove a font from the **Never Embed List:**

1. Click on the **Never Embed List:** check box, so that an x appears in the box.
2. Highlight the font(s) that you want to remove from the **Never Embed List:** list box.
3. Drag the font(s) to the **Available Fonts:** list box.

Or

1. Click on the **Never Embed List:** check box, so that an x appears in the box.
2. Highlight the font(s) that you want to remove from the **Never Embed List:** list box.
3. Press the **Remove** button which is located next to the **Never Embed List:** list box.

Case Study

PDF format allows you to create files that can be browsed and printed on any computer system. This allows organizations to distribute materials electronically and print them where they are used, rather than printing them in a central location and distributing them on paper. In Adobe's case, distributing documents electronically, instead of on paper, reduced their overnight shipping costs.

This case study shows another way Adobe saves money with Acrobat. Rather than shipping paper documents, Adobe employees send PDF documents by email. Since many people prefer to view these documents on the screen, fewer copies of the documents are printed, reducing paper usage and costs.

**From the
KPMG Audit:**
*KPMG analyzed copier
and paper use at
Adobe to see if the
widespread availability
of Acrobat software
was resulting in
reduced demand.
Roger gave us
historical data on both
copier and paper use,
as well as cost per copy
and cost per ream of
paper.*

Finance

Adobe's Shrinking Copier and Paper Costs

KPMG compared copier and paper use for the twelve months ending in June 1994 with the prior twelve month period. Since Adobe's workforce was increasing during this period, we normalized the results by determining per employee use of copying and paper. Based on our analysis, copier use per employee went down 16%, and paper use per employee went down 10%. The figure below shows cost impacts of these reductions.

Reductions in per employee copier and paper use since Acrobat software has been widely available have resulted in an annual savings of nearly $49,000 at current employment levels. Of the total savings, $45,000 is copier savings and $4,000 is paper savings. See the appendix for details of this cost analysis.

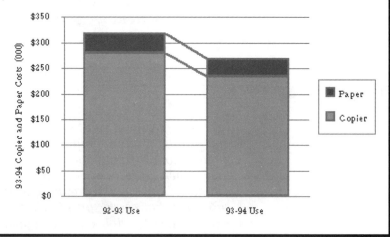

PART 2

Browsing
Interface
Navigating
Zoom
Features
Printing
Clipboard
Preferences
Creating
PDFWriter
PDF Files
Enhancing
Pages
Thumbnails
Bookmarks
Notes
Links
Articles
Web Publishing
Introduction
Getting On
Reader
Author
Publisher
Cool Sites
Advanced
Search
Catalog
Distiller

PDF Files

Managing Files: Choosing Options and Saving Files

Managing the documents you create is a particular concern when the documents are browsed by many people across a network. As a creator of a document, maybe you want to create a security password to open it, or set how a document is displayed when it first opens. Acrobat meets these demands by allowing you to set options when you save a file using Exchange.

In this chapter, you will learn how to:

- Enter Document Information
- Set Open File options
- Save a file
- Set Security Options for a document.

Document Info

PDF documents contain several pieces of information besides the document itself. These pieces of information can be divided into four categories: general information, font information, open information, and security information.

General Info

As discussed in Chapter 7, general information refers to the contents of the document, how it was produced, and when it was produced, including:

- **Title**: The name of the document. The title is different from the document's filename, but you can use a filename as a document's title.

- **Subject**: What the document is about.

- **Author**: The name of the person or organization that created the document.

- **Keywords**: Words that summarize the document's topic or that appear frequently in the document.

- **Creator**: The program used to create the document. This can be any application that can create PostScript files, or use PDFWriter to create a PDF file, such as: a word processor, a spreadsheet, or a presentation graphics program.

General Info

D:\USER\KATE\MAG1.PDF

Title:	
Subject:	
Author:	
Keywords:	
Creator:	Acrobat Capture 1.0b
Producer:	Acrobat PDFWriter 2.0 for Windows
Created:	6/8/95 10:42:03 AM
Modified:	6/9/95 10:16:37 AM

[OK]   [Cancel]

- **Producer**: The program used to create the PDF version of the document, either PDFWriter or Distiller.

- **Created**: The date and time when the PDF file was created.

- **Modified**: The date and time when the PDF file was last modified.

To display general information:

- Select the **Document Info | General** command. Acrobat will display the General Info dialog box.

You can edit the **Title**, **Subject**, **Author**, and **Keywords** fields with Exchange; the other fields cannot be modified.

To modify the fields:

1. Click on the field's edit box.
2. Edit the text in the edit box using your system's editing commands.

These four fields can be indexed with Catalog, and you can search for them with Exchange's indexed Search feature.

To close the General Info dialog box:

- Press the **OK** button.

If you have modified any of the fields in the dialog box, and you do not want the modifications to be recorded, press the **Cancel** button.

Open Info

Version 2.0 of Acrobat allows you to specify how a document will be displayed when it is first opened. The options you can specify include:

- Whether the document is displayed with bookmarks or thumbnails, or is displayed in Full Screen mode

- Which page of the document is displayed

- The magnification that is used to display the document.

To view or edit information about how the document is displayed when it is first opened:

- Select the **Document Info | Open** command. Acrobat will display the Open Info dialog box.

To change how the document is displayed, use the radio buttons in the **Show** frame:

- Click on the **Page Only** radio button to display the document page only

- Click on the **Bookmarks and Page** radio button to display the document page and bookmarks. This produces the same effect selecting the **View | Bookmarks and Page** command.

- Click on the **Thumbnails and Page** radio button to display the document page and

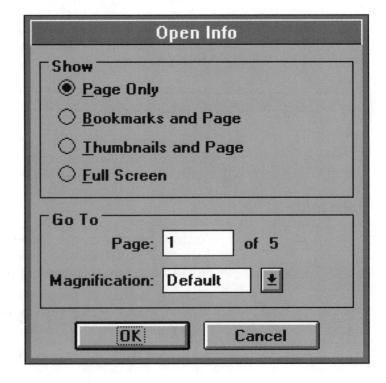

thumbnails. This produces the same effect as selecting the **View | Thumbnails** and **Page** command.

- Click on the **Full Screen** radio button to display the document in Full Screen mode.

To specify which page of the document will be displayed when the document is opened:

- Enter the page number in the **Page** edit box.

To specify the magnification Acrobat will use to display the document when it is first opened:

1. Click on the **Magnification:** drop-down list box. A list of magnification levels will appear.
2. Click on the magnification level you want Acrobat to use to display the document when it is first opened.

To close the Open Info dialog box:

1. Press the **OK** button. If you have modified any of the information in the dialog box, and you do not want the modifications to be recorded, press the **Cancel** button.

Security Info

Version 2.0 of Acrobat allows you to specify several security features for a document, including password protection and permission to print.

Security information is set when you save a file. To edit these options, use the **File | Save As...** command which is discussed in the next section of this chapter.

Saving a File

To save a file:

- Select the **File | Save** command.

If the file has a name, Exchange will save the file. If the file doesn't have a name, the Save As dialog box will appear. For information about the controls of the

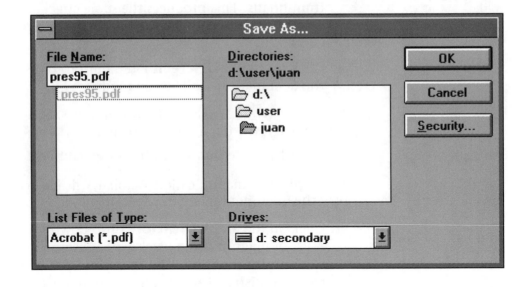

Save As dialog box, see the Saving a File Under Another Name section of this chapter.

If the current file is a read-only file, the **File | Save** command will be disabled.

When you try to close a file that has unsaved changes, Exchange will ask you if you want to save the changes. If you want to save the changes, press the **Yes** button; if you want to close the file without saving the changes, press the **No** button; if you decide not to close the file, press the **Cancel** button.

Saving a File Under Another Name

To save a file under another name:

1. Select the **File | Save As** command. When you select the **File | Save As** command, Exchange displays the Save As dialog box.
2. Use the controls of the Save As dialog box to specify the file's drive, directory, and filename.
3. Press the **OK** button. If you decide you do not want to save the file, press the **Cancel** button.

To save the file on a different drive:

1. Click on the **Drives:** drop-down list box. A list of the available drives will appear.

2. Double click on the drive name. The dialog box will then display the directory tree of the new drive in the **Directories:** list box and a list of the files in the new default directory in the **Files:** list box.

To select a directory to save the file in:

- Double click on the directory names in the **Directories:** list box.

To give the file a name:

- Enter the name of the file in the **File Name:** edit box, then press either the **<Enter>** key or the **OK** button.

You can specify that the file be saved as a PDF file, with the .pdf extension, or you can save the file with another extension. In either case, Exchange will write the file in the PDF format. If you do not give the file an extension, Exchange will give it the .pdf extension by default.

If the filename you specify already exists, Exchange will ask you if you want to overwrite the existing file. If you want to overwrite the file, press the **Yes** button; if you do not want to overwrite the file, press the **No** button.

File Security Options

As the number of sensitive electronic documents increases, the security of these documents becomes a greater concern. Unlike paper documents, there are no physical boundaries to keep prying eyes from electronic documents, and if a sensitive document falls into the wrong hands, the advantage of rapid electronic distribution becomes a liability; a sensitive document can be copied and distributed worldwide in seconds.

Electronic documents can also be changed without any visible traces; unlike a paper document, a PDF document will have no marks on its pages if it has been accidentally or deliberately modified. This has become a concern for PDF documents, since the latest version of Adobe's Illustrator program now supports limited editing of PDF documents.

To make PDF a viable format for sensitive documents, Adobe has added several security features to version 2.0. You can:

- Require a password to open a PDF document to keep unauthorized persons from looking at it

- Prevent Acrobat from printing a document or copying any information in the document to the Clipboard, to reduce the risk that unsecure copies of the document will be made

- Prevent people that view PDF documents from changing them.

Unfortunately, Acrobat's Print security features are easily circumvented, if the aim is simply to make a copy of the information the document contains. Illicit copies of the contents of PDF documents can be made by capturing the screen of the Acrobat or Exchange application when the file is being viewed. For instance, in Windows, any active window, including the Reader and Exchange application windows, can be stored in the Clipboard as a bitmap by pressing **<Alt> + <Print Screen>**. While the screen capture would be at a low, fixed resolution, and it would not have any of the intelligence of a PDF file, the contents of the document would be visible and printable. You should take this into account when distributing PDF files that contain sensitive information, and use caution when distributing such a document.

You set security options by selecting the **File | Save As** command, and pressing the **Security** button that appears on the Save As... dialog box. Acrobat then displays the Security dialog box. Use the controls of this dialog box to set the security options. If a password for changing security options has previously been set for the document, Acrobat will display the Password dialog box which prompts you to enter the password.

To enter the password:

1. Type the password in the **Password:** edit box.
2. Press the **OK** button. If you decide you don't want to change the document's security options, press the **Cancel** button.

Once you give a document's password for changing security options, you can change the security options for the document as many times as you wish without reentering the password.

To specify the password required to open the document:

1. Enter the password in the **Open the Document:** edit field. To prevent anyone else from seeing your password as you type it, Exchange will not display the characters you enter; instead, it will display an asterisk (*) for each character you type.
2. Press the **OK** button. Exchange will ask you to confirm the password by typing it again.
3. Type the password again in the **Confirm Password To Open the Document**: edit field dialog box.
4. Press the **OK** button. If you decide not to change the password, press the **Cancel** button.

To specify the password required to change security options:

1. Enter the password in the **Change Security Options**: edit field. To prevent anyone else from

---

Security

Specify Password To

Open the Document:

Change Security Options:

Do Not Allow

☐ Printing

☐ Changing the Document

☐ Selecting Text and Graphics

☐ Adding or Changing Notes

OK   Cancel

seeing your password as you type it, Exchange will not display the characters you enter; instead it will display an asterisk (*) for each character you type.

2. Press the **OK** button. Exchange will ask you to confirm the password by typing it again.

3. Type the password again in the **Confirm Password To Change Security Options**: edit field dialog box.

4. Press the **OK** button. If you decide not to change the password, press the **Cancel** button.

The Security dialog box contains four check boxes in the **Do Not Allow** frame that correspond to user actions: **Printing**, **Changing the Document**, **Selecting Text and Graphics**, and **Adding or Changing Notes**. To prevent people who view the document from doing any of those four things, click on the appropriate check box. Exchange will disable the toolbar buttons and commands that perform those actions.

Case Study

Distributing PDF files electronically results in significant time-savings. The time required to copy, collate, bind and distribute is often a surprisingly large cost hidden by the difficulties of tracking or auditing time.

From the
KPMG Audit:
KPMG interviewed Andy concerning Acrobat sofware's impact on engineering management. Andy's major Acrobat application is distributing the engineering project status report which tracks the progress of over 100 Adobe development efforts.

Engineering
Distributing the Engineering Project Status Report

The project data is stored in a database from which the 300-page status report is generated. The report is then distilled into PDF and bookmarked. Because of the sensitive nature of the report, it is made available to a closed list of 50 people for distribution, of which 12 printed copies are required. The entire process now requires one day.

Prior to using Acrobat software, an administrative assistant had to obtain hard copies of individual reports from every project manager. The administrative assistant then had to manually create an index, place the index and reports in a large binder, and have 50 copies of the full report made and distributed. This process required five work days to complete.

III

ENHANCING
Interactive
Documents

*Enhancing PDF
with Acrobat Exchange*

Manipulating Pages in an Interactive Document

One of the benefits of Acrobat is that the pages of a PDF document can be produced using almost any application, allowing you to choose the application best suited to creating the document. You can then use Acrobat Exchange's Page commands to tie together pages from different sources into one unified document. Also, you can easily create new documents by taking pages from one or more existing documents and rearranging them with the Page commands.

In this chapter, you learn how to:

- Insert pages from one PDF document into another
- Delete pages from a document
- Rotate pages
- Crop pages
- Replace pages from one document with pages from a second document
- Extract pages from a document to create a new document.

The narrative in this chapter describes how workgroups at a fictional financial services company can use the Page features of Acrobat to prepare a research report.

Mary, an analyst for a financial services firm, is responsible for tracking the performance of several stocks in the telecommunications industry and making buy, sell, or hold recommendations.

When a company's performance indicates its status should change, Mary and her staff prepare a report that gives an overview of the company and its performance, an analysis of the reasons for the change in status, and several charts and graphs that give a visual representation of the data.

Usually, Mary asks one member of her staff to prepare the overview material, assigns the task of creating the graphs to another staff member, and writes the analysis material herself. While Mary uses a Macintosh to do her work, the rest of the staff use PCs.

After Mary's staff members complete their sections of the report, they convert them into PDF files and submit them. Mary then uses Acrobat Exchange to combine the separate sections into one document.

Inserting Pages

To insert pages from one PDF file into another, select the **Edit | Pages | Insert** command. A dialog box appears. You use the controls of the dialog box to select the file to insert.

Selecting the File to Insert (Windows)

To select a file on a different drive, click on the **Drives:** drop-down list box. A list of the available drives will appear. Double click on the drive name. The dialog box will then display the directory tree of the new drive in the **Directories:** list box and a list of the files in the new default directory in the **Files:** list box. To move up and down the directory tree, double click on the directory names in the **Directories:** list box.

To select a file, double click on its name in the **Files:** list box, click on its name and press the **Select** but-

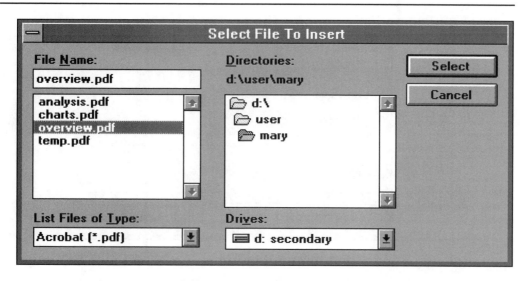

ton, or enter the name of the file in the **File Name:** edit box and press Enter.

 In Windows, you can ask the dialog box to list files that have the .pdf extension only, or to list files with any extension. Acrobat Exchange displays files with the .pdf extension by default. To switch between displaying files with the .pdf extension and all files, click on the **List Files of Type:** drop-down list box, and then double click on the file specification.

When you have specified the file that you want to insert into the document, press the **Select** button or press the **Enter** key. If you decide you do not want to insert the contents of the file, press the **Cancel** button or press the **Escape** key.

Specifying Where to Place the File

Once you have selected the file you want to insert, specify where you want to place its contents. Another dialog box appears with controls that specify where Acrobat will place the file.

You can place the contents of a file before or after any page in the document by clicking on the **Before** or **After** radio buttons. You specify the page using the **First** or **Last** radio buttons, or the **Page:** radio but-

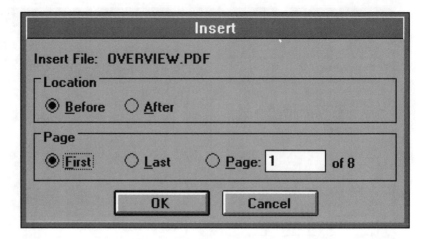

ton and its associated edit box. By default, Exchange sets the controls to place the contents of the file after the current page of the document.

When you have specified where you want to place the file, press the **OK** button or press the **Enter** key. If you decide you do not want to insert the contents of the file, press the **Cancel** button or press the **Escape** key. When Exchange inserts the file, the first page of the inserted file becomes the current page of the document.

*Mary wants to place the contents of the overview.pdf file before her analysis material, so she clicks the **Before** and **First** radio buttons, and then presses the **OK** button. Exchange inserts the analysis material into her document.*

*Mary repeats the process for the graphs and charts, placing the charts.pdf file after the analysis material by clicking the **After** and **Last** radio buttons and then pressing the **OK** button.*

After inserting the overview material in the beginning of the document, Mary places the charts and graphs at the end of the document. The staff member who prepared the charts made two versions of the material, on two separate pages, and placed a note on the document asking Mary to choose the format she prefers. Acrobat Exchange inserts entire files, rather than individual pages, so Mary inserts both pages into her document, and then deletes one of the pages.

Deleting Pages

You delete pages with the **Edit | Pages | Delete** command. When you select this command, a dialog box appears. You use the controls of the dialog box to delete pages.

Specifying a Range of Pages

You can delete one or more consecutive pages at a time. To specify a range of pages to delete, enter the beginning and ending page numbers in the **From:** and **To:** edit fields in the dialog box. By default, Exchange sets the controls to delete the current page of the document. You cannot delete every page of the document. If you attempt to do so, Acrobat Exchange will display an error message.

When you have specified which pages to delete, press the **OK** button or press the **Enter** key.

If you decide you do not want to delete the pages, press the **Cancel** button or press the **Escape** key. When Exchange deletes the pages, the page that followed the deleted pages becomes the current page of the document. If you delete the last page of the document, the page that preceded the deleted pages becomes the current page of the document.

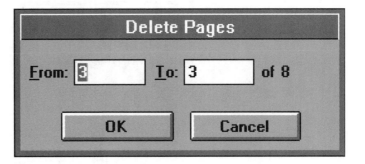

You will be given a final chance to confirm the pages you are deleting.

*Mary wants to delete the first of the two pages she inserted, so she enters 3 in the **From:** edit box and 3 in the **To:** edit box, and presses the **OK** button. Acrobat asks for confirmation before deleting pages, so Mary presses the **Yes** button in the dialog box that appears.*

Mary's co-worker printed the page of charts and graphs that Mary chose in landscape format, so she needs to rotate it to fit with the rest of the document.

Rotating Pages

You rotate pages with the **Edit | Pages | Rotate** command. When you select this command, a dialog box appears. You use the controls of the dialog box to rotate pages.

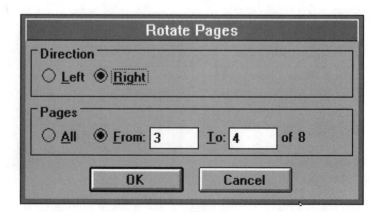

Methods of Rotating Pages

You can rotate pages in 90 degree increments, either to the left (counterclockwise), or to the right (clockwise). You can rotate every page of the document at once, or you can specify a range of pages. You specify the direction of rotation by clicking on the **Left** or **Right** radio buttons. The Page range is specified by clicking on the **All** radio button, or by clicking on the **From:** radio button and entering the page range limits in the edit boxes to the right of the radio button. Acrobat sets the controls of the dialog box to rotate the current page 90 degrees to the left by default.

When you have specified how to rotate the pages, press the **OK** button or press the **Enter** key. If you decide you do not want to rotate the pages, press the **Cancel** button or press the **Escape** key.

You will be given a final chance to confirm the pages you are rotating.

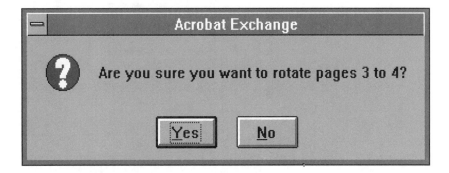

*Mary wants to rotate the charts and graphs to the right by 90 degrees, so she clicks on the **Right** radio button and presses the **OK** button. Acrobat offered to rotate the current page by default, so Mary did not have to specify the page to rotate. Acrobat asks for confirmation of page rotations, so Mary presses the **Yes** button in the dialog box that appears.*

As Mary takes a closer look at the document, she discovers that the overview page has larger margins than the other pages. She decides to crop the page to remove some white space.

Cropping Pages

You crop pages with the **Edit | Pages | Crop** command. When you select the command, a dialog box appears. You use the controls of the dialog box to specify which pages Exchange will crop and how much it will remove from each edge of the pages. The left, right, top, or bottom of pages can be cropped in any combination. You can crop all of the pages, or a range of consecutive pages.

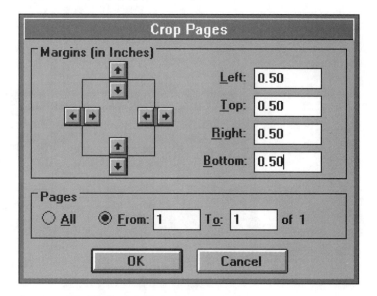

Using the Four Scroll Bars

The Crop Pages dialog box contains four scroll bars to adjust the margins, arranged on a rectangle that represents a page. There is one set of buttons each for the left, right, top, and bottom margins. The scroll bars are arranged so that you click on the button that moves the border of the page in the direction you want. For example, if you want to crop the top of a page, you click on the down arrow of the vertical scroll bar at the top of the rectangle.

Specifying the Exact Margin

You can also crop a margin by specifying the exact amount to be cropped in the edit box that corresponds to the margin. For example, the top of a page can be cropped by entering 0.10 in the **Top:** edit box. The length units used to express the crop amounts are selected with the **Edit | Preferences | General** command. Lengths may be expressed in points, inches, or millimeters.

As you adjust the amount that each margin will be cropped, crop lines appear on the current page, displaying the location of the edge of the page if the crops are made. These crop lines will appear whether or not the current page has been specified in the page range to be cropped.

Acrobat does not "cut off" the edges of a page it crops. Instead, it changes the size of a "window onto the page." This window is what you see when you view the page with Acrobat Exchange or Reader. When the page is not cropped, the window is the size of the page itself; when the page is cropped, the window is smaller.

Acrobat automatically senses the registration marks used by printers and publishers to mark the extent of a page, and crops the page accordingly. If Acrobat Distiller or PDFWriter are used to produce PDF files of pages that contain registration marks, the PDF file will contain the cropping information, and Acrobat Exchange and Reader will crop the page at the marks. You can display the area beyond the registration marks by reducing the size of the crops with the **Edit | Pages | Crop** command.

Specifying the Page Range

You specify the Page range by clicking on the **All** radio button, or by clicking on the **From:** radio button and entering the page range limits in the edit boxes to the right of the radio button. Exchange sets the controls of the dialog box to crop the current page by default.

When you have specified the page range and the amount to crop each margin, press the **OK** button or press the **Enter** key. If you decide you do not want to crop the pages, press the **Cancel** button or press the **Escape** key.

You will be given a final chance to confirm the pages you are cropping.

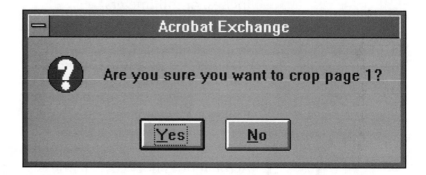

Tech Note

You cannot increase the size of pages with the **Edit | Pages | Crop** command, but a page that has been cropped can be restored to its original size.

Mary wants to remove one-half inch from each of the margins on the page of charts, so she enters 0.50 in the **Left**, **Top**, **Right**, *and* **Bottom** *edit boxes, and then presses the* **OK** *button. Acrobat offered to crop the current page by default, so Mary did not have to specify the page to crop.*

Acrobat asks for confirmation before cropping pages, so Mary presses the **Yes** *button in the dialog box that appears.*

After looking over the document she has assembled, Mary decides to include the page of charts she deleted from the document earlier instead of the current one. Mary could do this by deleting the page that is currently in the document, inserting the charts PDF file, and deleting the page she does not want; but there is a better way. Using the **Edit | Pages | Replace** *command, Mary can replace the page she no longer wants with the other page in one operation. In addition, as we will discuss in a later chapter, all hyper-*

links she created on the current page will be retained when it is replaced with the new one.

Replacing Pages

The **Edit | Pages | Replace** command takes pages from a file that you select and replaces pages in the current file with those pages. The name of the file that will be the source of the new pages is called the source file; the file whose pages will be replaced by those of the source file is called the target file.

When you select the **Edit | Pages | Replace** command, a dialog box appears. You use the controls of the dialog box to select the source file. The controls of this dialog box are identical to those of the file selection box displayed by the **Edit | Pages | Insert** command; see the "Inserting Pages" section of this chapter for an explanation of how the dialog box controls work.

Once you have selected the source file, you specify which pages of the target file to replace, and which pages of the source file will replace them. Another dialog box appears with controls that specify the page ranges for the source and target files.

Replace Pages

Original

Replace Pages: `3` **T**o: `3` of 8

In "ANALYSIS.PDF"

Replacement

With Pages: `1` To: 1 of 8

From "CHARTS.PDF"

[OK] [Cancel]

You specify which pages of the target file to replace by entering values in the **Replace Pages:** and **To:** edit boxes. You specify the pages that will replace them by entering values in the **With Pages:** edit box. By default, Exchange sets the controls to replace the current page of the target file with the first page of the source file.

Matching the Page Range

The **Edit | Pages | Replace** command always replaces consecutive pages in the target file with the same number of consecutive pages from the source file. Acrobat Exchange keeps track of the size of the page ranges you specify; if you change the size of a range, it adjusts the ranges automatically.

When you have specified the page ranges, press the **OK** button or press the **Enter** key. If you decide you do not want to replace the pages, press the **Cancel** button or press the **Escape** key. When Exchange replaces the pages, the first new page becomes the current page of the document.

*Mary wants to replace page three of the target document with page one of the source document. Acrobat Exchange sets the dialog box controls to do this by default, so Mary presses the **OK** button.*

Before Acrobat, Mary would print out the final analysis document and submit it for printing. When it was printed, the company would bundle it with other company docu-

ments in a weekly mailing that would be distributed to all the company's sales offices by first-class mail. Delays in the printing and mailing process often meant that the company's brokers did not have access to the document until nearly two weeks after it was completed. Now, when Mary finishes the document, she places it on a server on her company's wide-area network, and sends E-mail messages to the company's sales offices informing them of its location. The company's brokers have immediate access to the document through the network, and can read it on the different computer platforms used in the company.

David, a broker in the company's San Francisco office, sees the message about the new document later that same day. He downloads the document from the WAN server to his Macintosh and looks over the report. Because downloads from the server are occasionally slow, David likes to keep copies of these reports on his local disk, but keeping copies of them in their entirety is unnecessary. David's solution is to extract the analysis page from the PDF file, save it, and discard the rest of the information. That way, he keeps the conclusions of the report handy; if he needs more information later, he can download the file from the server again.

Extracting Pages

To extract pages from a PDF file, select the **Edit | Pages | Extract** command. To select the file to insert, you use the controls of the **Extract** command's dialog box.

You can extract one or more consecutive pages at a time, and you can delete the pages from the current

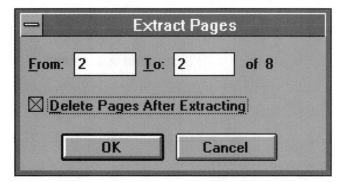

document after you extract them. To specify a range of pages to extract, enter the beginning and ending page numbers in the **From:** and **To:** edit fields in the dialog box. To specify whether or not to delete the pages from the original document, click on the **Delete Pages After Extracting** check box. By default, Exchange sets the controls to extract the current page of the document without deleting it.

If you ask Exchange to delete the extracted pages, Exchange asks for confirmation of the command.

You cannot delete every page of the document. If you attempt to do so, Acrobat Exchange will display an error message.

*David wants to extract the analysis page of the document but he does not want to delete the page from the original document, so he presses the **OK** button. Acrobat offers to extract the analysis page by default, since it is the current page, so David does not have to specify the page range.*

After extracting the pages, Acrobat Exchange opens a new document window, titled Pages from Filename-2, that contains the extracted pages. This new document is a distinct PDF file that you can alter, save, or discard.

David saves the file containing the extracted page and deletes the original report when he closes Acrobat Exchange.

Saving Money Managers Time and Money

Institutional money managers around the world have historically relied on a flood of hard-copy research reports developed by brokerage firms on companies, industries, and market trends to make critical investment decisions. First Call Corporation, a Thomson Financial Services company, found a way to give money managers "just-in-time," searchable equity research information that provides them with a more efficient way to manage this research. The company created First Call® RESEARCH DIRECT™, a new service that uses Adobe Acrobat software as one of the enabling technologies to distribute these research reports electronically.

"First Call RESEARCH DIRECT and Adobe Acrobat give money managers the research they want, when they want it, in a way they can use it," says Carolyn Mattimore, vice president of marketing and product development for First Call. "It enables money managers to make better decisions based on easier and more timely access to the information they need. Electronic distribution using Acrobat software provides a better way to manage the research—saving institutional money managers and brokerage firms time, money, and storage space."

As publishers of research reports, brokerage firms typically spend millions of dollars per year on printing and distribution. Using RESEARCH DIRECT, brokerage firms expect to reduce these costs and improve communication with their institutional clients by providing quick, easy access to up-to-date information without the time and money spent on hard-copy reports.

High-quality Reporting

According to Mattimore, distribution of reports as Acrobat Portable Document Format (PDF) files was responsible for much of the popularity of RESEARCH DIRECT. "This is the first time that we could offer the exact look, feel, and quality of original research reports," she says. "There was little demand for electronic reporting previously, because electronic reports differed substantially from the original hard-copy reports. Now that reports are distributed as PDF files, brokers are happy that their distinguishing corporate marks are apparent within the reports, and the clients are comfortable replacing their paper reports with electronic versions because they look just like what they were used to getting in hard copy."

Bruce Benedict, managing director at C.J. Lawrence Deutsche Bank Securities Corporation and one of the contributing brokerage firms, says, "Because of the significant benefit it will deliver to institutions, I believe RESEARCH DIRECT is the way research distribution will be done in the future."

Warren Shaw, head of equity management and managing director of Chancellor Capital Management, agrees. "As one of the pilot users of RESEARCH DIRECT, our team of portfolio managers and research analysts find the system to be an extremely valuable research tool," he says. "We believe that RESEARCH DIRECT will become as integral a part of our investment process as First Call Research Notes are today." First Call RESEARCH DIRECT is now being used at 50 institutional investment sites around the world.

First Call RESEARCH DIRECT uses Adobe Acrobat software to provide cross-platform viewing, navigation, and printing of electronic research reports. Says Roland Beaulieu, executive vice president of First Call and senior vice president of operations and technology for Thomson Financial Services, "We looked at many different options but selected Adobe Acrobat software because its Portable Document Format is an emerging, open standard. Some of the brokerage firms contributing research to the network had already standardized on Acrobat, so it was the natural choice."

Timely Access to Critical Data

Brokerage firms create the electronic reports, as they did the hard-copy reports, on PCs, Apple® Macintosh® computers, or UNIX® workstations using applications such as Microsoft® Word, FrameMaker,® and WordPerfect®. They then convert research reports into PDF files and send them over a network to one of several computers at First Call RESEARCH DIRECT. Subscribers store the most recent three to four weeks of market information on a local server, and less recent research is made available from the main database via a wide area network.

Now, instead of relying on paper documents that can take five to seven days to receive by mail, institutional investors have immediate access to real-time research information. Since reports are now PDF files, storing, retrieving, and searching the data is a more efficient process. RESEARCH DIRECT enables money managers to search on several criteria and to be alerted to new documents on the companies, industries and subjects they follow most. Money managers then use Adobe Acrobat to navigate through the reports.

Time and Money Saved; Productivity Improved

"The beauty of RESEARCH DIRECT is that we are solving a real need for investors," says Mattimore. "Money managers can set up their own specific profiles so that they can receive, retrieve, store, search, print, and obtain alerts about only those reports that interest them. This saves them an incredible amount of time and makes them more productive in their jobs."

"Not only will First Call RESEARCH DIRECT yield a reduction in printing and mailing costs, but it will also dramatically improve communications between research brokers and their customers—the institutional investors—by increasing critical research shelf life and usability," says Beaulieu.

CHAPTER

11

Thumbnails

Using Small-scale Document Views

Thumbnails are miniature page views; they provide a convenient way to view and manipulate pages, and to navigate through a document.

In this chapter, you learn how to:

- Create thumbnails
- Move pages using thumbnails
- Copy pages using thumbnails
- Replace pages using thumbnails
- Delete pages using thumbnails.

In this chapter, we also present a fictional example of how an executive of an advertising firm can use thumbnails to help him create a presentation for the company's financial backers.

Juan is an exec in a growing advertising firm. His responsibilities include periodic meetings with bankers to discuss the firm's performance. For the next meeting, he will create a presentation that contains information from the firm's annual report and several items from the firm's portfolio. Since a large portion of the presentation will consist of graphically-rich pages from other documents, Juan will make extensive use of Acrobat's thumbnail features.

Juan makes a copy of the annual report to use as the basis of his presentation and names it "pres_95.pdf."

Juan knows that the bankers will be most interested in the charts and graphs that illustrate the company's financial performance; the thumbnails of these pages stand out from the rest of the document. Rather than scroll through the pages of the report, Juan uses the **Thumbnails and Page** *toolbar button to display the report's thumbnails, then clicks on the first page of the graphs to move directly to it.*

Displaying Thumbnails

To view a document's thumbnails:

- Press the **Thumbnails and Page** toolbar button.

Or

- Select the **View | Thumbnails and Page** command. Acrobat will display the thumbnails on the left side of the active document's document window.

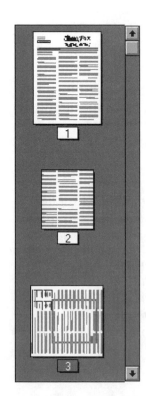

When you display a document's thumbnails, the current page view is marked with a rectangle on the thumbnail representing the current page; this rectangle is called the *page-view box*. A *page number box* appears below each thumbnail; the current page's thumbnail page number box has a gray background and the others are white.

If thumbnails do not exist for some or all of the pages of a document, they will be displayed as grey boxes. You can navigate and manage pages with these "placeholder" thumbnails as if they were thumbnails with page views.

Thumbnails of pages up to 11" x 11" are sized proportionally. Thumbnails of pages that are larger than 11" x 11" are scaled the size of a thumbnail of an 11" x 11" page; Acrobat places an asterisk in the page number box of thumbnails that it scales to a smaller size.

You can use thumbnails to do the same things you can do with Acrobat's navigation and magnification tools: move from page to page, select which portion of a page you view, and change the magnification of a page.

Next, Juan opens a file that contains all of the materials for a large advertising campaign. Among the contents of the file are charts and tables with demographic information, spreadsheets with budget information, and the final ad pages. The file does not have any thumbnails. Juan uses the **Edit | Thumbnails | Create All...** *command to create them so he can save time browsing the document.*

Creating Thumbnails

To create thumbnails, select the **Edit | Thumbnails | Create All...** command; if you are using Short Menus, select the **View | Full Menus** command first. Exchange will display a dialog box that displays its progress. If thumbnails already exist for certain pages of the document, Exchange will skip them.

If Exchange is creating thumbnails, and you want it to stop, press the **Cancel** button of the dialog box.

Adding thumbnails to your document can increase its size substantially. As an example, a document that was 104647 bytes without thumbnails increased in size to 122682 bytes after thumbnails were created, a 17% increase.

Tech Note

You can also create thumbnails as you distill a document with Distiller; for more information see Chapter 23.

Managing Pages Using Thumbnails

Adobe added page management features to thumbnails in version 2.0 of Exchange. You can use thumbnails to move, copy, replace, and delete pages in a document.

Selecting Thumbnails for Operations

To select a single thumbnail, click on the page number box.

To select several thumbnails simultaneously:

1. Click on the thumbnail area.
2. Drag to draw a rectangle around the pages you want to select.
3. Release the mouse button.

Exchange will mark all the pages that are wholly or partially inside the rectangle.

Or, you can:

1. Press and hold the **<Shift >** key.
2. Click on the page number boxes of the thumbnails you want to select, while keeping the **<Shift>** key pressed.

Juan needs to copy pages from a document that is being created for a current campaign. Lisa, the account manager in charge of the project, puts a write-protected copy on-line for him.

Juan uses the thumbnails to copy pages of Lisa's file and inserts them into the presentation.

As Juan reviews the presentation, he decides to reorganize it. Thumbnails help Juan to arrange the pages of his presentation simply and efficiently.

Moving Pages Using Thumbnails

To move pages using thumbnails:

1. Select the pages you want to move.
2. Click on the page number box of one of the selected pages; a page icon will appear at the mouse cursor.
3. Move the mouse cursor to the location to which you want the pages to be moved. As you move the cursor, Exchange will display a black bar to indicate where the page will be placed. This location can be a location in the current document, or it can be a location in another document (in which case you move the mouse cursor to that document's window).
4. Release the mouse button when the black bar is in the position where you want to place the pages.

Exchange will move the pages to the location that you selected. If you move the pages to another document, Exchange will keep the pages in the original document as well.

Copying Pages Using Thumbnails

To copy pages using thumbnails:

1. Select the pages you want to copy.
2. Click on the page number box of one of the selected pages; a page icon will appear at the mouse cursor.
3. Press and hold the **<Ctrl>** key; a plus sign will appear in the page icon at the mouse cursor.
4. Keeping the **<Ctrl>** key pressed, move the mouse cursor to the location where you want the copied pages to be placed. This location can be a location in the current document, or it can be a location in another document (in which case you move the mouse cursor to that document's window).
5. Release the mouse button.

Exchange will copy the pages to the location that you selected.

Marcia spoke with Juan at their morning meeting and mentioned that she has some documents from previous ad campaigns that may make his report more complete.

As Juan reviews the material, he discovers that the information is more useful than some of the other data that he had already included. He decides to replace some of the old material with the new pages he found in Marcia's documents.

He quickly selects and replaces the pages using the thumbnails, but finds that he has an extra page of redundant material. Juan uses the thumbnail of the page to delete the page from the document.

Replacing Pages Using Thumbnails

To replace pages:

1. Select the pages you want to replace the other pages with.
2. Click on the page number box of one of the selected pages; a page icon will appear at the mouse cursor.

3. Press and hold the **<Ctrl>** key; a plus sign will appear in the page icon at the mouse cursor.
4. Keeping the **<Ctrl>** key pressed, move the mouse cursor to the page number box of the first page you want to replace; Exchange will display an "R" in the page icon at the mouse cursor and draw the pages that will be replaced in inverse video. The replaced pages can be in the current document, or they can be in another document (in which case you move the mouse cursor to that document's window).
5. Release the mouse button.

Tech Note

Exchange can use non-consecutive pages as the source for a replacement, but can only replace consecutive pages. Exchange will only perform one-for-one replacements; the numbers of source and target pages will be the same.

Deleting Pages Using Thumbnails

To delete a single page from a document:

1. Click on the page number box of the page's thumbnail.
2. Press the **<Delete>** key. Exchange will display a rectangle around the thumbnail to indicate that it has been selected.

To delete more than one page from a document:

1. Press and hold the **<Shift >** key while clicking on the page number boxes of the thumbnails of the pages you want to delete.
2. Press the **<Delete>** key.

When you press the **<Delete>** key, Exchange will ask you to confirm the deletion, press the **Yes** button to delete the pages, or press the **No** button to cancel the deletion.

When Juan finishes creating his presentation, he stores two copies of the file: one on the company's network and one on his notebook computer. Since space on his notebook's hard drive is limited, Juan deletes the thumbnails from the copy that he saves on it; he can regenerate the thumbnails quickly when he meets with the bankers.

Deleting Thumbnails

To delete every thumbnail in the document, select the **Edit | Thumbnails | Delete All...** command. Exchange will ask you to confirm the command; delete the thumbnails by pressing the **Yes** button in the dialog box that appears, or cancel the deletion by pressing the **No** button.

When you rotate or crop pages, their thumbnails are deleted.

Improving Customer Relationships by Making Clients an Integral Part of the Creative Process

To improve customer service and streamline production processes, the Buck & Pulleyn advertising agency teamed up with a client to reengineer its process for bringing sales literature and brochures from concept to print. Adobe Acrobat software plays a key part in this collaboration and the result is lower costs, fewer meetings, improved time to market and greater customer satisfaction.

Eastman Kodak Company's marketing communications department initiated the idea for a reengineering project and decided to beta test it with a task force that comprised Buck & Pulleyn, Kodak print production, a local printer, and a business process reengineering consultant. Says Dick Patterson, communications director for Kodak Professional and Printing Imaging, "Acrobat is a key technology that has facilitated this new process by enabling a much higher frequency of communication."

Buck & Pulleyn is a 52-person, full-service, business-to-business advertising agency serving the needs of clients such as Bausch & Lomb, Eastman Kodak, Seneca Foods, and Xerox. The firm invested heavily in technology—currently having a network of 70 PCs running Microsoft® Windows™ for Workgroups—to find new ways to improve client service and boost productivity. "We have a lot of sophisticated technology," says Cathy Rubino Hines, account supervisor at Buck & Pulleyn and co-leader of the task force, "but we were not using it to shorten the lengthy routing and approval process. Before Acrobat, we set up meetings or messengered layouts and copy to clients. This process was very expensive, inefficient, and time consuming."

Challenge: An Integrated, Cost-effective Review Process

The goals of the task force were aggressive: cut production time by 50 percent, reduce costs by 30 percent, ensure profitability for agency partners, and preserve or improve the firm's well-known quality of work and service.

Each step in the creative and production processes was examined, and the task force immediately discovered that everyone on the team—the agency, the client, and outside vendors—worked in a vacuum. "Ours was not a collaborative effort. Each group had its own process, and groups often duplicated efforts," says Dick VanGaasbeck, Buck & Pulleyn's technical director.

Solution: Electronic Design Review

The task force decided it was essential to expose clients and outside vendors to creative concepts early on to get feedback during the process. The agency now converts concepts and production comps (mechanicals) into the Adobe Acrobat software Portable Document Format (PDF) and then sends PDF files to members of the team via CompuServe® or posts them internally on Microsoft Mail. With Acrobat, all team members can access PDF files at any time. Electronic proofs—frequently including specialty fonts—can be routed without requiring the recipient to have the exact software or fonts used to create the piece.

The agency chose Acrobat primarily because of its annotation capabilities. "We need two-way communication and the ability to capture comments in context," says VanGaasbeck.

"Acrobat helps us keep control of the process," says Hines. "We can maintain the integrity of the creative comp [copy and layout] and still let everyone make comments."

Benefit: Reduced Costs and Faster Time to Market

According to Hines, the results of the new electronic process using Acrobat are "phenomenal." Working with Kodak, the agency completed two full-color sell sheets and achieved its 50 percent time-reduction goal. "Even though we are still in the pilot phase," says Hines, "we have met our time-savings goal and are working for the rest of this year to track our complete cost savings." Time is saved, in part, because the process of reaching consensus during the concept phase is now quicker. "By getting clients' early, active involvement, the concept becomes their idea," says VanGaasbeck. "We all buy into the ideas and reach consensus more quickly, because the finished concept combines everyone's thoughts."

A Collaborative Effort

The new electronic process eliminates duplication of effort and promotes easy collaboration during the concept and proofing phases. "By sending PDF files through e-mail, we can route files swiftly to all team members," says VanGaasbeck. "E-mail has a greater sense of urgency than hard-copy, so people respond to it earlier. In addition, we collaborate easily and effectively, even though we might be separated physically."

The final production phase is also much smoother. Says VanGaasbeck, "Our printers are more efficient. They know the details of a job right from the beginning, preventing last-minute surprises that could result in a delay or costly reprint.

Kodak is equally enthusiastic. "As the program sponsor, we immediately saw the merits of this reengineering effort in reducing excessive time and money spent while still ensuring quality results," says Marianne Samenko, manager of marketing communications for Kodak Professional and Printing Imaging in the U.S.A. and Canada.

"It is a thrill to be able to visualize a job early on, in spite of the fact that we use the Macintosh® and Buck & Pulleyn uses the PC," says Patterson. "The new process dramatically reduces revisions, brings a job to fruition much sooner, ends unnecessary meetings, and saves an incredible amount of time and money."

Expanded Business Opportunities

Hines believes using Acrobat software to communicate electronically has changed Buck & Pulleyn's business in many ways. "We are able to communicate so much faster and easier," she says.

Using Acrobat, Buck & Pulleyn plans to start communicating electronically with its other clients, as well as with potential new clients in remote locations. Says VanGaasbeck, "One of the goals of this agency is to spread its client base geographically. Acrobat will break down barriers to conducting long-distance business."

CHAPTER

12
Bookmarks

Viewing and Managing the Hyperlinks

Bookmarks are hyperlinked labels to sections of a document or to external files. They are similar to an outline or table of contents with hyperlinks. When you select a bookmark, Acrobat will move to the location in the document the bookmark refers to, or open the external file specified by the bookmark.

In this chapter, you learn how to:

- Create bookmarks
- Modify bookmarks
- Delete bookmarks.

This chapter also includes a fictional example that focuses on the ways that bookmarks help a company develop an employment/human resources guide.

Creating Bookmarks

Kim Wu is the human resources director for a consulting firm in Boston. Since the company's founding several years ago, it has added offices in Atlanta, Dallas, and Phoenix, and the number of employees has increased significantly.

Kim has decided to update the company's human resources' documents and to combine them into a single file that will be placed on the company's network server in PDF format. This will benefit the company in several ways. First, this will save the company money by conserving paper resources.

PART 3

Browsing
Interface
Navigating
Zoom
Features
Printing
Clipboard
Preferences
Creating
PDFWriter
PDF Files
Enhancing
Pages
Thumbnails
Bookmarks
Notes
Links
Articles
Web Publishing
Introduction
Getting On
Reader
Author
Publisher
Cool Sites
Advanced
Search
Catalog
Distiller

Second, because the content will be hyperlinked, the document will be more convenient to those people who access it; they can use bookmarks to move automatically to the material they are interested in.

Third, the on-line version is easier to update than its paper counterpart. These updates can be viewed as soon as the new version is placed on the network, eliminating problems with obsolete versions of the document.

When Kim first creates his PDF file, it does not have any bookmarks, so Kim must create them.

Like an outline, the document is organized by topic and subtopic. Instead of scrolling through the document, Kim understands that the fastest way for others to find information about a topic is to create a bookmark hyperlinked to the page where the topic is discussed.

Creating a Bookmark that Refers to a Location Within the Document

To create a bookmark that refers to a location within the document:

1. Use Exchange's navigation tools to move to the location to which you want the bookmark to refer.

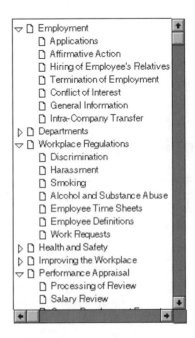

2. Use Exchange's magnification tools to create the page view you want.

3. If the bookmark list is not displayed, press the **Bookmarks and Page** toolbar button or select the **View | Bookmarks and Page** command to display it.

4. Click the bookmark under which you want to place the new bookmark. If you do not click on a bookmark, Exchange will place the new bookmark at the bottom of the list by default.

5. Select the **Edit | Bookmarks | New** command, or Press the **<Ctrl > + <B>** keys. Exchange will place a new bookmark page icon and the book-mark name "Untitled" in the bookmark list.

6. Enter the name of the bookmark, or paste it from the Clipboard.

Some policy information changes periodically, such as tax and benefits information. To allow for these changes, Kim places this information in separate PDF documents that he connects to the main document with bookmarks. This allows Kim to change the tax and benefits information without affecting other sections of the document.

Tech Note

Changing Magnification with Bookmarks. Exchange allows you to define a zoom level when you create a link or bookmark, so that the destination page view that appears when you select the link or bookmark is exactly as you define it. Besides the **Fit View**, **Fit Page**, **Fit Width**, and **Fit Visible** zoom levels that were discussed in Chapter 4, you can also define the **Fixed**, **Fit Height**, and **Inherit Zoom** levels for a bookmark. The **Fixed** zoom level allows you to set a custom zoom level for the bookmark; **Fit Height** adjusts the zoom level so that the height of the page you are viewing fits in the document win-dow; and **Inherit Zoom** keeps the zoom level that was in effect when the bookmark was selected.

Creating a Bookmark that Refers to a Location in another PDF File

To create a bookmark that refers to a location within a different PDF document:

1. If the bookmark list is not displayed, press the **Bookmarks and Page** toolbar button or select the **View | Bookmarks and Page** command to display it.
2. Click the bookmark under which you want to place the new bookmark. If you do not click on a bookmark, Exchange will place the new bookmark at the bottom of the list by default.
3. Select the **Edit | Bookmarks | New** command, or Press the **<Ctrl> + <B>** keys. Exchange will place a new bookmark page icon and the bookmark name "Untitled" in the bookmark list.
4. Enter the name of the bookmark or paste it from the Clipboard.
5. Right click on the bookmark's page icon to display the Bookmark pop-up menu, and select the **Properties...** command from the pop-up menu. You can also select the **Edit | Properties...** command. The Bookmark Properties dialog box will appear.
6. Open the destination document with the **File | Open** command.
7. Press the **Edit Destination...** button. The document that contains the bookmark will reappear.
8. Use the Window menu commands to display the document that contains the destination view.
9. Use Exchange's navigation tools to move to the location to which you want the bookmark to refer.
10. Use Exchange's magnification tools to create the page view you want.
11. Select a magnification from the **Magnification:** drop-down list box.
12. Press the **Set Action** button to make the modification, or press the **Cancel** button to cancel the modification.

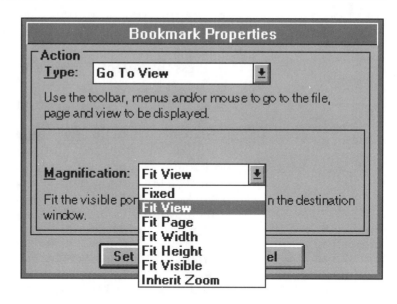

Creating a Bookmark that Refers to Another File

To create a bookmark that refers to another file:

1. If the bookmark list is not displayed, press the **Bookmarks and Page** toolbar button or select the **View | Bookmarks and Page** command to display it.
2. Click the bookmark under which you want to place the new bookmark. If you do not click on a bookmark, Exchange will place the new bookmark at the bottom of the list by default.
3. Select the **Edit | Bookmarks | New** command, or press the **<Ctrl> + <B>** keys. Exchange will place a new bookmark page icon and the bookmark name "Untitled" in the bookmark list.
4. Enter the name of the bookmark, or paste it from the Clipboard.
5. Right click on the bookmark. The Bookmark Properties dialog box will appear.
6. Select **Open File** from the **Typography:** drop-down list box.
7. Press the **Select File** button. The Select File to Open dialog box will appear.

8. Use the controls of the Select File to Open dialog box to select the file to which you want the bookmark to refer.
9. Press the **Select** button. The Select File to Open dialog box will close.
10. Press the **Set Action** button.

Bookmarks to external files can only refer to filenames; you cannot store any other information in the bookmark. While you can start an application by creating a bookmark that refers to its filename, you will have to load data files into the application manually; you cannot give a data filename to an application as a command line argument.

Exchange uses relative pathnames to represent the location of a file. If you move a PDF document that contains bookmarks to external files, Acrobat will not be able to find the files to which the bookmarks refer. Relative pathnames also make it necessary to put all files that you refer to with bookmarks on the same volume—in other words, on the same floppy disk, hard disk drive partition, or tape.

Since the headings of the sections were organized like an outline, Kim uses the text in the headings as the names of the bookmarks.

Using Document Text as a Bookmark Name

To use document text as a bookmark name:

1. Press the **Select Text** toolbar button or select the **Tools | Select Text** command. The mouse cursor will turn into the Text Selection cursor (an I beam with a small horizontal line in the center).
2. Select the text you want to use as the bookmark's name.
3. Create the new bookmark, following the steps in the "Creating a Bookmark that Refers to a Location Within the Document" section.
4. When "Untitled" appears as the bookmark name, paste the text into the bookmark using the **<Ctrl>**

+ **\<V>** keys, the **\<Shift>** + **\<Ins>** keys, or the **Edit | Paste** command.

You cut or copy text from any source into the Clipboard and paste it into a bookmark, including text in notes.

Altering Bookmark Properties

To alter a bookmark's properties:

1. Click on the bookmark's page icon to select the bookmark.
2. Select the **Edit | Properties** command, or right-click (as shown below) and select the **Properties** command from the pop-up menu that appears. When you select the **Properties** command, the Bookmark Properties dialog box will appear.

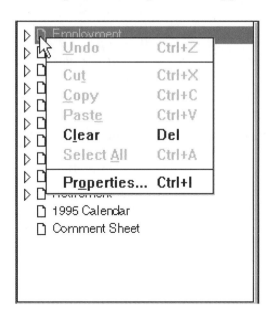

3. Use the controls of the Bookmark Properties dialog box to alter the properties of the bookmark. You can alter all of the bookmark's properties with this dialog box, including both the action Acrobat takes when the bookmark is selected and the destination of the bookmark.

You cannot alter the position of the bookmark in the bookmark list or its level in the bookmark hierarchy with the **Properties** command. If you want to change the bookmark's position or its hierarchy level, see *Modifying Bookmarks* below.

Modifying Bookmarks

Kim notices that a table, called "TaxInf 94", in one of the pages he inserted is outdated. After inserting the page with the updated table, Kim changes the bookmark name to "TaxInf 95" to reflect the changes in the date of the document.

Some of the files Kim is using have bookmarks with links to other files. These files are located in other directories. To consolidate the project, Kim moves the files into the human resources directory. He updates the bookmarks that link to these files; if he did not, Acrobat would not be able to find the files and would be unable to link to the information.

Changing Bookmark Names

To change bookmark text:

1. Click on the bookmark page icon. The page icon and bookmark text will be highlighted, and the cursor will turn to an I-beam when you move it over the bookmark text.
2. Click on the bookmark text. The bookmark text will be highlighted.
3. If you want to replace all of the bookmark text, start typing or paste the new text into the bookmark using the **<Ctrl>** + **<V>** keys, the **<Shift>** + **<Ins>** keys, or the **Edit | Paste** command.
4. If you want to edit the bookmark text, click on the bookmark text again to place the text cursor within the bookmark text.

Users of Acrobat 1.0 will note that, in version 1.0, clicking on the bookmark name allowed you to edit the bookmark name. This is no longer possible; in version 2.0, you must follow the procedure above to edit a bookmark name.

Changing the Destination of a Bookmark

In Acrobat Exchange 1.0, the **Edit | New Destination...** command was used to change the destination of a bookmark. In version 2.0, the command has been renamed **Edit | Reset Destination...**, but the operation of the command is the same.

To refer a bookmark to a different location:

1. Use Exchange's navigation tools to move to the location to which you want the bookmark to refer.
2. Use Exchange's magnification tools to create the page view you want.
3. Click on the bookmark page icon. The page icon and bookmark text will be highlighted.
4. Right click on the bookmark's page icon to display the **Bookmark** pop-up menu. Select the **Properties...** command from the pop-up menu. The Bookmark Properties dialog box will appear. You can also select the **Edit | Properties...** command.
5. Press the **OK** button to associate the new page view with the bookmark.

To refer a bookmark to a different file:

1. Use Exchange's navigation tools to move to the location to which you want the bookmark to refer.
2. Use Exchange's magnification tools to create the page view you want.
3. Click on the bookmark page icon. The page icon and bookmark text will be highlighted.
4. Right click on the bookmark's page icon to display the Bookmark pop-up menu.
5. Select the **Properties...** command from the pop-up menu. The Bookmark Properties dialog box will appear.
6. Press the **Select File** button. The Select File to Open dialog box will appear.

7. Use the controls of the Select File to Open dialog box to select the new file to which you want the bookmark to refer.
8. Press the **Select** button. The Select File to Open dialog box will close.
9. Press the **Set Action** button.

To refer a bookmark to a file instead of a location:

1. Click on the bookmark page icon. The page icon and bookmark text will be highlighted.
2. Right click on the bookmark's page icon to display the **Bookmark** pop-up menu.
3. Select the **Properties...** command from the pop-up menu. The Bookmark Properties dialog box will appear.
4. Select **Open File** from the **Type:** drop-down list box.
5. Using the controls of the Select File to Open dialog box, select the file to which you want the bookmark to refer.
6. Press the **Select** button. The Select File to Open dialog box will close.
7. Press the **Set Action** button, or press the **Cancel** button to cancel the modification.

To refer a bookmark to a location instead of a file:

1. Use Exchange's navigation tools to move to the location to which you want the bookmark to refer.
2. Use Exchange's magnification tools to create the page view you want.
3. Click on the bookmark page icon. The page icon and bookmark text will be highlighted.
4. Right click on the bookmark's page icon to display the **Bookmark** pop-up menu.
5. Select the **Properties...** command from the pop-up menu. The Bookmark Properties dialog box will appear.
6. Select **Go To View** from the **Type:** drop-down list box.
7. Select a magnification from the **Magnification:** drop-down list box.

8. Press the **Set Action** button to make the modification, or press the **Cancel** button to cancel the modification.

As Kim renames a few of the bookmarks, he decides to restructure the bookmark list by dragging the bookmarks to a better location in the list.

While creating the bookmarks for each topic, Kim changes their level in the bookmark list's hierarchy to match the topic's position in the document's hierarchy.

Changing the Position of a Bookmark in the Bookmark List

To change the position of a bookmark in the Bookmark List:

1. Click on the bookmark page icon. The page icon and bookmark text will be highlighted.
2. Drag the bookmark to its new position. As you drag the bookmark, a black line will appear below the page icons in the bookmark list; when you

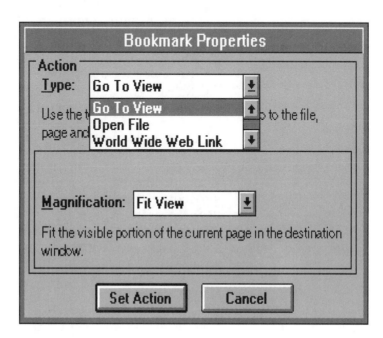

release the mouse button, the bookmark will be placed under the bookmark marked with the black line.

3. Release the mouse button.

Users of Acrobat 1.0 will note that this is a different procedure than the one for version 1.0. The **Edit | Bookmark | Move Up** and **Edit | Bookmark | Move Down** commands and the **<Ctrl> + <Up>** and **<Ctrl> + <Down>** keyboard shortcuts no longer exist; the new procedure must be used at all times.

You cannot move a bookmark to the first position in the bookmark list; the highest you can move it is to the second position. If you want to move the bookmark to the first position, move the bookmark to the second position, and then move the bookmark that is in the first position down one position.

Changing the Level of a Bookmark in the Hierarchy

To change the level of a bookmark in the hierarchy:

1. Click on the bookmark page icon. The page icon and bookmark text will be highlighted.
2. Drag the bookmark up slightly and to the left or right. As you drag the bookmark, a black line will appear below or to either side of the page icon of the preceding bookmark, indicating the level of the current bookmark.
3. Release the mouse button. Exchange will move the bookmark in the hierarchy.

Note: A bookmark can be no more than one level higher or lower than the preceding bookmark.

Users of Acrobat 1.0 will note that this is a different procedure than the one for version 1.0. The **Edit | Bookmark | Move Left** and **Edit | Bookmark | Move Right** commands and the **<Ctrl> + <Left>** and **<Ctrl> + <Right>** keyboard shortcuts no longer exist; the new procedure must be used at all times.

Deleting Bookmarks

In a final review of the document, Kim realizes that the information in one section of the files is superseded by newer material in other portions of the document. This section is in a separate file and is hyperlinked to the rest of the document with a bookmark. Kim removes the bookmark that refers to this section, effectively removing the section from the on-line policies manual.

To delete a bookmark:

1. Click on the bookmark's page icon.
2. Press the **<Delete>** key. Exchange will display a dialog box asking you to confirm the deletion.
3. Press the **Yes** button. If you decide not to delete the bookmark, press the **No** button.

To delete a bookmark and its subordinates:

1. Click on the bookmark's page icon while pressing the **<Ctrl>** or the **<Shift>** keys. The bookmark and all of its subordinate bookmarks will be highlighted.
2. Press the **<Delete>** key. Exchange will display a dialog box asking you to confirm the deletion.
3. Press the **Yes** button. If you decide not to delete the bookmarks, press the **No** button.

To delete several bookmarks at once:

1. Click on each bookmark's page icon while pressing the **<Shift>** key. Each bookmark and its subordinate bookmarks will be highlighted.
2. Press the **<Delete>** key. Exchange will display a dialog box asking you to confirm the deletion.

3. Press the **Yes** button. If you decide not to delete the bookmarks, press the **No** button.

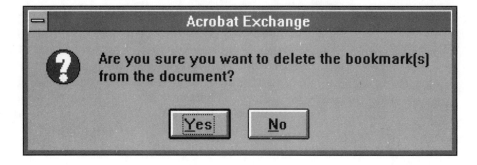

Intel Embraces More Cost-Effective, Efficient Electronic Communications

In support of Intel's vision that the PC is rapidly becoming the center of communications, the company is using electronic means to distribute and access information. Increasingly, Intel uses Adobe Acrobat software to distribute documents electronically, disseminating information to a wider range of individuals more quickly and cost effectively than it can with printed material.

"The combination of the new capabilities of Adobe Acrobat software and the ability to broadly distribute Acrobat Reader are a major step in freeing the computer industry from the ASCII jungle," says Clif Purkiser, manager of Intel Business™ Marketing Programs. "The ability to universally distribute graphically rich electronic documents, coupled with widespread availability of high-performance Pentium™ processor-based computers, will help make the PC the centerpiece of the information superhighway."

Intel is a leading supplier of microcomputer components and modules. The company introduced the world's first microprocessor, a development that changed not only the future of the company but also much of the industrial world. Intel's mission is to supply the electronic building blocks for the new computer and communications industry.

Adobe Acrobat software is being adopted in several areas at Intel. For example, the advertising department has chosen the Acrobat family of products to save time and money producing ads, and it is publishing these ads as Portable Document Format (PDF) files on-line, enabling them to reach new audiences. "Adobe Acrobat software has made it possible for Intel to develop, review, produce, and deliver ads to a wider audience at a lower cost with all of the rich, compelling, graphical information intact," says Purkiser. In addition, Intel is beginning to convert literature fulfillment to PDF, and the technical documentation department is starting a pilot program to convert technical documentation to PDF as a more effective means of electronic distribution.

Streamlining Advertising Production

Intel uses Acrobat software to save time and money in developing its Technology Briefings advertisements. Its Salt Lake City-based advertising agency develops the monthly four-page educational documents that appear in BYTE, InfoWorld,

PC Magazine, and PC Week, covering the Pentium processor, the PCI local bus, and other topics.

Previously, the agency could only work up to midday prior to the day a proof or concept was due. The agency printed the proof—usually taking several hours depending on the complexity—and sent it to Intel in California by overnight mail or courier services. The agency and Intel then arranged a teleconference to review the materials. Waiting to print proofs and relying on overnight mail and courier services reduced the agency's valuable production time.

With Acrobat software, the agency converts ad proofs to PDF files, preserving the Technology Briefings' information-intensive visuals. PDF files are e-mailed to Intel's Windows™ based PCs for point-by-point review on-screen via video conference. Says Purkiser, "Using Acrobat, we eliminate the considerable time and expense of express mail services, leaving the agency more time to devote to creation. Acrobat software enables this new process, preserving document fidelity perfectly and freeing us from the worry of having different computer platforms and applications."

On-line Distribution of Ads, Fulfillment Literature, and Technical Documentation

As a way to cost-effectively reach new audiences, the company has taken these traditional 8.5" x 11" briefings and redesigned them for on-line viewing on America Online SM and CompuServe®. Says Purkiser, "Intel chose the Acrobat family of products for several reasons. Acrobat software's linking capabilities let us easily create compelling interactive documents. Adobe's PDF is extremely flexible and can describe the content and appearance of documents created with virtually any application. The broad distribution of Acrobat Reader means that we can reach any audience. In addition, Acrobat compresses documents extremely well, saving our customers time and money in downloading documents." In one case, Intel converted a 5.8 MB file into a 567K PDF file.

"Acrobat is the key to effective on-line advertising, letting us create information-rich ads that really educate the consumer," says a designer at Intel's agency. "Creating 'hot links' using Acrobat makes ads more interesting and better controls the flow of information to the consumer. The ability to open PDF files in full-screen mode as stand-alone files lets us make a more aesthetic electronic presentation and gives us more design control. Acrobat does a great job of facilitating on-line advertising."

Says Purkiser, "In addition to Technology Briefings, we are planning to make a wide variety of documentation available electronically, including fulfillment literature. This will be more convenient for our customers and will significantly reduce costs." Ninety percent of the Technology Briefings have corresponding fulfillment materials, such as white papers, that Intel is converting to PDF for on-line distribution.

Distributing advertising and fulfillment materials using Acrobat software is one small part of Intel's plan for using Acrobat. Intel's technical documentation department has initiated a pilot program to distribute its technical manuals in PDF on the Internet worldwide network using Adobe Acrobat software. Intel's goal for the pilot program is to serve its developer community and technical customers better by providing more accessible information that can be searched quickly and conveniently.

"Intel is moving ahead very quickly with several programs involving Acrobat," says Purkiser. "Now, all of the necessary technologies are available to help Intel make visually rich, cost-effective electronic communications with its customers, vendors, and developers a reality."

CHAPTER

13
Notes

PART 3

Browsing
Interface
Navigating
Zoom
Features
Printing
Clipboard
Preferences
Creating
PDFWriter
PDF Files
Enhancing
Pages
Thumbnails
Bookmarks
Notes
Links
Articles
Web Publishing
Introduction
Getting On
Reader
Author
Publisher
Cool Sites
Advanced
Search
Catalog
Distiller

Managing and Using Notes

Acrobat's annotation features allow you to attach comments to a PDF document—similar to writing notes in the margin of a paper document.

In this chapter, you will learn how to:

- Attach annotations to a document

- Export notes from a document into a new document

- Import notes into a document from another document

- Search for the next annotation in a document

- Read an annotation

- Delete annotations from a document

- Summarize the annotations in a document.

In this chapter we also present a fictional example that describes how employees of a software company, working in offices throughout the world, review marketing literature for a new product by e-mail, using PDF documents.

John is the leader of a marketing communications group for a software company whose customers and partners span the globe. John's group produces marketing materials for each new software release and arranges for their worldwide distribution and translation. When John and his co-workers

have developed the initial concept for a set of marketing materials, they send PDF files of the drafts to sales offices in Europe and the Far East by e-mail. The sales offices then attach their comments about the concept to the drafts and return them to John.

John's group has just finished work on a new brochure that describes customers' success stories with the latest release of one of the company's products. Before he leaves for the day, John e-mails copies of the brochures in PDF format to marketing managers in several of the company's offices in the US and overseas.

George is the marketing director for the company's London office. John values George's comments on the marketing group's work, but the time difference between London and the company's California headquarters makes it difficult for them to schedule telephone conversations. To overcome the time difference, they started using Acrobat to transfer marketing material for review and comments. They found that Acrobat made the review process more convenient and reduced turn-around time, so John now sends PDF documents to all his reviewers. Acrobat combines the best features of two other methods the company had used for reviews in the past; the high quality of paper documents sent by express mail and the immediacy of faxes.

George finds the brochure waiting for him when he arrives at work the next morning. As George looks it over, he notices that one of the graphics John's group had used does not have the impact of the others. He attaches a note next to the graphic, suggesting that John replace it, and goes on to make several comments about the document, each in its own separate note.

Placing Notes in Documents

To place a note in a document, select the **Notes** button from the toolbar or select the **Tools | Note** command, then click on the spot where you want to place the note. A *note window* will appear.

Note Windows

Note windows have a title bar, a system button, a scroll bar, a resizing handle, and an edit field. Note windows contain the note text within their edit field. The title bar of a note window contains a label. When you install Acrobat Exchange, it sets this label to the name of the person who registered the software, but you can change it to any text string (see the *Changing the Default Properties of All Notes* section of this chapter for more details).

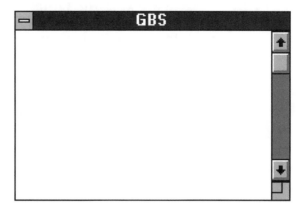

Placing Text in a Note

To place text in the note, start typing; the text will appear at the cursor. The note window's edit field is fully functional; you can move around the note text with the cursor control keys, select text, and cut, copy, and paste text. If you want to add text to the note, move the text cursor to the appropriate text within the note and start typing.

The comments George is making tend to fall into two categories: general comments about the tone and style of the document and specific suggestions to correct mistakes in it. To make it easier for John to understand the nature of specific comments, he color codes the notes by category and gives the two categories different labels.

Changing a Note's Properties

You can change the label text and the color of a note. To change these properties, double click on the note's title bar. The Note Properties dialog box appears. You use the controls of this dialog box to change the note's properties. To change the label text, enter the new text in the **Label:** edit box. To change the note's color, click on the **Color:** drop-down list box, and then double click on the new color.

When you have finished changing the note's properties, press the **OK** button or press the **<Enter>** key. If you decide you do not want to change the note's properties, press the **Cancel** button or press the **<Escape>** key.

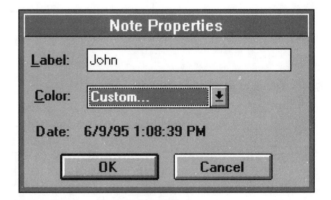

Changing the Default Properties of All Notes

You can change the default properties of notes and the font that Acrobat uses to display them with the **Edit | Preferences | Notes** command. When you select this command, the Note Preferences dialog box appears. You use the controls of the dialog box to change the default note properties.

To change the default note label, enter the new text in the **Default Label:** edit box. To change the default note color, click on the **Default Color:** drop-down list box, and then double click on the new color. When you change the default label or the default color, existing notes are not affected.

To change the font that Acrobat uses to display note text, click on the **Font:** drop-down list box, and then double click on the new font. To change the point size of the text:

- Click on the **Point Size:** drop-down list box, and then double click on the new point size.

Or

- Enter the new point size in the list box with the keyboard.

When you change the font or point size, existing notes are affected. Acrobat can display font sizes between 8 and 24 points in notes. Unfortunately, Acrobat does not have a text previewer in its Note Preferences dialog box, so you will have to use trial and error when changing fonts and point sizes.

Managing Notes

When George finishes reviewing the document, he exports his notes to a new PDF file, and sends the file back to John. The PDF file containing only the notes is much smaller than the PDF file containing the entire document; by sending John just the notes, George reduces the load on his mail system.

Exporting Notes to a New PDF File

Acrobat Exchange's note export feature creates a blank page for each page of the source document and places the notes from the source document onto the blank pages. This results in a much smaller PDF file than the original. This feature has two major benefits:

1. It reduces the amount of work and time the electronic mail system must take to send the message.

This is also known as reducing the bandwidth needed to send a message.

2. It reduces the amount of disk space required to store the annotations. Rather than storing multiple copies of a document, you can store one copy of the document and multiple copies of the notes.

Tech Note

As an example, a twelve page PDF file that is 70K in size and contains twelve notes can have all of its notes exported to a file of less than 3K, for a reduction of almost 96 percent!

To export the notes in a document to a new PDF file, select the **Edit | Notes | Export** command. When you select this command, the Export Notes As: dialog box appears. You use the controls of this dialog box to select the file that will contain the exported notes. The controls of this dialog box are identical to those of the file selection box displayed by the **Edit | Pages | Insert** command. See the "Inserting Pages" section of the "Pages" chapter for an explanation of how the dialog box controls work.

When you have selected the file that you want Acrobat to export the notes to, press the **OK** button. Acrobat Exchange creates the new file and returns you to the current document. If you decide not to export the notes to a new file, press the **Cancel** button.

When John arrives at the office the next morning, George's notes on the brochure are in his mail program's in box, along with other notes that he has received from other reviewers. To make it easier to see everyone's comments, John imports each reviewer's notes into his copy of the brochure, then creates a summary of the notes in a new PDF document.

Importing Notes into a PDF Document

By simplifying the collection and display of comments from multiple reviewers, Acrobat's note import, export, and summarization features make it easier for workgroups to review documents. Rather than examining several paper copies of a document with marginal notes, sticky notes, or added pages of comments, the person collecting the reviews can place all of the comments into one PDF document and then create another PDF document that lists the source and text of each note.

To import notes from a PDF file into the current document, select the **Edit | Notes | Import** command. When you select this command, the Select File Containing Notes dialog box appears. You use the controls of this dialog box to select the file with the notes you want to import. The controls of this dialog box are identical to those of the file selection box displayed by the **Edit | Pages | Insert** command; see the "Inserting Pages" section of the "Pages" chapter for an explanation of how the dialog box controls work.

When you have selected the file that contains the notes you want to import, press the **OK** button. Acrobat Exchange will import the notes. If you decide not to import notes from another file, press the **Cancel** button.

Creating a Summary of Notes in a New PDF Document

With Acrobat Exchange, you can extract the text from each note in a document and place it in a new document. The new document contains the name of the source document and lists the text in each note; along with its author, creation date, and creation time; arranged by the page number of the source document. To extract the notes from a document, select the **Tools | Summarize Notes** command. Exchange will create a new PDF document that contains the notes and make the new document the current document.

To get a quick idea of the success of the draft brochure, John spends a few minutes reading the summary of the notes the reviewers have submitted. The response to the brochure was generally positive, but the reviewers suggested several small improvements John's group could make for the next draft of the document. Many of these suggestions concern specific parts of the brochure. To better

understand the comments, John looks at the copy of the draft brochure that contains the imported notes.

John decides which of the suggestions he should act upon and asks the members of his group to work on them. The total turn-around time for the review: less than 24 hours.

Deleting Notes

You can only delete a note when it is minimized.

To delete a note:

1. Click once on its icon to make it active.
2. Press the **<Delete>** key.

Acrobat Exchange will ask you to confirm the deletion. If you want to delete the note, press the **OK** button. If you decide you do not want to delete the note, press the **Cancel** button.

You can only delete an *active* note from the document. You must click on an inactive note to make it active before you delete it.

Reducing Higher Education Costs

With a population of almost 24,000 students and 5,500 faculty and staff members, Virginia Polytechnic Institute and State University (Virginia Tech) found that consistent, timely distribution of key course information was an arduous and expensive task. This is no longer the case for the Department of Chemical Engineering, where one professor conducted a pilot program that almost completely replaced hard-copy document distribution with on-line access. Adobe Acrobat software figured prominently in the success of this project.

"As soon as I saw what Acrobat could do, I knew it would benefit my students as well as the university immensely," says Peter Rony, a professor in the Department of Chemical Engineering. "Distribution of course materials, software manuals, and other university documents involves a great deal of time and money for paper, printing, and duplication. The department cannot assume all of these costs, so many are passed on directly to our students."

Reduced Costs

As is the case with most universities, students incur significant costs purchasing software and hard-copy textbooks, manuals, and lecture notes. The faculty also gets caught up in the paper chase, keeping track of the many reports, technical articles, and other documents written by students or colleagues.

To save costs, Rony publishes software manuals and other key course materials electronically as Portable Document Format (PDF) files using Adobe Acrobat software. These files are made available on servers in the chemical engineering controls laboratory where students can view, copy, or print whatever files they need. "I save about 5 cents per page distributing materials electronically," says Rony. "With typical documents varying from 50 to 200 pages each, that's a substantial savings that I can pass on to my students."

More Effective Communication

Virginia Tech has more than 8,000 PCs running DOS and Windows™, as well as Apple® Macintosh® computers, Sun™ work-stations, and an IBM® mainframe system. "We are a very computer literate university, but we need to be able to exchange information more effectively between many different kinds of computers," says Rony. "Acrobat allows us to provide that exchange electronically, independent of the computing platform or software and font configuration. I can create a single, high-quality text and graphic document that can be accessed by anyone."

According to Rony, Acrobat software makes it easier for him to communicate with students and colleagues, and vice versa. "I can provide richer information to students, because the PDF files I create contain elements such as color images and color screen captures—much richer information than can be found on the black-and-white printed page."

During the 1993–94 pilot project, Rony encouraged students to submit technical papers in electronic form. He converted the documents into PDF files and transmitted several of them to colleagues who wanted examples and information on technical report writing.

In addition, very few students have modems to dial into the university network, so being able to take files home on a diskette can be very helpful. Documents that are hundreds of pages long and include multiple images and graphics can fit on a single 1.44 MB floppy diskette. "Adobe Acrobat is very helpful for information distribution," says Rony. "It compresses most files by an impressive factor of five."

Rony is using Adobe Acrobat to communicate with students and colleagues in other innovative ways. November 1994 marks the 25th anniversary of the CACHE (Computer Aids in Chemical Engineering) Corporation, a not-for-profit corporation serving chemical engineering departments nationwide. To honor the event, Rony is publishing a CACHE CD-ROM containing information about the application of computers in chemical engineering education, including lectures and software manuals in PDF. The CD-ROM will contain copies of Acrobat Reader for DOS, Windows, and Macintosh so that Rony's department colleagues can have access to the information.

Rony also contributes manuals and other documentation in PDF to the Virginia Tech Engineering CD-ROM which goes to the more than 1,000 freshmen in the College of Engineering.

Creating a Standard

The pilot program has convinced Rony to adopt Acrobat software as the department standard for electronic distribution. Starting in the 1994–95 school year, he plans to distribute key course materials—including software manuals, assignments, and laboratory experiment procedures—only as PDF files. Students will be required to submit all technical reports as PDF files as well. "Once I started producing Acrobat PDF files for my students," says Rony, "I developed more creative ideas for how to get electronic information to my students at a very low cost. Using Adobe Acrobat to communicate information provides the additional benefit of helping me introduce my students to the new world of electronic communications. I find that they are now starting to use their computers more often and in more interesting ways."

"Acrobat is part of the growing, exciting movement of electronic communications. I would even like to see text-books published electronically so students could adapt them to their individual learning needs," Rony says. "For example, a student could create a duplicate PDF textbook and anno-tate it, or pull out key material and insert pages from other PDF files that the professor provides. This would make the information more useful and give professors a wider range of instructional materials to choose from."

"As the dissemination and retrieval of electronic informa-tion catches on," Rony says. "Acrobat will play an important part in my ability as a professor to share volumes of impor-tant information without being burdened by the cost of paper."

CHAPTER

14
Links

Creating Hyperlinks

Links are hypertext elements in a PDF document. They allow you to move to related material by clicking within a rectangle that contains text or graphics. You define these *link rectangles* in your PDF document using Acrobat Exchange.

In this chapter you learn how to:

- Create links

- Specify link attributes

- Modify link attributes

- Delete links.

The fictional narrative in this chapter describes a hospital that uses links to aid in organizing information sheets that are printed for patients.

Yvonne is a hospital administrator whose responsibilities include outpatient care. The hospital typically gives out printed information sheets to patients when they are discharged. These information sheets describe steps patients need to take to fully recover from their illnesses. The hospital is also developing short audio and video clips that supplement the information sheets.

Yvonne wants to place these information sheets on-line to reduce inventory and distribution problems with the paper forms. She decides to create a menu system, based on hyperlinks, to make it easy for hospital personnel to find the forms they need quickly.

Yvonne uses her word processing program to create several pages specifically for the menu system. For the hyperlinked menu items and topics, she uses a distinct color and text style that matches the hypertext help system the hospital employees are accustomed to using. She adds button graphics to each page as navigation aids; she will hyperlink the buttons to common starting points in the system.

After creating PDF versions of the menu system and forms, Yvonne adds hyperlinks to connect the documents in the system. Since her link text has a distinct style, she doesn't need to highlight the link with a visible link rectangle; she uses an invisible link rectangle instead. For the navigation buttons, she uses a visible link rectangle whose color matches the link text.

Creating Links

You can make hypertext links to other locations in a document, to other PDF documents, and to other types of external files and applications. You create links by drawing a *link rectangle* on the document and specifying the location or file to which the link will point. When you click the mouse within the rectangle, Acrobat will jump to the location or file.

To create a link:

1. Activate the **Link** tool by selecting the **Tools | Link** command or by pressing the **Link** toolbar button. Exchange will place link rectangles around every link in the document (even those links that you previously made invisible), and the mouse cursor will turn into a crosshair.
2. Click the mouse where you want to place the link and drag it to create a link rectangle. The Create Link dialog box will appear.
3. Specify the appearance of the link rectangle and the type of link to make in the dialog box.
4. Use Exchange's navigation tools to move to the part of the document where you want the link to point, or specify the name of the file to which you want the link to point.

5. If the link points to another location in the same document, select a zoom level in the **Magnification:** drop-down list box

6. If you selected the **Fixed zoom** level, use Exchange's magnification tools and scroll bars to create the view of the document that you want to appear when the link is selected.

7. Press the **Set Link** button to set the link. If you decide you don't want to set the link, press the **Cancel** button.

Once you create the link, Exchange deactivates the **Link** tool. If you want the **Link** tool to remain active after you set a link, press the **<Ctrl>** key while selecting the **Tools | Link** command or press the **Link** toolbar button. The **Link** tool will remain active until you select another tool.

Acrobat's hypertext links are different from those of some other hypertext systems, such as HTML files and Windows Help. Acrobat does not base its hypertext links on tagged text, but on locations within a document (link rectangles). This means that Acrobat cannot automatically change the appearance of hyperlinked

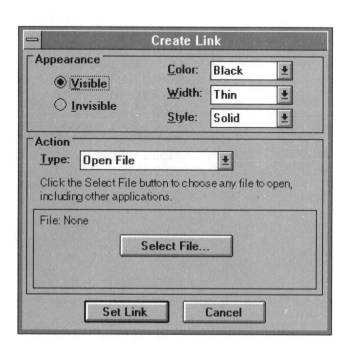

text. If you want to underline your hyperlinked text or give it a different color, as HTML documents and Windows Help do, *you must give the text these attributes in the original document.*

You may place link rectangles anywhere in a PDF document—you can even place them on the background of the document, outside the page boundaries. There does not seem to be any reason to do this, though, since there would be no indication of where the link points.

Specifying the Appearance of a Link Rectangle

The link rectangles you create may be visible or invisible. To specify a visible or invisible link rectangle, click on the **Visible** or **Invisible** radio buttons in the Create Link dialog box. If your document uses a specific format for linked text, or you are creating links on graphics embedded in the document, you may want to use invisible link rectangles to reduce screen clutter.

If you create a visible link rectangle, you can specify the color, thickness, and style of the rectangle. The default values are a black rectangle with thin, solid lines. To choose a color for the link rectangle, click on the **Color:** drop-down list box, then click on a color name. You can choose from a variety of colors. To choose a line thickness, click on the **Width:** drop-down list box, then click on **Thin**, **Medium**, or **Thick**. To choose a line style, click on the **Style:** drop-down list box, then click on **Solid** or **Dashed**.

Yvonne has to make two different types of links for the information sheets. She makes links between locations in the menu system document to link together menus and their submenus. She also makes links between the menu system document and locations in the PDF forms.

Links to Another Location in the Document

To create a link that points to another location in the current document:

1. Select **Go To View** from the **Type:** drop-down list box. Exchange displays the **Magnification:** drop-down list box.
2. Select a **Magnification** option from the **Magnification:** drop-down list box.
3. Using Exchange's navigation tools, move to the section of the document that you want Acrobat to display when the link is selected. The Create Link dialog box will remain visible.
4. Press the **Set Link** button.

Tech Note

The **Magnification:** drop-down list box contains options for the magnification that the hyperlinked page will have. The options are: **Fixed**, **Fit View**, **Fit Page**, **Fit Width**, **Fit Height**, **Fit Visible**, and **Inherit Zoom**. All of the magnification options except **Inherit Zoom** use a predefined zoom level to display the hyperlinked page. With **Inherit Zoom**, the hyperlinked page will maintain the zoom level in effect when the link was selected.

With the **Fixed** magnification option, the hyperlinked page will be displayed at the zoom level in effect when the link was created. You can use the **Fixed** option to define precisely how Acrobat will display a hyperlinked page. To define the page view, change the zoom level and use the scroll bars while the Create Link dialog box is displayed.

Links to Another PDF File

To create a link that points to a location in another PDF document:

1. Select **Go To View** from the **Type:** drop-down list box. Exchange displays the **Magnification:** drop-down list box.

2. Select a **Magnification** option from the **Magnification:** drop-down list box.
3. Open the PDF document that you want the link to point to.
4. Using Exchange's navigation tools, move to the section of the document that you want Acrobat to display when the link is selected. The Create Link dialog box will remain visible.
5. Press the **Set Link** button.

For the audio and video clips, Yvonne makes links to the sound and movie files. In the Select File to Open dialog box, Yvonne chooses the name of the file that contains the audio or video information. When a hospital employee selects the link, the computer's operating system determines which media player to use; the application is opened automatically with the media file already loaded.

Links to Other Types of Files

To create a link that points to another file:

1. Select **Open File** from the **Type:** drop-down list box.

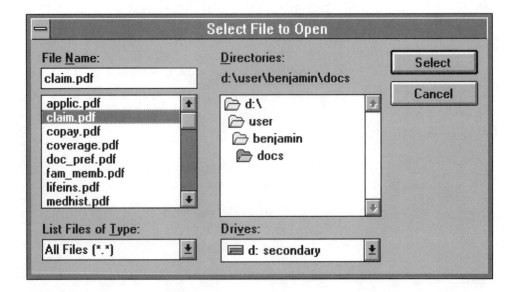

2. Press the **Select File...** button that Exchange displays in the Create Link dialog box. Exchange will display the Select File to Open dialog box.

3. Use the controls of the Select File to Open dialog box to select the file you want to open.

Managing Links Across Multiple Files

File Associations and External Applications

To open a linked file in Windows, the extension of the file must be associated with an application. If you plan to use PDF documents with file links in the Windows environment, make sure:

- Your filenames conform to the DOS filename conventions

- The file extensions are associated with the proper applications.

Links to external files can only point to filenames; you cannot store command line options or any other information in the link. While you can start an application by creating a link to its filename, you will have to load data files into the application manually; you cannot give a data filename to an application as a command line argument.

Relative and Absolute Pathnames

Exchange uses *relative* pathnames to represent the location of a linked file. If you move a PDF document that contains file links to another directory, Acrobat will not be able to find the files to which the links point. Links can point to files on different volumes.

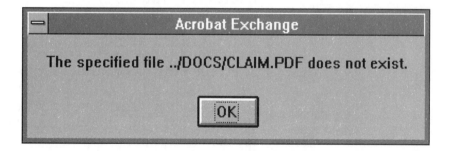

As long as the relative path between the files is the same, Acrobat can preserve the links of files that you move to a different volume. For instance, if a PDF document stored in c:\userguid\toc.pdf points to the file c:\userguid\chap1\chap1_1.pdf, the link will be preserved if you move the files to d:\userguid\toc.pdf and d:\userguid\chap1\chap1_1.pdf, or to d:\pub\userguid\toc.pdf and d:\pub\userguid\chap1\chap1_1.pdf. If the relative position of the two files is changed by moving either the file that contains the link or the file that the link points to, you must modify the link. For instance, if you moved the files to d:\userguid\toc.pdf and d:\userguid\chapters\chap1_1.pdf, however, you would have to modify the link.

Acrobat uses absolute pathnames when you point a link to a file on a different volume.

Modifying Links

You can modify all the properties of a link, including:

- The size and position of a link rectangle
- The properties of a link rectangle (its visibility, color, thickness, and style)
- Whether the link points to another section of the document or to a file
- The location a link points to within a document; the file to which a link points.

Modifying Link Properties

To modify a link's properties:

1. Click on the toolbar's **Link** tool button, or select the **Tools | Link** command.
2. Click within the link rectangle of the link you want to alter to select the link. When the link is selected, handles will appear on the link rectangle.
3. Select the **Edit | Properties** command, or right click and select the **Properties** command from the pop-up menu that appears. When you select the Properties command, the Link Properties dialog box will appear.

4. Use the controls of the Link Properties dialog box to alter the properties of the link.

You cannot alter the size or position of the link rectangle with the **Properties** command.

Modifying the Size of a Link

To modify the size of a link:

1. Activate the **Link** tool by selecting the **Tools | Link** command or by pressing the **Link** toolbar button.
2. Click inside the link rectangle of the link you want to modify. Exchange will display handles at the corners of the rectangle. Handles are small squares that you use to move the corners of a rectangle.
3. Place the mouse cursor on the handle of the corner you want to move, click on the handle, and drag it to its new position.

The **Link** tool will remain active after you have modified the size of the link.

Modifying the Position of a Link

To modify the position of a link:

1. Activate the **Link** tool by selecting the **Tools | Link** command or by pressing the **Link** toolbar button.
2. Click inside the link rectangle of the link you want to modify, and drag the link to its new location.

The **Link** tool will remain active after you have modified the position of the link.

Pointing a Link to a Different Location or File

To point a link to a different location:

1. Activate the **Link** tool by selecting the **Tools | Link** command or by pressing the **Link** toolbar button.

2. Double click inside the link rectangle of the link you want to modify. The Link Properties dialog box will appear.

3. Press the **Edit Destination...** button. Exchange will display the **Magnification:** drop-down list box in the Link Properties dialog box.

4. Use Exchange's navigation tools to move to the part of the document to which you want the link.

5. Select a zoom level in the **Magnification:** drop-down list box.

6. If you selected the **Fixed** zoom level, use Exchange's magnification tools and scroll bars to create the view of the document that you want to appear when the link is selected.

7. Press the **OK** button to make the modification, or press the **Cancel** button to cancel the modification.

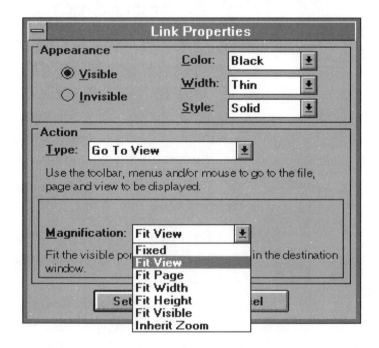

PART 3

Browsing
  Interface
  Navigating
  Zoom
  Features
  Printing
  Clipboard
  Preferences
Creating
  PDFWriter
  PDF Files
Enhancing
  Pages
  Thumbnails
  Bookmarks
  Notes
  Links
  Articles
Web Publishing
  Introduction
  Getting On
  Reader
  Author
  Publisher
  Cool Sites
Advanced
  Search
  Catalog
  Distiller

Exchange deactivates the **Link** tool after you point a link to a different location.

To point a link to a different file:

1. Activate the **Link** tool by selecting the **Tools | Link** command or by pressing the Link toolbar button.
2. Double-click inside the link rectangle of the link you want to modify. The "Link Properties" dialog box will appear.
3. Press the **Edit Destination...** button. Exchange will display the **Magnification:** drop-down list box in the Link Properties dialog box.
4. Press the **Select File...** button. The Select File to Open dialog box will appear.
5. Use the controls of the Select File to Open dialog box to select a file, then press the **Select** button. The Select File to Open dialog box will disappear.
6. Press the **OK** button to make the modification, or press the **Cancel** button to cancel the modification.

Exchange deactivates the **Link** tool after you point a link to a different file.

To point a link to a file instead of a location or to a location instead of a file:

1. Activate the **Link** tool by selecting the **Tools | Link** command or by pressing the **Link** toolbar button.
2. Double click inside the link rectangle of the link you want to modify. The Link Properties dialog box will appear.
3. Select **Open File** or **Go To View** from the **Type:** drop-down list box, as appropriate.
4. Select the location or file that the file will link to, as appropriate. See the rest of this section for more details on selecting locations and files.
5. Press the **OK** button to make the modification, or press the **Cancel** button to cancel the modification.

Exchange deactivates the **Link** tool after you change the destination of a link or the file opened by a link.

Deleting Links

To delete a link:

1. Activate the **Link** tool by selecting the **Tools** |
   Link command or by pressing the **Link** toolbar
   button.
2. Click inside the link rectangle of the link you
   want to modify.
3. Press the **<Delete>** key. Exchange will display a
   dialog box with a prompt to confirm the delete.
4. Press the **Yes** button to confirm the deletion, or
   press the **No** button to cancel the deletion.

After you delete a link, the **Link** tool remains active.

Adding Functionality to Sales Information System and Reducing Product Development Time

When Siebel Systems began developing the Siebel Sales Information System for its corporate customers, the company needed a cost-effective electronic document solution to integrate into its application that gives salespeople immediate on-line access to their entire repository of sales tools. Siebel selected Adobe Acrobat software, cutting the company's product development time and costs and offering its customers much more competitive, feature-rich sales information systems.

"Acrobat is the only electronic document software that can handle the various kinds of sales literature that our customers want to include in our system, while preserving the documents' look and feel," says Tom Siebel, president of Siebel Systems. "No other program provides an open, published file format with more than 500 documented Application Programming Interfaces [APIs] and support for Microsoft® Object Linking and Embedding [OLE] 2.0. Without Acrobat software, integrating electronic documents into our Windows™ based product would have been so expensive and time-consuming to develop that we could not have succeeded."

Siebel Systems, located in Menlo Park, California, develops sales force automation software for field sales, telesales, telemarketing, and third-party distribution for large sales organizations that are focused on increasing sales productivity. The company's client-server sales automation software supports both mobile and stationary sales representatives and is currently being piloted at several corporate customer sites.

"Acrobat enabled Siebel to build an on-line marketing encyclopedia that offers significant productivity increases and can fundamentally change the way customers manage sales information," says Siebel.

"From a sales representative making a customer proposal to a telesales representative knowing the latest product information, having quick and easy access to the right information at the right time is a competitive advantage. Using Adobe Acrobat software is the easiest, most cost-effective way that we can build this advantage into our customers' applications."

Cross-document Searches Boost Productivity

Adobe Acrobat includes support for interapplication communication (IAC), using Microsoft OLE automation and Dynamic Data Exchange (DDE) calls. Using this functionality, Siebel Systems seamlessly integrated Acrobat into its application, providing access to a ready repository of sales information in Adobe's Portable Document format (PDF) and adding all the functionality of Acrobat software.

The integration of Adobe Acrobat software into the Siebel system substantially reduces the time to locate pertinent information and eliminates the need to carry often out-of-date and cumbersome paper copies. A sales representative can browse a list of sales documents from within the Siebel application or preview documents in a separate window. Clicking a document launches the Acrobat application, letting users do full-text searches, find any document on a particular subject using Acrobat software's cross-document linking capabilities, or read Acrobat annotations that provide helpful hints on how to sell a particular product or service. Adobe Acrobat software's file-compression capabilities make it possible for field sales representatives to store literally hundreds of electronic sales documents including annual reports, brochures, datasheets, competitive comparisons, and more on a laptop computer.

Delivering the Optimal Sales Information System

Siebel Systems had several technical and user-related requirements for its electronic document software. Technically, it had to have fully documented APIs and support Microsoft OLE. It also had to manage the complete document cycle, from converting source documents to producing high-quality PostScript™ language output. For end-user productivity, the document management system had to support full-text searches, cross-document links, and previews of documents to save salespeople valuable time in locating the right information.

"Once we specified the functionality of our application, we needed to decide whether to build our own or integrate another company's electronic document software," says Siebel. "After an in-depth technical evaluation, our engineering department concluded that building our own electronic document software wasn't technically or economically feasible. We evaluated all the commercially available software products and found that Adobe Acrobat was the only product that met all of our requirements. Using Adobe Acrobat software is truly the fastest, most economical way to integrate electronic documents into any business solution."

"Using Acrobat as a core enabling technology for our application has given us a clear competitive advantage and has expanded our business opportunities. Not only has it saved years and hundreds of thousands of dollars in our product development effort, it has greatly enhanced our ability to offer our customers a sales automation system that gives them a competitive advantage."

CHAPTER

15
Articles

Viewing Complex Text Flows

If you have documents that are in a multi-column format, or if you have documents with articles that continue on non-consecutive pages, it can be difficult to browse through the document with a simple page view. In version 2.0, Acrobat makes reading such documents easier. You can mark sections of a document that go together as *articles*, and Acrobat will scroll through the article for you, moving from column to column or from page to page.

In this chapter, you learn how to:

- Create articles
- Add sections to articles
- Modify articles
- Delete articles or sections of articles.

Also in this chapter is a fictional example that shows how articles help a college's arts and literary magazine place its publication on the World Wide Web.

A well-known engineering school has a computing system where student organizations can place their Web pages. Katherine, the editor of the college's literary publication, wants to publish an electronic version of the magazine on the Web. She decides to use Acrobat because on-line readers will be able to print copies of the magazine and pass them on to others.

As Katherine proofreads the PDF version of the magazine, she finds that it is difficult to read. To follow an article from beginning to end often involves excessive scrolling and jumping between pages. Articles, which automatically link together the sections of writing, are Acrobat's solution to the problem.

Creating Articles

To create an article in Exchange, you define a series of boxes that contain the article's text in the order that the text should be read. Acrobat will draw an *article box* around each area you define. An *article box* has a label at the top of the box, sizing handles, and a plus tab at the lower right corner of the box. In the label, Exchange displays an article number and section number; the article number refers to which article the text within the box is associated with, and the section number refers to the order in which Acrobat will view the sections of text that make up an article. The sizing handles allow you to resize the article box. The plus tab allows you to add new sections to the article.

To create an article:

1. Select the **Tools | Article** command. The mouse cursor will change to a crosshair, and all existing article boxes will be displayed.

2. Click on one corner of the section of the page that includes the article.

3. Drag the mouse to the opposite corner of the section.

4. Release the mouse button. Exchange will change the mouse cursor to the link tool icon.

5. Repeat steps 2–4 for the other sections of the article.

6. When you have placed article boxes around each section of the article, press the **<Return>** key or select another tool. Acrobat will display the Article Properties dialog box.

7. Enter the article information in the edit fields of the Article Properties dialog box and press the **OK** button, or press the **Cancel** button if you decide you don't want to create the article.

If you use the **<Return>** key to mark the end of an article, the **Link** tool will still be active; select another tool to deactivate it.

Modifying Articles

At the last minute, Katherine decides to add biographical information at the end of each author's work. She wants to maintain the structure of the existing articles, so she enters the information in a separate file and distills it to PDF format. She copies the new pages into the magazine and adds a section to the end of each author's article.

Adding Sections to Articles

To add a section to an article, you place an article box around the section. To add a new article box to an article:

1. Select the **Tools | Article** command. The mouse cursor will change to a crosshair, and all existing article boxes will be displayed.

2. Click on the section of the article after which you want the new section to be viewed. You can place new sections after any section in an article.

Exchange will display the article box's label, handles, and plus tab.

3. Click on the plus tab. When the mouse cursor is placed over the plus tab, it changes to the article tool icon.

4. Click on one corner of the section of the page that you want to add.

5. Drag the mouse to the opposite corner of the section.

6. Release the mouse button; Exchange will add the new section. If you have added the section to the middle of the article, Exchange will renumber the sections that follow the new section.

7. Repeat steps 4–6 for any other sections that you want to add to the article.

8. When you have placed article boxes around each new section of the article, press the **<Return>** key or select another tool.

If you use the **<Return>** key to indicate that you are finished adding sections to an article, the article tool will still be active; select another tool to deactivate it.

Deleting Article Boxes from Articles

To delete an article box from an article:

1. Select the **Tools | Article** command. The mouse cursor will change to a crosshair, and all existing article boxes will be displayed.

2. Click on the article box that you want to delete.

3. Press the **<Delete>** key. Exchange will display a dialog box, asking you if you want to delete the article box or the entire article.

4. Press the **Box** button to delete the article box; if you decide you don't want to delete the article box, press the **Cancel** button.

The article tool will remain active after you delete the article box; to deactivate it, select another tool.

Moving an Article Box

To move an article box from an article:

1. Select the **Tools | Article** command. The mouse cursor will change to a crosshair, and all existing article boxes will be displayed.
2. Click on the article box that you want to move. The mouse cursor will change to a four-arrow cursor.
3. Drag the article box to the new location.
4. Release the mouse button. Exchange will display the article box in the new location.

The article tool will remain active after you move the article box; to deactivate it, select another tool.

Changing the Size of an Article Box

To change the size of an article box:

1. Select the **Tools | Article** command. The mouse cursor will change to a crosshair, and all existing article boxes will be displayed.
2. Click on the article box that you want to move. Exchange will display the article box's resizing handles.
3. Click on the resizing handle you want to move. When the mouse cursor is placed over the resizing handle, it changes to a diagonal two-arrow cursor.
4. Drag the resizing handle until the article box has the size you want.
5. Release the mouse button. Exchange will resize the article box.

The article tool will remain active after you move the article box; to deactivate it, select another tool.

Changing an Article's Properties

To change an article's properties:

1. Select the **Tools | Article** command. The mouse cursor will change to a crosshair, and all existing article boxes will be displayed.

CHAPTER 15

2. Double click on any article box of the article whose properties you want to change. Exchange will display the Article Properties dialog box.
3. Enter the new information in the edit fields of the Article Properties dialog box.
4. Press the **OK** button to confirm the changes you made; if you decide you don't want to make the changes, press the **Cancel** button.

The article tool will remain active after you change an article's properties; to deactivate it, select another tool.

Deleting Articles

To delete an article:

1. Select the **Tools | Article** command. The mouse cursor will change to a crosshair, and all existing article boxes will be displayed.
2. Click on the section of the article that you want to delete.
3. Press the **<Delete>** key. Exchange will display a dialog box, asking you if you want to delete the article box or the entire article.
4. Press the **Article** button to delete the article; if you decide you don't want to delete the article, press the **Cancel** button.

The article tool will remain active after you delete the article; to deactivate it, select another tool.

Easy Access to a World of Information

What started out as a project to provide students and faculty with easy access to computer documentation has evolved into an extensive on-line information network, with formatted electronic documents published across the Internet worldwide computer network. It is called the Wharton Information Network, and Adobe Acrobat software is an integral part.

"Adobe Acrobat is a powerful tool for sharing information across the Wharton School campus or around the world via the Internet worldwide network," says Kendall Whitehouse, associate director of publishing and media technologies at Wharton. "Providing information on the network in a single format—Acrobat software's Portable Document Format (PDF)— has enabled us to expand the Wharton Information Network far beyond our initial expectations."

The Wharton School of the University of Pennsylvania is one of the leading and most innovative global business schools in the world. Every year, Wharton provides top-rated management education to nearly 5,000 undergraduate, MBA, and doctoral students. In the process, students and faculty need access to volumes of information. The Wharton computing system is typical of the complex, multiplatform computing environments of businesses and universities today, with several computer labs containing a series of Novell® NetWare® file servers, more than 110 PCs, several Apple® Macintosh® computers, and a network of high-performance UNIX® workstations.

Wharton first developed an archive of electronic documents in PDF and made it available over the school's local area network, accessible from the DOS/Windows™ and Macintosh labs throughout the Wharton campus. The second phase of the information system will enable Wharton to publish information across the worldwide Internet network.

Phase I: Local Area Network Document Archive

Wharton publishes TechBriefs, information to help its students and faculty access the diverse information systems on campus. Wharton Computing and Information Technology wanted these TechBriefs to be available on-line so users could view and print needed documents. "The prospect of maintaining all of this documentation on-line in different file formats was daunting," says Whitehouse. "Because we frequently update our TechBriefs, it would have required a lot of overhead to manage different electronic versions."

Using Acrobat software, Whitehouse has one simple automatic conversion process. Whatever needs to be published is created as a PostScript™ language file that is then converted into PDF. The same files are accessible and viewable—with all the original formatting—from either PCs or Macintosh computers within the labs.

Since the introduction of Acrobat software, the Wharton Information Network has expanded to contain not only technical documentation but also undergraduate and MBA publications and documents collected from other Internet archive sites.

Benefit: Improved Access to Information

Whitehouse says that Acrobat software makes managing and accessing information on the network easier. He plans to use cross-document links between PDF files to simplify viewing and browsing of information on the network. For example, cross-document links would enable users to click on a publication title and view the document instantly.

The ability to make touch-up edits on PDF files within Adobe Illustrator™ 5.5 for the Macintosh will be a big plus, simplifying the process of making minor changes to a document once it has been converted to PDF. "There have been times when minor errors were detected in a published document," says Whitehouse. "Being able to make quick, clean fixes to a file will save a lot of time and effort."

Phase II: Internet-wide Document Archive

Once the local area network document archive was completed, Whitehouse began investigating how to make this information available outside of Wharton. He recently implemented an Internet-based version of the Wharton Information Network. Faculty and students can still browse information in the campus document archive, or they can share information published by colleagues and others via the Internet.

"We have a highly distributed computing environment, with a large number of people publishing documents created many different ways," says Whitehouse. "Acrobat plays an integral role in expanding the Wharton Information Network." Acrobat software promotes sharing ideas and information throughout the university, because no one has to worry about the originating application or platform.

"By making documents available as PDF files either on the campus or worldwide networks, users can access them regardless of the available platforms or applications," says Whitehouse. "Acrobat was the enabling technology that made all this feasible."

IV

PUBLISHING
Interactive
Documents

*The Easiest Way To Publish
On The World Wide Web*

An Introduction to the World Wide Web

What Is the World Wide Web?

The World Wide Web (affectionately called "the Web" by those who use it) is a collection of information stored on computers all over the world (hence the World Wide) that are connected to the Internet. Each piece of information on the Web, known as a *resource*, can be associated with other resources via hyperlinks, so that you can move from topic to topic easily, according to your interest. The links between resources do not have to follow any specific pattern; as links between pieces of information are added, the links start to resemble a dense mesh (hence the Web). Any type of information can be a Web resource, including text, graphics, audio, and video.

Why Should I Care?

The Web is the largest, most comprehensive, and widely used electronic information system in the world. It is popular and easy to use; you move to a new topic by pressing a key or clicking a mouse button. It is organic; there is no central authority that decides what will or will not be on the Web. This means that you, or anyone, can add information to the Web—all you need to do is place your information in the proper format and store it on a properly connected computer, known as a *Web server*; you will see how to do this in the following chapters. If the information you provide is particularly useful, other people will link their information to yours, increasing the potential audience for your information. The Web, in short, is the most convenient and powerful way to publish your PDF documents.

History of the World Wide Web

In 1990, Tim Berners-Lee of CERN, the European Center for Nuclear Physics Research, developed the World Wide Web hypertext system. His goal was to improve the flow of information between members of the high-energy physics research community. At the time, a large amount of information was available in electronic form, but there were obstacles that prevented it from being used to its fullest. Information was distributed among many individual machines without sufficient means to tie related materials together. Furthermore, each type of resource was associated with a different protocol and could only be retrieved by a program that "spoke" that protocol. If you wanted to download a file, you had to learn a file transfer program; if you wanted to participate in a Usenet newsgroup, you had to learn a newsreader program, and so on.

The World Wide Web uses the following components to solve these problems:

- The *URL*, a naming system that compactly describes the location of every resource on the Internet, and the protocol used to retrieve it.

- *HTML*, a language for "marking" hypertext links and other important features of a document.
- *HTTP*, a protocol for transferring hypertext documents and other resources.
- *Web clients* or *Web browsers*, programs that combine a variety of information retrieval abilities under one interface, making it easier to use resources.
- *Web servers*, programs that send resources to Web clients on request.

The system Berners-Lee created grew slowly; in May of 1993, there were only 50 Web sites worldwide, concentrated at physics research institutions. But the Web was about to take off, because of a decision made the previous year.

In 1992, *CERN* released much of its WWW technology into the public domain; this spurred development of Web servers and browsers at other organizations. A team led by Marc Andreessen at the National Center for Supercomputing Applications (*NCSA*) at the University of Illinois-Urbana/Champaign took advantage of this technology to create Mosaic, the first graphical Web browser, which was released in 1993. Mosaic has thousands of users and has spawned a legion of imitators, not least of which is Netscape's Navigator, also created by Andreessen and other members of the original NCSA Mosaic development group. Millions of people use graphical browsers, and they have changed the face (and the size) of the Web.

Graphical Web browsers make it easier than ever before to retrieve Internet resources. You can activate a hyperlink, download a file, or read a Usenet news article with a single mouse click. Surfing, the word used by Web fans to describe the use of the Web with a graphical browser, conjures the appropriate images; browsing the Web with a graphical browser gives you the feeling of gliding on top of a wave of information.

Another key feature of Mosaic and other graphical browsers is that they are designed to work in partnership with *helper applications*. Any type of information can be a Web resource: sound, graphics, animation, even interactive computer sessions. It would be difficult to write a browser that could handle all of these data types by itself; most browsers can only understand text in HTML and plain ASCII formats and graphics in GIF format. *Helper applications* are separate programs that handle data the browser cannot understand.

When a Web server responds to a browser's request for a resource, it transmits the *MIME* type of the data to the browser. If the browser is unable to interpret data of that MIME type, it passes the data to a helper application that can interpret it. The helper application interprets the data and opens its own program window to display it. Helper application support has encouraged information providers to add graphics, animation, and sound to their Web sites, making the Web a true multimedia system. Acrobat Reader and Exchange can be used as helper applications for viewing PDF files that are published on the Web; instructions for configuring your browser to launch Reader or Exchange as a helper application are found in chapter 18.

In the time since NCSA released Mosaic, the growth of Web traffic has been phenomenal, as reflected in the number of Web servers world-wide, illustrated in the following table:

June 1993	130 sites
December 1993	623 sites
June 1994	1265 sites
December 1994	11576 sites
June 1995	30000 sites

There are currently over 30,000 Web servers, with 50 to 100 more connecting every day.

At present, there are two major trends that are shaping the future of the Web. The major commercial on-line services are making the Web available to their subscribers, and corporations are installing Web servers and creating an on-line presence. These two trends, which are reinforcing each other, are changing the purpose of the Web from a repository of scientific and technical information to an interactive medium that combines information, entertainment, and advertising.

Web access via CompuServe™, Prodigy™, and AOL™ is bringing the Web to a different—and much larger—audience than ever before. In the beginning, the Web was the exclusive province of scientists and engineers, and the content of the Web reflected the needs of that technically proficient audience. As an ever greater percentage of the population gains access to the Web, its content is shifting to serve a more general audience. Some of the most popular Web sites are related to music, photography, gardening, movies, and games. There are sites covering almost any topic imaginable—there is even a site that is devoted entirely to information about llamas! (Llama fans can find this site at http://www.webcom.com/~degra-ham/.)

The promise of an inexpensive mass-market presence —and the high-tech appeal of the Internet—has drawn corporations of all sizes to the Web. Naturally, computer and technology companies are at the forefront of this trend, but many companies in other industries are staking their claim on the Web as well. While most of these companies are placing product information, marketing materials, and technical support information on the Web, a growing number of them are using the Web to conduct electronic transactions. These transactions are of two types: one is a Web-based on-line service, where subscribers pay for the privilege of access to a Web site; the other is on-line ordering, where people can transmit an electronic order for a product.

Web Concepts

Pages and Home Pages

Web documents are known as *pages*. Unlike paper documents, a Web page has no size; it is a unit of information and can correspond to any number of paper pages.

When placing a collection of pages on a Web site, an author usually creates one page that is a starting point for exploring the other pages; this type of page is known as a *home page*. Home pages are often a combination of a title page and a table of contents. There are some standard methods of writing the address of a home page that make it easier to find them; these methods are discussed in the "URLs" section.

Hypertext/Hyperlinks

The links between resources are known as *hyperlinks*, and the documents that contain them are known as *hypertext* documents. The author of a hypertext document marks the words of the document that refer to related topics, and embeds the locations of the related materials in the document. The hypertext viewing program sets the marked words apart from the rest of the text, using underlining, different colors, or reverse video (white on black, for instance). When you activate the hyperlink with a keystroke or mouse click, the hypertext viewing program displays the material to which the link refers.

URLs

URLs, or Uniform (or Universal) Resource Locators, have three parts: transfer mechanism names, domain names, and location names.

- **Transfer mechanism names**, or scheme names, are abbreviations of the transfer protocol that is used to retrieve the resource. For instance, http is the name for the HyperText Transfer Protocol, which is used to transfer Web pages. The most common transfer mechanism names, and the transfer mechanisms they correspond to, are shown in the following table:

http	HyperText Transfer Protocol
gopher	Gopher Protocol
ftp	File Transfer Protocol
file	For retrieving files on local systems
news	Network News Transfer Protocol
nntp	Usenet news (for local NNTP access only)
mailto	Electronic mail address
mid	Message identifiers for electronic mail
cid	Content identifiers for MIME body part
prospero	Access using the prospero protocols; prospero is a Net-wide virtual file system
telnet	Interactive session using telnet
rlogin	Interactive session using rlogin
tn3270	Interactive session using tn3270
wais	Wide Area Information Server protocol

- **Domain names** refer to the computer on which the resource is stored. Optionally, a user name /

password combination and an IP port number may be added to the domain name.

- **Path names** refer to the location of the resource within the computer's storage system. The path name is written from the perspective of the computer where the resource is stored, and is usually a full path name.

The URLs for most organizations' home pages follow this convention:

http://www.*organization_domain_name*.

For instance, Adobe Systems' domain name is adobe.com, and the URL for their home page is:

http://www.adobe.com

There is also a convention for the URL of an individual's home page on a UNIX system. It is:

http://www.*organization_domain_name*/~*user_name*

HTML

Most of the information available on the Web today is formatted in HTML, the HyperText Markup Language. A markup language is a set of symbols that specify the structure of a document, as opposed to its contents. HTML defines different document *elements*, such as titles, headings, body text, ordered (numbered) lists, unordered (bulleted) lists, and hyperlinks. The elements of an HTML document have a hierarchical structure, like an outline. Each element is marked by a *start tag* at the beginning of the element, and an *end tag* at the end of the element. Start tags are enclosed within the < and > characters; <TITLE> is an example of a start tag. End tags are enclosed within the </ and > characters; </TITLE> is an example of an end tag.

In general, HTML does not define the format of a document. The format is defined by the reader of the document who configures a browser program to associate different typographical attributes to different document elements. For instance, headings are often in boldface and in a larger type size than body text.

A Sample HTML Page

```
<!DOCTYPE HTML PUBLIC '-//W30//DTD WWW
      HTML 2.0//EN'>
<HTML>
   <HEAD>
      <TITLE>Designing Interactive
      Documents with Acrobat Pro</TITLE>
   </HEAD>
   <BODY>
      <H1>About This Site</H1>
      <P>
      Welcome to the Designing Interactive
      Documents with Acrobat Pro Web Site.
      This site is a model for making PDF
      documents available to readers via
      the World Wide Web. It contains the
      information needed to "serve" PDF
      documents from three perspectives:
      that of the Author, Publisher, and
      Reader.
      </P>

      <HR>

      <H2>The Author</H2>
      <P>
      The Author is the person who creates
      a document in PDF format. He is
      responsible for the text, graphics,
      and layout of the document, and its
      conversion to the PDF format using
      PDFWriter or Distiller.
```

```
</P>

<H2>The Publisher</H2>
<P>
The Publisher is the person who
maintains the Web server, the
computer that sends the information
on the Web site to the Internet.
Publishers are responsible for:
</P>

<UL>
<LI>
Associating the PDF file extension
with the application/PDF MIME type,
so the Web server informs Web
clients that the incoming data is a
PDF file.
</LI>
<LI>
Restricting access to all or part of
the Web site to authorized
users or domains.
</LI>
<LI>
Configuring the CGI (Common Gateway
Interface) and cgi-bin programs and
scripts. This allows Readers to use
interactive features, such as
keyword searches.
</LI>
</UL>
```

```
<P>

The Publisher is not responsible for
the content of the documents that
are stored on the Web server. While
the Author and the Publisher may be
the same person, we do not make that
assumption here.

</P>

<P>

An example of a link to a PDF file
would be:

<UL>

   <LI>

      <A HREF="http://www.adobe.com/
      PDFs/PR/9508/
      950821.acro.21.pdf">

<IMG SRC="pdfmid.gif" >Test PDF
File(using Viewer)</A>

</UL>

</P>

<H2>The Reader</H3>

<P>

The Reader is the person who views
the documents. Readers are
responsible for properly configuring
their WWW clients, or browsers, to
view PDF files.

</P>

<P>
```

To configure a browser to view PDF files, associate the PDF file type with a helper application, such as Acrobat Reader or Exchange, that can display them. You may have to enter values in dialog boxes, or edit your browser's configuration files.
`</P>`

`<HR>`

`</BODY>`
`</HTML>`

Netscape - [Designing Interactive Documents with Acrobat Pro]

File   Edit   View   Go   Bookmarks   Options   Directory   Help

Back   Forward   Home   Reload   Images   Open   Print   Find   Stop

What's New!   What's Cool!   Handbook   Net Search   Net Directory   Newsgroups

About This Site

Welcome to the Designing Interactive Documents with Acrobat Pro Web Site. This site is a model for making PDF documents available to readers via the World Wide Web. It contains the information needed to "serve" PDF documents from three perspectives, that of the Author, Publisher, and Reader.

The Author

The Author is the person who creates a document in PDF format. He is responsible for the text, graphics, and layout of the document, and its conversion to the PDF format using PDFWriter or Distiller.

The Publisher

The Publisher is the person who maintains the Web server, the computer that sends the information on the Web site to the Internet. Publishers are responsible for:

- Associating the PDF file extension with the application/PDF MIME type, so the Web server informs Web clients that the incoming data is a PDF file.
- Restricting access to all or part of the Web site to authorized users or domains.
- Configuring the CGI (Common Gateway Interface) and cgi-bin programs and scripts. This allows Readers to use interactive features, such as keyword searches.

The Publisher is not responsible for the content of the documents that are stored on the Web server. While the Author and the Publisher may be the same person, we do not make that assumption here.

An example of a link to a PDF file would be:

- Test PDF File(using Viewer)

The Reader

The Reader is the person who views the documents. Readers are responsible for properly configuring their WWW clients, or browsers, to view PDF files.

To configure a browser to view PDF files, associate the PDF file type with a helper application, such as Acrobat Reader or Exchange, that can display them. You may have to enter values in dialog boxes, or edit your browser's configuration files.

Client-server Systems and Protocols: Buying a Sack of Potatoes

The Web is built on a client-server model. A server is like the proprietor of a general store; it waits for a client to come in with a request, just like a grocer waits behind a counter. A client is like a customer who walks into the store and asks for one or more items on a grocery list.

Clients and servers communicate with each other using a common protocol. A protocol is like a collection of sentences the general store owner and his customers agree to speak when conducting business. For instance, the client may announce its presence to the server; this is a like a customer walking into a store and greeting the owner, saying "Hello, Mrs. Hatfield. How are you today?" The server then acknowledges the client and asks for the request; in the store, the owner might say "I'm fine, Mr. McCoy. What can I get for you?" The client then gives its request, "I'd like a sack of potatoes," and the server transfers the resource to the client; "Here are your potatoes, Mr. McCoy. Have a nice day." Of course, programs don't converse in human language; most protocols are codes that are designed to efficiently handle a very small set of situations in a standard manner. It's as if Mrs. Hatfield and Mr. McCoy used the same sentences every time Mr. McCoy bought supplies, except for the name of the supplies.

The Web is a *stateless* system; in essence, this means that the server is unusually forgetful. Unlike Mrs. Hatfield in the general store, the server will not remember any previous requests you made, even if you made them only seconds earlier. Each transaction you make is discrete, unrelated to any previous ones. This has its advantages and disadvantages. While stateless systems can't always give you the good old-fashioned customer service you would like, they are relatively easy to write.

Why Use PDF on the Web?

The goal of establishing a Web site is to have people view the information you publish on it. PDF can help you achieve that goal by allowing you to produce electronic documents that are as readable—and as good-looking—as the best paper documents.

Using PDF on the Web has become even more exciting with the recent release of a beta version of the WebLink plug-in for Macintosh and Windows versions of Exchange. The WebLink allows you to place links to URLs in PDF documents; when you select a URL link, the plug-in asks an installed Web browser to retrieve the resource to which the link points. Before the WebLink was released, PDF documents on the Web were dead-end points; since there was no way to link a PDF document to another Web resource, it was necessary to use HTML for all pages that required links. The WebLink makes it possible to experiment with PDF pages in a greater variety of situations, and to use the complimentary features of PDF and HTML to communicate your message most effectively.

To achieve your Web viewership goal, it is important to keep in mind the software tools that your target audience will be using to browse your site. At present, many more people have Web browsers than have Exchange, for the following reasons:

- While several Web browsers can be obtained free of charge, Exchange must be bought.

- Exchange is only available for the Macintosh and Windows platforms; Web browsers are available for many more platforms.

Furthermore, only two browsers currently work with WebLink: Netscape Navigator 1.1 and later and Spyglass Enhanced Mosaic 2.0. This means that many more people will be able to activate Web hyperlinks in HTML documents than will be able to activate them in PDF documents, at least in the near future.

The number of people who can activate URL links in PDF documents will increase, however. Adobe is developing a new version of Reader with built-in URL link capability, and making Reader available for other platforms besides Windows and Mac. The WebLink includes a plug-in driver architecture that simplifies the task of adding support for a particular browser; it is likely that other browsers will support the WebLink plug-in in the future.

Until the WebLink is available to a wider audience, it is not a good idea to completely replace HTML pages with PDF pages—you risk reducing the potential audience for your information. If you plan to introduce more PDF on your site, you should duplicate as much of the content as possible in HTML. Then, analyze the preferences of the people who visit your site to determine which format is most appropriate for each situation.

PDF vs. HTML: Strengths and Weaknesses

As you start to introduce more PDF content on your Web site, you should keep in mind the different advantages of PDF and HTML. The two formats have different strengths and weaknesses in the areas of typography, document preparation, document maintenance, and document reuse. By taking all of these factors into account, you will be able to produce the best possible content—and the highest viewership—at the least cost.

Typography

PDF was designed to describe pages with a high degree of flexibility. With PDF, you can place graphics and text at arbitrary locations on a page, limited only by the capabilities of the software you use to produce the document. This allows you to easily produce complex page layouts, tables, and equations with the tools that are best suited to producing them. HTML, on the other hand, is designed to describe the structure of a document, and its typographical capabilities are limited. While HTML support for tables and equations is being developed, most Web browsers cannot display them.

PDF gives you precise control over the typefaces in a document. It allows you to use as many typefaces as you wish in a document, to embed them in documents, and to use them in any way you see fit—this ensures that the document your readers see looks exactly like you want it to look. HTML, on the other hand, does not specify typographical attributes precisely, and gives control over typefaces to the reader. Most of the typographical attributes of text in an HTML document are determined by the browser, according to the document element in which the text is contained; for instance, text in a heading element is generally boldface and larger than the text in a body text element. Browsers will often limit the number of typefaces in an HTML document to two, one proportional and one non-proportional, which are selected by the reader of the document.

PDF allows you to specify the width and height of a document's pages, making it possible to design a document for either on-line viewing or printing. This is an advantage if your audience is using a specific display device, such as a VGA monitor or laser-printed 8.5" x 11" pages, but it is a challenge to design a document that will be easy to read on every display. HTML pages do not have sizes, they simply fill whatever display area is available. HTML's formatting vagueness makes it versatile; it will do a decent job with just about every display.

Many zines (electronic magazines) have adopted the PDF format because it allows them to design their publications to be printed on common printers. PDF allows publishers of zines to distribute them electronically while retaining the distinctive look and readability associated with paper publications. These magazines are often devoted to publicizing their content, rather than building a paid subscriber base; they encourage their readers to print copies of the zine and share it with friends. This is a classic case of the "distribute and print" model, one of the main concepts behind Acrobat.

Document Preparation

Page Creation

One of the reasons that PDF has become popular on the Web is that it simplifies the transition between paper and on-line documents. Many organizations have found Acrobat to be an effective solution for putting existing documents on-line. These documents were often created in less-portable formats, such as a desktop publishing format, and then printed. If the documents are already in electronic form, publishing them on-line is simple; they need only to be printed to PDF (using PDFWriter or Distiller) and placed on a Web site.

To convert existing documents to HTML format often requires much more effort. HTML does not support tables, equations, or many of the graphical and typographical elements used in typical documents. As a result, many documents must be reformatted when they are converted to HTML.

Also, there are not many software packages that allow you to produce HTML output directly. A growing number of software vendors are including HTML output capability in their products, but these tools are immature compared to the standard word processors, desktop publishers, and spreadsheets available in the typical office. In contrast, you can produce PDF output from almost any software package with PDF-Writer and Distiller.

One company that uses Acrobat to convert documents to electronic form is the *New York Times*. The *Times* produces a daily news digest, TimesFax, that is faxed to thousands of subscribers worldwide. This document is designed to be easily read when printed by a fax machine; it is in 8.5" x 11" format, in black and white, and it has three columns. Instead of making a separate HTML version of the digest, the *Times* simply converts it to PDF format and places it on their Web server, greatly increasing the potential readership of the digest with little additional cost. PDF has two main benefits over HTML for the Web version of TimesFax: the additional cost of producing the on-line version is negligible, since there is no reformatting; PDF allows the *Times* to maintain its brand identity, with a masthead on the first page and the traditional column format of a newspaper.

HTML is more evenly matched with PDF when it comes to creating new electronic documents for the Web, but PDF does have a significant advantage in one area, which stems from its being a page description language: it is independent of the tools you use to create a document. This allows you to create a document using the tool that is best suited to the task—you can even create different sections of a document with different tools, and then combine them with Exchange. You may decide, for instance, to create some pages of a PDF document with a desktop publishing package that has sophisticated layout capabilities. Other pages may lend themselves to the strong text processing features in your word processor, and still others may require tables of figures that are best handled by a spreadsheet. While this benefit of PDF may not be an overriding concern for all documents, it may be important for certain complex ones.

Hyperlink Creation

In HTML, hypertext links and the link text associated with them are part of the document's structure, while in PDF, they are simply rectangular areas of a page. This has consequences for the ease of hyperlink generation that give the advantage in this area to HTML.

In many hypertext systems, link text is distinguished from static text by underlining it and giving it a different color. This is true of many Web browsers, of Windows help—and even of Adobe's PDF help files for Acrobat products. Because hyperlinks and link text are part of the structure of an HTML document, Web browsers can automatically highlight link text in them. Since PDF's hyperlinks are not associated with the link text, the text is not automatically highlighted. Creating a hyperlink with highlighted link text in a PDF document takes two steps, as opposed to HTML's one: first, you highlight the link text in the document creation tool, and then you create the hyperlink in Exchange.

HTML's advantage in hyperlink generation will diminish in the future. Already, several desktop publishing software packages, such as FrameMaker and

PageMaker, allow you to create the hyperlink and highlight the link text in one step. As other document creation software adds this support, it will become easier to create PDF documents whose link text is automatically highlighted.

Document Maintenance

There are three aspects to maintaining a document you place on the Web: maintaining its content, its formatting, and its hyperlinks. Because it is easier to maintain the formatting and hyperlinks of an HTML document, HTML is the better choice for those documents that you expect to undergo many revisions.

The same advantages and disadvantages that PDF and HTML show when you create a document will also be in effect when you revise it. You can find out more about these advantages and disadvantages in the "Document Creation" section of this chapter. PDF documents require the extra step of converting the revised document to PDF format using either PDF-Writer or Distiller. This is usually a trivial extra step, but it is an extra step, nonetheless.

Since HTML pages do not have fixed boundaries or rigid formatting, it is unlikely that revisions to the content of a document will make it necessary to reformat it. In many cases, PDF documents will require reformatting. For instance, if you want to add new items to a list on an HTML page, you just add the new items; since the page has no boundaries, there is nothing further to do. Adding the new items to a PDF document, however, may take a significant amount of effort. Since a PDF document will have boundaries, you may have to change the page size or make other adjustments to the document to accommodate the larger list. To minimize the need for reformatting and the effort it takes to do it, you should structure your documents well and rely on style sheets or templates for formatting decisions rather than manual layout.

HTML has an edge in hyperlink maintenance, for the reasons listed in the "Hyperlink Creation" section of this chapter. PDF has a marked disadvantage in this area when the software used to create the document does not support PDF hyperlink generation; in such cases, all of the hyperlinks must be regenerated each time a document is reprinted. Unless you work with a software package that generates PDF hyperlinks automatically, you should use HTML for documents you will revise frequently.

Document Re-use

HTML marks the structure of a document, while PDF does not. This is an important point to consider if you plan to re-use, combine, or index documents. You may, for instance, find it necessary to extract link text, headings, or certain sections of text from documents that you place on the Web. HTML's structure makes this is a relatively straightforward task; while it is possible to manipulate PDF files in this manner, it is far from straightforward.

CHAPTER

17

Getting On

How to Access the World Wide Web

Okay—you've heard that the Web is the hottest thing going, and you're dying to give it a try. What do you do? To surf the Web, you need two things: a Web browser, and a connection to the Internet. In this chapter, you'll see how to get both.

The Web Via On-line Services

If you are a beginner, the easiest way to take a look at the Web is via one of the major on-line services, such as America Online, Compuserve, Prodigy, or Delphi. These services have made getting on the Web easier by integrating a Web browser and Internet connection support into their navigation software. As we write this, Compuserve and Prodigy provide Web browsers, AOL is beta testing their Web browser, and Delphi information service supports the text-based Lynx browser. Compuserve and AOL consider Web surfing a premium service, and you will have to pay an extra hourly charge; Prodigy and Delphi do not add any extra charges. The on-line service route is convenient if you already subscribe to a service, since you do not have to pay for another service.

Unfortunately, there are some disadvantages to gaining Web access through an on-line service. Most on-line services offer relatively slow data transfer rates, typically 9600 baud or less. Also, the major on-line services do not allow you to place your own pages on the Web without restriction; if your aim is to publish information on the Web, you will need to find another solution. In which case, you need to get on the Net yourself, using an Internet service provider.

The Web Via Internet Providers

Compared to on-line services, most Internet providers keep things simple; they don't provide stock quotes, weather information, or friendly interfaces—they just get you on the Net. The services offered by an Internet provider can vary widely, ranging from support for a plug-and-play solution, to dial-up shell accounts, to dedicated high-speed connections that connect your entire local network to the Net.

The increased power and flexibility that Internet providers offer doesn't come without a price, however. The more advanced your connection to the Net is, the more complicated and costly it is to establish and maintain it. You will be responsible for installing and configuring the software on your side of the connection, such as communications software and client programs such as Web browsers.

Plug-and-play Internet Solutions

Next to the on-line services, plug-and-play Internet solutions, such as Spry™'s *Internet in a Box* and Netcom™'s *Netcruiser*, are the next-easiest way to see what the Web is all about. Plug-and-play Internet solutions are commercial packages of Internet client software that offer automatic subscription to one or more Internet providers. Some of these packages offer a full suite of client software, such as e-mail, FTP, Usenet newsreader, telnet, and gopher; others offer only a Web browser. These solutions are most appropriate for home users or small companies who are interested in the Web but do not want to subscribe to one of the major on-line services.

Plug-and-play Internet solutions have the advantage of being easy-to-use, but some of them lock you into a particular provider, and there's no guarantee that any of the service providers you can choose from will meet your needs. In particular, some of the Internet service providers that support plug-and-play solutions offer Web publishing services, and others do not. You should make sure that you can get the Internet services you want from a plug-and-play solution before buying it.

Shell Accounts and SLIP/CSLIP/PPP Accounts

There are two ways that an Internet provider can connect you to the world: *shell accounts* and *serial line connections*. A *shell account* is simply a user account on the Internet provider's computer, which is usually a UNIX system. The name shell account comes from the fact that you are using the command prompt of a UNIX *shell,* a program that interprets the commands you type. You use a communications program on your computer to operate the shell on the service provider's machine.

Shell accounts provide indirect Internet access; the provider's computer is connected to the Net, but yours is not. Data from the Net stops at the service provider's computer; only the communication between your computer and the service provider's computer travels through the telephone line. You can't use a graphical browser with a shell account, but you can run a text-based browser, such as Lynx, if it is installed on your provider's computer.

Serial line connections are direct connections to the Internet via a telephone line, which is, as you may have guessed, a serial line. When you use this kind of account, you "borrow" an Internet address from your provider while you are on-line, and the provider redirects the Internet traffic for that address to your computer. This means that your computer is directly connected to the Net; data from the Net is transmitted to your computer through the telephone line. A direct connection to the Net is necessary if you want to run a graphical Web browser.

Serial line connections will use either the SLIP/CSLIP (Serial Line Internet Protocol / Compressed Serial Line Internet Protocol) or PPP (Point-to-Point Protocol) to manage the communications between your computer and the Internet provider's computer. When you use PPP, your computer and your Internet provider's computer will "negotiate" how the communication between the two will take place. SLIP and CSLIP do not provide that service, so you will have to set certain configuration parameters yourself; this makes these protocols somewhat more difficult to use and somewhat less reliable. Once you have established the connection to your Internet provider's computer, however, the two protocols will perform nearly identically.

Some Internet providers offer Web publishing services to their customers, and others do not. If you want to publish on the Web, your Internet provider will need to provide Web server capability, the ability to furnish Web resources when they are requested, and disk space, so you can store the PDF and HTML files you want to publish on the Internet provider's computer. Many Internet providers will provide a certain amount of disk space as a part of your subscription. If you need more space than the standard allotment, you will have to pay an extra fee for it.

Heavy-Duty, Big-League Web Sites

Busy, extensive Web sites consume large amounts of computing resources, and take time and effort to maintain. If you are planning to create a Web site for a business or non-profit organization, with large amounts of information and many visitors, neither on-line services, nor plug-and-play solutions, nor single-user Internet access will be sufficient. You should consider either working with a company that specializes in Web publishing or installing your own Web server. We won't cover these topics here, as there are plenty of books about the Web that do cover them—we will discuss several of the mechanics of using PDF with the Web in the next chapter, though.

CHAPTER

18

The Reader

Browsing PDF Documents on the Web

The reader is the person who retrieves PDF and HTML documents from the Web and views them. Readers are responsible for:

- Configuring their Web browser to use Acrobat Reader or Exchange as a helper application for PDF files

- Obtaining and installing the Weblink plug-in

- Obtaining and installing a Web browser that works with the Weblink plug-in

PDF, URLs, and the MIME Protocol

URL links can point to a variety of file types besides HTML, including several types of graphics, audio, and video files — and PDF, of course. How do Web browsers know what type of information they are receiving? They determine the file type of an incoming file through the MIME (Multipurpose Internet Mail Extensions) protocol. Using this protocol, the Web server sends information about the file to the browser, so the browser can decide whether to display the data by itself or to open a helper application that will display it.

The MIME protocol defines several different types of data, such as audio, video, and application data. For each type, there are subtypes that correspond to individual data formats. To encourage consistent use of the type and subtype names throughout the Internet, MIME types and subtypes are recorded in a central registry. To be registered, a data format must be an *open* format; the format must be published and publicly available. PDF is an such an open format, and it has been registered with the MIME type of *application* and the subtype of *pdf*.

Some Web servers do not indicate the MIME type of the resources they send. If you retrieve a resource from a server that does not provide the MIME type of the resource, your browser will use the file's extension to determine the file type.

Browsing PDF on the Web

You can use Acrobat Reader and Exchange as helper applications to Web browsers. When you configure Reader or Exchange as a helper application, the browser will launch them whenever it receives a PDF file. If you have Acrobat Exchange, you can also use the Weblink plug-in (described in Chapter 19) and your Web browser to retrieve URL links in PDF files. This allows you to browse both the PDF and the HTML documents.

Configuring Acrobat Reader or Exchange as a Helper Application

As an example of how to configure Reader or Exchange as a helper application to your Web browser, we will demonstrate the procedure for the Netscape browser. Netscape maintains a list of MIME file types, MIME subtypes, filename extensions, and associated viewers. We will add the PDF MIME type and subtype, filename extensions, and the path to Acrobat Reader to this list.

To configure Acrobat Reader or Exchange as a helper application to Netscape Navigator:

1. Select the **Options | Preferences**... command. Netscape Navigator's **Preferences** dialog box will appear.
2. Select **Helper Applications** from the list box that appears at the top of the **Preferences** dialog box. A list of MIME types appears in the **Prefer-**

ences dialog box, along with controls to specify the action the browser should take when it encounters a file of a specific MIME type.

3. Press the **New Type:** button to define a MIME type and subtype. The **Configure New MIME Type** dialog box appears, with edit boxes labeled **Mime Type:** and **Mime Sub Type:**.
4. Enter **application** in the **Mime Type:** edit box.
5. Enter **pdf** in the **Mime Sub Type:** edit box.
6. Press the **OK** button. The **Configure New MIME Type** dialog box will disappear.
7. Enter **pdf** in the **Extensions:** edit box.
8. Click on the **Launch Application:** radio button and enter the path and filename of your Acrobat Reader; if you do not know the path to your Reader, press the **Browse** button and use the controls of the dialog box that appears to select the path.
9. Press the **OK** button.

Netscape will now launch Acrobat Reader when it encounters a PDF file in a hyperlink or with FTP.

Obtaining and Installing the Weblink Plug-In

You can obtain the Weblink plug-in from Adobe Systems's Web site. Here are the URLs to download the Macintosh version of the plug-in directly:

- http://www.adobe.com/Acrobat/PlugIns/ WebLink/Mac/WebLink.bin (MacBinary format)
- http://www.adobe.com/Acrobat/PlugIns/ WebLink/Mac/WebLink.hqx (BinHex encoded)
- http://www.adobe.com/Acrobat/PlugIns/ WebLink/Mac/Web_Link_1.0b0a.sit.hqx (Stuffit archive - BinHex encoded)

Here is the URL to download the Windows version of the plug-in directly:

- http://www.adobe.com/Acrobat/PlugIns/ WebLink/Windows/wwwlink.api

You can also obtain the plug-in from Adobe's anonymous FTP server, ftp.adobe.com. The Macintosh version can be found in:

- /pub/adobe/Applications/Acrobat/Macintosh/ PlugIns/Weblink/WebLink.bin (MacBinary format)

- /pub/adobe/Applications/Acrobat/Macintosh/ PlugIns/Weblink/WebLink.hqx (BinHex encoded)

The Windows version can be found in:

- /pub/adobe/Applications/Acrobat/Windows/ PlugIns/Weblink/wwwlink.api

To install the plug-in under Windows, copy the plug-in to Exchange's plug_ins subdirectory. On a Macintosh, copy the plug-in to Exchange's Plug-Ins folder. Once you have installed the plug-in, you must indicate the location of your Web browser. To do this:

1. Start Exchange.
2. Select the **Edit | Preferences | WWW Link** command. The **WWW Link Preferences** dialog box will appear.
3. Enter the full path and filename of your Web browser in the **WWW Browser Application** edit box. If you do not know the location of your Web browser application, press the **Browse** button and select the file with the controls of the dialog box that appears.
4. Press the **OK** button.

Browsers that Work with the Weblink Plug-In

The Weblink plug-in works by sending commands to a running Web browser. The plug-in sends these commands via a *driver*, a program that translates high-level commands such as "retrieve this URL" to low-level commands that another program can understand. Adobe has written a standard Web driver, whose commands are a part of an emerging standard for controlling Web browsers; they are sent using DDE (Dynamic Data Exchange) in Windows and AppleEvents on the Macintosh. Currently, only two Web browsers support this standard: Netscape Navigator 1.1 and higher and Spyglass Enhanced Mosaic 2.0. These two browsers, therefore, are the only browsers that support the

Weblink plug-in, though this list will undoubtedly grow as more browser developers adopt standard protocols for accepting commands from external programs.

19

The Author

Authoring PDF Documents on the Web

The author is the person who creates the PDF and HTML documents that are published on a Web site. Authors are responsible for the text, graphics, and layout of the documents, conversion of documents to PDF format using PDFWriter or Distiller, and maintaining the links between the documents on the site. For the information that you publish to be effective, you, as the author, must create a navigable Web site with readable HTML and PDF pages.

Creating a Navigable Site

Much of the time, the information you place on the Web will be there to serve a particular need, whether it is to educate the world about a particular subject, to provide customer service or product information, or to entertain visitors. To meet your readers' needs, your site must be navigable—your readers must be able to find the information it contains and move among the pages that interest them without difficulty.

Site Organization

For your information to be effective, it must be organized in a way that your readers can understand. There are several structures that you can use to organize your documents, including:

- **Linear structure**: In a linear structure, pieces of information are in a serial order, like the chapters in a novel.

- **Tree structure**: In a tree structure, your information is organized into topics and subtopics, like an outline. This is a common structure for technical documents.

- **Star structure**: The star structure is related to the tree structure. In a star structure, you have a central piece of information and then one level of subtopics, none of which refer to each other. Many sites have a structure that is basically a star structure; for instance, a corporate site may have a "home page" and pages devoted to company overviews, product line, and customer service.

- **Grid structure**: In a grid structure, your information is organized in a table or spreadsheet format; each piece of information is linked only to adjacent entries in the table. This structure is rarer than the linear or tree structures, but it is sometimes used for reference data.

Information "Chunking"

After you organize the information on your site into a structure, you may add cross-references between topics. Authors of other Web sites may also make links to your site, and those links may be to any page on your site, not just the home page. This will transform your original document structure into a Web structure, where your documents may be linked together through many paths. There is no way to ensure that your readers will look at the pages you publish in any particular order. As a result, you cannot assume that your readers will see introductory material before they reach more detailed information.

To increase reader comprehension in the Web's hypertext environment, you should organize your data into understandable "chunks," and you should place links to introductory material in every "chunk" that relies on it. As an example, imagine we create a "History of WWII" site. We may have a first-level document that is a chronology of the war, a second-level document about the Pacific Theater, and third-level documents about the battles at Pearl Harbor, Iwo Jima, and Okinawa. It is possible for a reader to follow a link from one site to, say, the Okinawa page. Since we cannot assume that the reader knows anything about the Pacific Theater or the chronology of World War II, we should place links to those topics on the Okinawa page.

"Dead End" Pages

All too often, following a link to a new topic leads to a "dead end" page—a page with a high level of detail, without links to more general explanations of the topic. To prevent this from happening to your readers, make links that bring them to the home page of the site and to the topic level above the current level, if it exists. Here is an example of a text "navigation bar" that we use in our sample pages to do this:

```
<P>

|

<A HREF="index.html"> Home </A>

|

<A HREF="acromain.html"> Up </A>

|

</P>
```

Creating Readable Pages

To create readable pages on your Web site, you must take into account the computer hardware, browser software, and Internet connections that your audience will use to view the pages. You must also take the final use of the documents into acccount; for instance, if the PDF documents you place on your Web site are meant to be downloaded and printed, you do not want to design them for the screen.

Creating Readable HTML Pages

HTML specifies the structure and contents of a document, but does not specify its formatting. Web browsers format HTML documents according to their structure; by setting the Web browser's display options, the reader has final control over the appearance of your document on the screen. While this relieves you of the responsiblity of formatting the document for the screen, you must also be careful not to make any assumptions about the size of the document. One of the most common mistakes authors make is to use <BR> tags to enforce hard line breaks in those places where they look best on *their* screen. If the reader of the document uses different window or font sizes than the authors, this will result in misplaced line breaks. Use the <P></P> tags instead, to let the browser determine where the lines of a paragraph should end.

Creating Readable PDF Pages

In contrast to HTML, PDF gives you—not the reader—precise control over the page layout and formatting of a document. You must control them carefully, however, and with an eye to the different types of video hardware your readers may be using. You should design your pages to be easily readable with the lowest grade of video hardware you expect your audience to have.

Here are some guidelines that will help you create readable PDF pages.

- Use a screen oriented (landscape) page layout; to read a portrait page layout on most computer screens requires excessive scrolling. Alternatively, you can use PDF's article threads to provide automatic scrolling.

- Use larger text for documents that you view on the screen than for documents that you print. 12 to 14 point body text and 24 point headings are good sizes for a 14" VGA monitor.

- Use fonts that are easily read on a computer screen.

- Reduce the margins. The window border acts as a margin.

- Use whitespace as a visual aid to the organization of the document. While whitespace increases the cost of paper documents, it adds virtually no cost to an online document.

Taking Character-based Browsers into Account

Browsing
Interface
Navigating
Zoom
Features
Printing
Clipboard
Preferences
Creating
PDFWriter
PDF Files
Enhancing
Pages
Thumbnails
Bookmarks
Notes
Links
Articles
Web Publishing
Introduction
Getting On
Reader
Author
Publisher
Cool Sites
Advanced
Search
Catalog
Distiller

As graphical browsers have become more sophisticated, many Web authors have created HTML pages that are designed expressly for them, with heavy emphasis on in-line images, image maps, and graphical links. While there are many situations where graphics-heavy pages are the most effective means of communicating, you should make sure that your page design does not unintentionally prevent readers with less sophisticated browsers from using the information on your site.

There are two ways you can make the HTML documents on your site accessible to both character-based and graphical browsers:

1. Create two sets of documents with identical content, where one set is designed for graphical browsers and the other set is designed for character-based browsers.
2. Create one set of documents that has a mixture of graphical and text content, readable with both graphical and character-based browsers.

Here are some ways you can mix graphical and text content:

- Use the ALT attribute whenever you use the <IMG SRC> tag to place an image on the page or within a link.

- Use text-based navigation bars in addition to image maps. Microsoft's site, at http://www.microsoft.com, has several pages with both image maps and identical text-based links.

Taking Non-standard Tags into Account

Some commercial Web browsers use non-standard HTML tags to implement features that are unique to their browser. Perhaps the most famous is the <BLINK> tag; text within this tag will blink on and off when you view the document with Netscape Navigator. Other non-standard tags give you greater control over text style or text justification. These tags can improve the look of your documents when viewed with the browser software that understands them, but your documents may not look as good when viewed with other browsers. You can minimize the possibility of your documents looking strange when viewed with certain browsers by test-viewing them with several different browsers before you publish them.

Taking Low-bandwidth Connections into Account

A document that takes too long to download will not be read. When designing your Web site, take the connection speed of your intended audience into account, and adjust the file size of your documents accordingly.

There are many different ways of connecting to the Internet, from dialup SLIP connections to Ethernet to fiber optic cable, with connection speeds that vary from a few hundred or thousand characters per second to tens of millions of characters per second. The speed at which a data connection can transfer information is often referred to as bandwidth; low-speed connections are known as low-bandwidth and high-speed connections are known as high-bandwidth. While many corporate networks offer relatively high-speed Ethernet connections, most people using the Internet from home have slower connections.

Graphics and Bandwidth

One way to make sure your documents do not hog bandwidth is to minimize the amount of graphics that they contain. Images contain much more information than text; as a picture is worth a thousand words, image files can be thousands of times larger than the text that accompanies them! This is true for both PDF and HTML documents. While images in PDF files can be compressed by a large percentage, they will still consume more bandwidth than plain text. Judicious use of graphics and smart PDF compression choices will enhance the impact of your documents while keeping file sizes small enough for them to be downloaded quickly.

Document Size and Bandwidth

Another way to speed up the response time for a site is to keep document size small. Because HTML documents have no page boundaries, it is easy to create a large document without even realizing it. If the information you are placing in an HTML document will fill several paper pages, consider breaking up the information into sections and placing links between them. With PDF, gauging document size is easier because the document is split into pages. When you split a PDF file into sections, make sure that you have a link for each section on an HTML page, so that people that do not have the Weblink plug-in can still download each section (See the "Making Links to PDF files" section).

Marking Links to Large Files

You are likely, at one time or another, to create documents that are too large to download quickly, yet cannot be "cut." When you publish these documents on the Web, you can make life much easier for readers with low-bandwidth connections by following a simple courtesy: place the size of the file next to the link.

Making Links Between PDF and HTML Documents

There are two levels at which PDF and HTML can be mixed. At the first level, PDF files do not have links to URLs; readers can download the PDF documents, but they cannot use them to link back to the Web. At the second level, PDF files do have links to URLs, and readers can use PDF pages in a manner similar to HTML pages. You can use Acrobat Reader for the first level, viewing PDF files that you retrieve from the Web, but you cannot link back to the Web. For the second level, linking back to the Web from a PDF file, you need Acrobat Exchange and the Weblink plug-in, which is described in the "Web Intro" chapter.

Making Links from HTML to PDF

To make a link from an HTML document to a PDF document, you use the anchor <A> tag, just as you would when making a link from an HTML document to another HTML document. The only difference is that you name a PDF file as the target of the link:

<A HREF="acroauth.pdf">Retrieve a PDF document that does not contain any URL links</A>

An HTML link to a PDF document will be the same, whether the PDF document contains URL links or not. The difference between the two is in the PDF document, where the Weblink plug-in is used to define a link to a URL, rather than to another view in the PDF document. You can prove this for yourself by looking at this example link to a PDF document that contains a URL link.

<A HREF="acroaut2.pdf">Retrieve a PDF document that contains a URL link</A>

Making Links from PDF to URLs

The Weblink plug-in extends Acrobat Exchange's link creation tool to include support for URL links. You can make hypertext links from PDF to URLs of any type: HTML documents, graphics, audio files, Usenet news, ftp sessions, even telnet sessions.

The procedure for making a link to a URL is similar to making links to PDF document views or to external files. You create links by drawing *link rectangles* on the pages of the document and specifying the URL to which the link will point. When you click the mouse within the rectangle, Acrobat will ask the installed Web browser to retrieve the URL. If you are unfamiliar with creating links with Acrobat Exchange, you can refer to the Links chapter for more information.

To create a link to a URL:

1. Activate the Link tool by selecting the **Tools | Link** command or by pressing the **Link** toolbar button. Exchange will place link rectangles around every link in the document (even those links that you previously made invisible), and the mouse cursor will turn into a crosshair.
2. Click the mouse where you want to place the link and drag it to create a link rectangle. The **Create Link** dialog box will appear.

PART 4

Browsing
   Interface
   Navigating
   Zoom
   Features
   Printing
   Clipboard
   Preferences
Creating
   PDFWriter
   PDF Files
Enhancing
   Pages
   Thumbnails
   Bookmarks
   Notes
   Links
   Articles
Web Publishing
   Introduction
   Getting On
   Reader
   Author
   Publisher
   Cool Sites
Advanced
   Search
   Catalog
   Distiller

3. Specify the appearance of the link rectangle with the controls in the **Appearance** frame.
4. Specify a World Wide Web link in the **Type**: list box.
5. Press the **Edit URL** button. The **WWW Link Edit URL** dialog box will appear.
6. Enter the URL in the edit box of the **WWW Link Edit URL** dialog box.
7. Press the **OK** button. The **WWW Link Edit URL** dialog box will disappear, and you will return to the **Create Link** dialog box. If you do not want to enter a URL, press the **Cancel** button.
8. Press the **Set Link** button to set the link. If you decide you don't want to set the link, press the **Cancel** button.

When you enter URL links in PDF documents, you should always use full URLs, not relative URLs. A full URL includes the protocol name, the domain name, and the full path to the file. The Weblink plug-in cannot process relative URLs. When you attempt to follow a relative URL link, the Weblink plug-in will display an error message.

Specifying the Appearance of a Link Rectangle

The link rectangles you create may be visible or invisible. To specify a visible or invisible link rectangle, click on the **Visible** or **Invisible** radio buttons in the **Create Link** dialog box. If your document uses a specific format for linked text, or you are creating links on graphics embedded in the document, you may want to use invisible link rectangles to reduce screen clutter.

If you create a visible link rectangle, you can specify the color, thickness, and style of the rectangle. The default values are a black rectangle with thin, solid lines. To choose a color for the link rectangle, click on the **Color**: drop-down list box, then click on a color name You can choose from a variety of colors. To choose a line thickness, click on the **Width**: drop-down list box, then click on **Thin**, **Medium**, or **Thick**. To choose a line style, click on the **Style**: drop-down list box, then click on **Solid** or **Dashed**.

Links to Another Location in the Document

To create a link that points to another location in the current document, select **Go To View** from the **Type**: drop-down list box. When you select **Go To View**, Exchange displays the **Magnification**: drop-down list box below it. This drop-down list box contains options for the magnification that the hyperlinked page will have. The options are: **Fixed**, **Fit View**, **Fit Page**, **Fit Width**, **Fit Height**, **Fit Visible**, and **Inherit Zoom**. All of the magnification options except **Inherit Zoom** use a predefined zoom level to display the hyperlinked page. With **Inherit Zoom**, the hyperlinked page will maintain the zoom level in effect when the link was selected.

With the **Fixed** magnification option, the hyperlinked page will be displayed at the zoom level in effect when the link was created. You can use the **Fixed** option to define precisely how Acrobat will display a hyperlinked page. To define the page view, change the zoom level and use the scroll bars while the **Create Link** dialog box is displayed.

Links to Another File

To create a link that points to another file:

1. Select **Open File** from the **Type**:drop-down list box
2. Press the **Select File...** button that Exchange displays in the **Create Link** dialog box. Exchange will display the **Select File to Open** dialog box.
3. Use the controls of the **Select File to Open** dialog box to select the file you want to open.

Making Sample Pages

A Sample Page with Links to PDF Documents

Here is an example of a page on our site that contains HTML links to PDF files. The first link is to a PDF file that does not contain URL links, and the second link is to a PDF file that does contain URL links.

```
<!DOCTYPE HTML PUBLIC '-//W30//DTD WWW
HTML 2.0//EN'>

<HTML>


    <HEAD>
        <TITLE>Experiments in Interactive
        Document Design with Acrobat Pro:
        The Author</TITLE>

    </HEAD>


    <BODY>
        <H1>The Author</H1>
        <P>
        There are two levels at which PDF
        and HTML can be mixed. At the first
        level, PDF files do not have links
        to URLs; readers can download the
        PDF documents, but they cannot use
        them to link back to the Web.

        At the second level, PDF files do
        have links to URLs, and readers can
        use PDF pages in a manner similar to
        HTML pages.
        </P>
        <P>
        Any reader who has the Acrobat
        Reader can view PDF documents that
        they retrieve from the Web, but
        Acrobat Exchange and the Weblink
        plug-in are required to use URL
        links in PDF files. Acrobat Exchange
```

is a combination viewing/authoring program for PDF files; unlike Acrobat Reader, Acrobat Exchange is <EM>not</EM> free. The Weblink plug-in enables Exchange to work with the Web; it is available free from <A HREF="http://www.adobe.com>Adobe</A>.

If you get to the Weblink plug-in directly, you can follow this <A HREF="http://www.adobe.com/Acrobat/Weblink.html>link to the Adobe Weblink page</A>.

</P>

<P>

Once you have downloaded the Weblink plug-in, copy it to your <CODE>plug_ins</CODE> directory, if you are using a PC, or to the <CODE>Plug-Ins</CODE> folder, if you are using a Mac. Exchange will load the plug-in automatically the next time you start it.

</P>

<P>

Now that you have your viewing software in order, we can take a look at some examples of how the links between PDF and HTML documents work. Here is what a link to a PDF document looks like. Like a link to

an HTML document, you use the
`<CODE>&ltA HREF&gt</CODE>` tag to
create the link.
`</P>`

`<P>`
`<CODE>`
`&ltA HREF="acroauth.pdf"&gtRetrieve`
a PDF document that does not have
any URL links`&lt/A&gt`
`</CODE>`
`</P>`

`<P>`
`<A HREF="acroauth.pdf">Retrieve a`
PDF document that does not contain
any URL links`</A>`
`</P>`

`<P>`
A link to a PDF document that
contains URL links is the same as a
link to a PDF document that does
not. The difference between the two
is in the PDF document, where the
Weblink plug-in is used to define a
link to a URL, rather than to
another view in the PDF document.
This PDF document has one URL link.
The link text is drawn in red and
underlined to make it easier to
find. See where it leads you...
`</P>`

```
<P>

<A HREF="acroaut2.pdf">Retrieve a
PDF document that contains a URL
link</A>
</P>


<HR>
<P>

As the &quotExperiments&quot in the
title implies, the things that you
see here may be a bit on the rough
side. If you have any comments,
suggestions, bug reports,
<A
HREF=mailto:holfep@readme.com>send
them to me</A>.
</P>


<HR>
<P>
|
<A HREF="index.html"> Home </A>
|
<A HREF="acromain.html"> Up </A>
|
</P>


<HR>
<ADDRESS>
Peter Holfelder<BR>
holfep@readme.com<BR>
```

```
                    July 31, 1995
              </ADDRESS>



              </BODY>

        </HTML>
```

File Permissions for Web Resources

To access a Web resource, you must have read permission for the resource. We will use UNIX file permissions as an example; the file permissions and the means of specifying them may be different on your system. On a UNIX system, a Web resource cannot be retrieved unless all others (as opposed to user and group) have read permission. The UNIX command that sets this permission is:

    chmod go+r filename

where *filename* is the name of the Web resource you want to make available.

Using PDF Icons to Mark PDF Files

Adobe has created small, medium, and large PDF file icons in GIF format that you can use to identify your PDF documents. They can be found on the "Serving PDF on the Web" page of Adobe's Web site, at:

    http://www.adobe.com/Acrobat/ServingPDF.html

You can download the GIFs directly from these addresses:

    http://www.adobe.com/GIFS/PDFicon.gif

    http://www.adobe.com/GIFS/PDFmid.gif

    http://www.adobe.com/GIFS/PDF4.gif

You use the <IMG SRC> tag to place the PDF icons in your document. The <IMG SRC> tag tells your browser to download an image from a URL that you specify. You can reference the icons that are stored at Adobe's site, or you can download local copies of the icons and reference those. The <IMG SRC> tag has the following syntax:

```
<IMG SRC="URL_for_the_graphics_file"
ALT="Descriptive text">
```

The ALT attribute is optional; character-based browsers place the text defined in the ALT attribute on the page. Surround the <IMG SRC> tag with the <A HREF></A> tags to create the graphical link; we show two examples of this in the following sample pages.

The PDF icons themselves do not give any information about the contents of a document, so you will have to include some text in your HTML document that describes the file. Remember to include alternate text for users of character mode browsers, and make sure that your alternate text and file description read properly when both are displayed.

Here is the HTML for a link that references the medium-sized icon on Adobe's site:

```
<A HREF="http://your.domain.name/your_path/
your_file.pdf">
<IMG SRC="http://www.adobe.com/GIFS/
PDFmid.gif"
 ALT="Acrobat PDF file:">A description of your
PDF file</A>
```

Here is the HTML for a link that references a local copy of the medium-sized icon:

```
<A HREF="http://your.domain.name/your_path/
your_file.pdf">
<IMG SRC="/local_icon_path/icon_file_name.gif"
 ALT="Acrobat PDF file:">A description of your
PDF file</A>
```

A Sample Page that Uses PDF Icons to Mark PDF Files

Here is a sample page that uses PDF icons to mark PDF files.

```
<!DOCTYPE HTML PUBLIC '-//W30//DTD WWW
HTML 2.0//EN'>

<HTML>



<HEAD>
```

```
<TITLE>Using PDF Icons to Mark PDF
Files</TITLE>

</HEAD>


<BODY>
  <H1>A Sample Page that Uses PDF Icons
  to Mark PDF Files </H1>
  <P>
  Here are two links to PDF files that
  are marked with PDF document icons.
  The first link references a local
  copy of the icon, and the second
  link references a copy of the icon
  on Adobe's site.
  </P>


  <HR>


  <P>
  <A HREF="http://www.readme.com/
  pdficon.pdf">
  <IMG SRC="PDFmid.gif" ALT="Acrobat
  PDF file:">
  Select this link and see what you
  get.</A>
  <A HREF=" http://www.readme.com/
  pdficon.pdf>
  <IMG SRC="http://www.adobe.com/
  GIFS/PDFmid.gif" ALT="Acrobat PDF
  file:">
  Then, select this link and see what
```

```
you get.</A>
</P>


<HR>


<P>
<A HREF=" http://www.readme.com/
index.htm> Home </A>
|
<A HREF="http://www.readme.com/
acromain.htm> Up </A>
```

```
</BODY>
```

```
</HTML>
```

This is what this page looks like on a PC running Netscape Navigator 1.1:

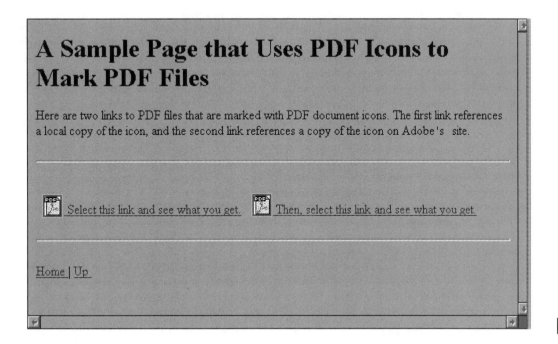

This page can be found at the URL: http://www.readme.com.

20

The Publisher

Serving PDF Documents on the Web

PART 4

Browsing
Interface
Navigating
Zoom
Features
Printing
Clipboard
Preferences
Creating
PDFWriter
PDF Files
Enhancing
Pages
Thumbnails
Bookmarks
Notes
Links
Articles
Web Publishing
Introduction
Getting On
Reader
Author
Publisher
Cool Sites
Advanced
Search
Catalog
Distiller

Setting the PDF MIME Type

It is advisable to include the **.pdf** file extension when you place a PDF file on an ftp or WWW server, for two reasons:

1. The most widely used Web servers determine the MIME type of a resource by examining its file extension. These servers then send the MIME type to the Web browser that requested the resource, so the browser can decide how to handle it.

2. If a Web browser does not receive the MIME type of a resource from the server, it will use the file extension of the resource to determine the resource's MIME type, provided the browser is properly configured.

Web servers that indicate the MIME type of the resources they send refer to a configuration file that associates file extensions with MIME types. The name of the configuration file and the syntax of the association command vary from server to server. Many servers include an association of the .pdf extension with the application/pdf MIME type in their configuration files, but some do not, and some older servers may have been obtained before the application/pdf MIME type was registered. We will demonstrate the configuration process for application/pdf with two of the most popular Web servers, CERN httpd and NCSA httpd.

Configuring CERN httpd for application/pdf

CERN httpd has one configuration file, named **httpd.conf**, which may be located in the **/etc** directory or in another directory you have defined. To add the application/pdf MIME type to the CERN httpd configuration, add this line to the **httpd.conf** file:

```
AddType  .pdf  application/pdf  8bit  1.0
```

Configuring NCSA httpd for application/pdf

NCSA httpd has a separate configuration file, **ServerRoot/conf/mime.types**, for specifying the associations between MIME types and file extensions. To add the application/pdf MIME type to the NCSA httpd configuration, add this line to the file:

```
application/pdf           pdf
```

Displaying the PDF Icon in Server-Generated Directory Listings

Web browsers are often used as FTP clients, allowing readers to download files from remote locations. When an FTP session is started via the Web, the Web server will generate a directory listing in HTML format with links to each file in the directory. You can configure your Web server to place the PDF icon before each PDF in a directory listing.

CERN httpd

To display the PDF icon before PDF files in server-generated directory listings:
1. Copy the PDFmid.gif icon to your system
2. Add this line to the **httpd.conf** file:
```
AddIcon  /icons/PDFmid.gif  PDF  application/pdf
```
3. Make sure the **DirShowIcons** option is set.

NCSA httpd

To display the PDF icon before PDF files in server-generated directory listings:
1. Copy the PDFmid.gif icon directory on your system

2. Add the line:

```
AddIcon   /icons/PDFmid.gif   .pdf  .PDF
```

to the **srm.conf** file, where **/icons** is the directory in step 1 where you stored the icon.

3. If you would like a description to appear after all PDF file names, add the lines:

```
AddDescription "description text" .pdf
AddDescription "description text " .PDF
```

to the **srm.conf** file, where **description text** is the description that you want to appear.

21
Cool Sites

PART 4

Browsing
Interface
Navigating
Zoom
Features
Printing
Clipboard
Preferences
Creating
PDFWriter
PDF Files
Enhancing
Pages
Thumbnails
Bookmarks
Notes
Links
Articles
Web Publishing
Introduction
Getting On
Reader
Author
Publisher
Cool Sites
Advanced
Search
Catalog
Distiller

Web Sites With
Cool PDF

PDF is being used on the Web to publish all sorts of information. Fortune™ magazine uses it to publish the Fortune 500 list, and the IRS uses it to put tax forms on-line. Many organizations are using it to place educational information, technical information, annual reports, and newsletters on the Web. A former photojournalist has even used it to produce an on-line "book" of his work. By browsing some of these sites, you can get a good idea of what you can do with PDF on the Web.

Kinds of Cool Sites

Business and Financial Information

Ernst & Young Canada

URL: http://www.inforamp.net/ey/#INDEX6

On this site, Ernst & Young Canada has placed PDF versions of several reports that are of interest to Canadian investors and taxpayers, such as *Managing Your Personal Taxes - An Ongoing Process*, *Ernst & Young's Analysis of the 1995 Canadian Federal Budget*, and *Your Connection to India*. These reports are electronic versions of 8.5" x 11" format paper reports, and include embedded fonts, full color (in some reports), and thumbnails.

Schlumberger 1994 Annual Report in PDF

URL: http://www.slb.com/ar94/index.html

Schlumberger, a company specializing in oil drilling services and measurement systems, is one of several companies that have placed their annual reports on the Web in PDF format. The report is a PDF version of the paper report, with all the snazzy fonts, color, graphics, charts, tables, and photographs you would expect in the annual report of a large company. The file includes thumbnails as a navigation aid. They were nice enough to break the report into sections for faster downloading; each section is in a file of ~365Kb or less. Schlumberger's earnings information is also available in PDF.

IRS Taxforms from the US Department of the Treasury

URL: http://www.ustreas.gov/treasury/bureaus/ irs/taxforms.html

The IRS, as we all know, is not cool. But they have done a remarkably good job with their Web site. There is a search mechanism that allows you to find the form you need easily, and PDF is perfect for reproducing the paper forms, many of which are in 8.5" x 11" format. In most cases, the PDF version forms are official; you can print them, fill them out, and submit them to the IRS.

Fortune 500 - Fortune Magazine at Time Warner's Pathfinder

URL: http://www.pathfinder.com/ then navigate to the Fortune 500 for several PDFs

Fortune magazine put essentially the entire Fortune 500 section of its Fortune 500 issue on-line in PDF. This latest list marks two historic, and related, firsts. For the first time, both manufacturing (industrial) and service businesses are combined on the list; before now, the two were tabulated on separate lists, the Fortune 500 and the Service 500. This is also the first time Fortune published the list in both print and electronic form simultaneously. Both firsts have deep roots in information technology like Acrobat.

The famed list, several other related lists, and articles about the performance and prospects of companies in the Fortune 500 are available. The serious businessperson may want to download them all, for their electronic viewing and word-searching pleasure. Fortune seems to have used Acrobat for a quick and inexpensive method to put their pages on-line. The files use PDF's page layout and color support (including blends), but they do not include font embedding or any of PDF's navigation or hypertext abilities—no thumbnails, bookmarks, article threads, or links.

Investment Dealers' Digest IDD magazine

URL: http://nestegg.iddis.com/nestegg/idd/mags.html#iddmag

IDD publishes information about the financial industry, focusing mainly on the professional investor. The company has placed a PDF version of the latest IDD magazine on the Web. The PDF version is the same as the printed version; it is a 39-page document with complex page layout, photographs, color graphics, tables, and lists. It uses thumbnails, but does not use bookmarks or article threads.

First Martin Corporation real-estate info

URL: http://BizServe.com/FMC/index.html

First Martin, a real estate company in Michigan, has placed floor plans and maps for several properties in PDF format. The floor plans appear to have been scanned from a paper document; they do not use color. Each building is one document, each floor is one page. Thumbnails and bookmarks have been added to the documents.

Magazines and Newsletters

InterText Magazine

URL: http://www.etext.org/Zines/InterText/

InterText is a magazine devoted to fiction writing. Like most of the PDF on the Web, *InterText* uses an 8.5" x 11" format; this format does not lend itself to screen readability, but makes it easier to distribute the magazine by printing it. *InterText* uses article threads to facilitate on-screen reading, and hyperlinks the entries table of contents to their locations in the magazine. The entire cover page is hyperlinked to the table of contents, a neat feature. There is a bookmark list of all of the articles in the magazine as well. The entire magazine is in black and white, which helps keep the file size small. The magazine uses a tasteful page layout consistently throughout, with no illustrations; this makes thumbnails relatively useless as a navigation aid, and they are not used.

InterText uses the Adobe Base 14 fonts only. Using the Base 14 fonts ensures that the document looks exactly like the original—since every installation of Acrobat includes those fonts—while making font embedding unnecessary, which keeps the file size to a minimum.

Technical Support Information

Bay Networks Customer Support

URL: http://support.baynetworks.com/marcom.htm

Bay Networks, a manufacturer of network switching and routing products, has placed all of their Technical Library documents on-line in PDF format. Bay Networks is using PDF as a convenient way to place these documents on-line; the PDF files do not use any of Acrobat's navigation features, and they only use the Base 14 fonts. This Web site is interesting because Bay Networks has placed all of its technical support library there, and because it uses PDF as its primary language—the tech support documents are not available in HTML format.

Quantum Corporation

URL: http://www.quantum.com/support/support.html

Quantum has placed technical support tip sheets on the Web using PDF; these are the same documents that Quantum sends to customers via their fax-back service. Quantum also offers the material in HTML format; you can see some of the advantages and disadvantages of PDF and HTML by examining the pages on this site.

Adobe Systems Application Notes and Technical Notes

URL: http://www.adobe.com/Support/Service.html

Adobe Systems places their technical support library on the Web in PDF format. As is the case with Bay Networks, the extensive and exclusive use of PDF for these documents is more interesting than the use of PDF's features—only the font embedding feature is used.

Kai's Power Tips and Tricks for Adobe Photoshop

URL: http://the-tech.mit.edu/KPT/

If you are a Photoshop geek, you should check this site out. MIT's campus newspaper, *The Tech*, obtained permission from Swanson Tech Support to place their Photoshop newsletter on the Web in PDF. These documents are good examples of how well Acrobat handles scanned images within a document. The documents are in 8.5" x 11" format, with complex page layout; they do not use font embedding. Thumbnails are the only navigation aid used in these files; they are very helpful in this case, as the documents are graphics-intensive.

Educational Information

Princeton University Press

> URL: http://aaup.pupress.princeton.edu:70/1/books/presses/princeton/catalogs

Princeton University Press publishes a variety of scholarly reading and textbooks. They have placed several of their catalogs on the Web in PDF format, with HTML pages listing all of the documents available. These catalogs include two or more colors, and often incorporate black and white photographs of each book's cover and author. The pages are attractively composed for an 8.5" x 11" format, but a screen-oriented format would be better for this application. No navigational aids are used; font embedding is used.

Great Lakes Collaborative / Explorer Educational Resources

> URL: http://server2.greatlakes.k12.mi.us/glc-www/WNew.html

> URL: http://server2.greatlakes.k12.mi.us/glc-www/Membership.html

The Great Lakes Collaborative is a group that produces and publishes educational materials, such as lesson plans and student projects, for primary and secondary schools. A plan for a field trip to the Kansas City Zoo is one of the PDF files available at the site. The document, which is 68% smaller in PDF than in Claris Works format, contains color maps of the zoo and outlines for activities, zoo etiquette, and related lessons. This document shows off Acrobat's color and graphics support, and uses bookmarks for navigation aids.

A membership information brochure is also available in PDF format. It contains color line art and images, font embedding, bookmarks, and thumbnails.

Miscellaneous Information

Oregon Department of Forestry

URL: http://salem10nt.odf.state.or.us/news.htm

The ODF maintains PDFs of several reports and for-estry-related newsletters on its pages. They are PDF versions of paper documents with different fonts, graphics, and images. If you want some information on outdoor Christmas tree lighting or living Christ-mas trees, the *CommuniTree News* newsletter is where to get it.

Kev's World—a newspaper cartoonist uses PDF

URL: http://www.cris.com/~mppa/s2f/kevin.html

Kevin Nichols, a freelance cartoonist/illustrator, places cartoons on this site in PDF. Use them for free, as long as you give Kevin credit. They have good high-resolution.

The McLuhan Probes from The Herbert Marshall McLuhan Foundation

URL: http://www.mcluhan.ca/mcluhan/issues.html

The folks at the McLuhan Probes were nice enough to put the file sizes of their PDF. It looks like a slick paper magazine placed in PDF. Each page has a nice back-ground, but it is hard to read them. These pages show off the sophisticated capabilities of PDF to the detri-ment of their readability.

Time-Life's Complete Gardener Series

URL: http://www.timeinc.com/vg/TimeLife/
Project

The PDFs in the Complete Gardener series are electronic versions of the Time-Life books. The layout is complex, the illustrations are detailed. Two color. Sidebars. Designed for 8.5" x 9" book pages, not the screen. There are links, some of them to other files (they need to be downloaded before you can execute the links). There are bookmarks, but no thumbnails.

Electric Gulker Land has a photo book in PDF

URL: http://www.gulker.com/gulker/portfo-
lio.html

Chris Gulker, a former photojournalist with the *Los Angeles Herald Examiner* and photo editor with the *San Francisco Examiner*, used PDF to create an electronic book of his finest photos. The book contains black and white photos with captions; a separate section contains a smaller copy of the photo with notes about the events surrounding it and the equipment used to capture the image. The full-page photo and the notes are linked to each other. The page sizes vary according to the dimensions of the picture where appropriate. There are thumbnails, which are very useful for graphical pages such as these; there are no bookmarks.

Gulker shows the size of the file, and how it was formatted for the screen. He also includes instructions for navigating through a document with Acrobat Reader.

PDF Samples from USC

A collection of PDF files at the University of Southern California.

http://www.usc.edu/Cool/USCpdf.html

Many departments at USC use PDF to post catalogs, schedules and other information on the Web. For the most part, the documents are designed to be printed; they are using PDF to make an easy transition to electronic documents. They place the file size on the Web page. One course schedule we looked over had thumbnails, but no bookmarks.

Tandem Computers

URL: http://www.tandem.com

Tandem is going all-out with PDF on its Web site. They publish market backgrounders, white papers, product descriptions, and brochures on the site, and each of them is available in PDF. This site also publishes the information in HTML format, making it a great place to compare the two formats. This site is a good example of how to use PDF extensively, but it still uses HTML to ensure maximum viewership for its information.

One product information sheet we downloaded was a 446Kb file. It was mostly black and white (the title and the Tandem logo had color), and contained photographs, numerous diagrams, and tables showing the product specifications. No bookmarks, article threads, hyperlinks, or thumbnails were used in the document.

WindoWatch

A zine devoted to the MS Windows operating environment.

URL: http://www.channel1.com/users/win-watch/WindoWatch.html

This zine is two-color, and light on the graphics and page layout. But it does use hyperlinks, and has one article thread for the editorial. If you also choose, of course, to print this zine before you read it (it is in 8.5" x 11" format).

V

ADVANCED Interactive Documents

Advanced Topics in Acrobat

CHAPTER

22
Search

The Acrobat Search Plug-in

Acrobat Search is a Plug-in module, included in version 2.0 of Exchange, that provides indexed searching capability to Acrobat. The searches you can perform with the Search Plug-In have several advantages over the word-by-word searches you perform with the **Tools | Find** command:

- They are faster

- You can search several documents at once

- You can construct advanced search queries, including searches for words in proximity to each other, searches for words with a common stem, searches for words with similar meanings, and searches for sound-alike words.

- You can restrict searches based on the contents of **Document Information** fields

- You can restrict searches based on the date that a document was created and/or modified

- The Search Plug-In indicates the likelihood that a document that matches the query actually contains the information that you are looking for.

In this chapter, you will learn how to:

- Select an Index to Search
- Construct Queries
- Enter a Query
- View Search Results.

The Search Plug-In uses the indexes created by the Acrobat Catalog program; for more information about Acrobat Catalog, see Chapter 17.

Searching Basics

There are many ways to search documents using Acrobat's Search Plug-In, and their results are immediate. These elements are the basis for creating more complex searches, but they can be used alone to make simple searches effective. The following lists the elements that form the basis for searches and how each of them performs in a search.

Queries

A search query is a combination of one or more conditions that a document must meet in order to match a search.

Searching for text within a document is a simple form of query, with one condition: "Does the document contain this text?" These are the only type of queries you can construct with the **Tools | Find** command.

The Search Plug-In, however, allows you to construct complex search queries that have one or more conditions. Search queries may include:

- **Search Text**. Like the **Tools | Find** command, this is the text string that you are looking for.

- **Wildcards**. Wildcards are place holder characters that allow you to look for several different strings with one query.

- **Boolean Expressions**. Boolean expressions allow you to broaden or narrow your search by linking together several pieces of search text.

Search Terms

A search term is a piece of text that Search will look for. A search term can be:

- A word, such as document

- A word fragment with wildcards, such as electr*. Wildcards are placeholders for one or more characters.

- Any combination of letters, numbers, and symbols, such as AP#7622A.

The maximum length a search term can be is 128 characters.

Search looks in document indexes for exact matches to the search terms you enter. As a result, you cannot use prefixes or word fragments as search terms. If you want to perform a search on a word fragment, you must use wildcards with the fragment, or use the **Word Stemming** option to find words that begin with the fragment.

Wildcards

Wildcards allow you to use one query to look for all words and phrases that have certain letters in common. The two wildcards are:

- **The question mark (?):** The question mark matches any single character. For instance, the search term ??ll will match "bill," "pull," "fall," "toll," and "well."

- **The asterisk (*):** The asterisk matches zero or more characters. For instance, the search term anti* would match "antipathy," "antibody," "antimacassar," "anti," and any other word that starts with "anti."

You can combine several wildcards in a search term to search for a variety of patterns. For instance, the search term d?l* will match the words "deluge," "dilate," "dullness," "dole," "dilettante," and "dalliance."

Boolean Expressions

Boolean expressions are combinations of one or more search terms that are modified or linked by the Boolean logical operators. You can use the following Boolean operators to construct Boolean expressions:

- OR
- AND
- NOT.

Separator Characters

Separator characters are the characters that Search and Catalog use to mark breaks between words.

When Catalog creates an index, it considers the text between each pair of separator characters it finds to be a separate word, and places it in the index. Most punctuation characters and all symbols are separator characters. The most common separator characters are spaces, tabs, periods, commas, colons, semicolons, exclamation points, question marks, parentheses, and double-quotes. The punctuation characters that are not separator characters are:

- single quote [']
- right apostrophe [']
- grave [`]
- acute [´]
- cedilla [¸]
- diereses [¨]
- macron [¯]
- breve [˘]
- dotaccent [˙]
- ring [°]
- hungarumlaut [˝]
- ogonek [˛]
- caron [ˇ]

You cannot use wildcards to represent separator characters. If the term you are searching for has a separator character in it, as hyphenated words do, place a space between the words or use the separator character you suspect is between the words. For instance, if the document text reads "undo/redo," your query should read undo redo or undo/redo. The query undo?redo will not work.

Stopwords

Stopwords are common words such as: the, and, than, and to. Stopwords are excluded from indexes because they do not give any evidence about the topic of a document and because they would make the index too large. There is a drawback to excluding stopwords from an index, however; excluding stopwords prevents Search from finding phrases that contain the stopword. For instance, if "the" is excluded from an index, Search can find neither the phrase "The medium is the message," nor the phrase "medium is message." To find the phrase, you would have to use the query medium and message to find it.

A list of typical Acrobat stopwords may be referenced in Appendix A.

Relevance Rankings

Search assigns a relevance ranking to each document that matches a query. Relevance rankings give you an indication of the likelihood that a document contains the information you want. Relevance rankings are displayed to the left of the document's title in the Search Results dialog box. There are five relevance rankings, each signified by an icon:

- **Very high relevance:** This document almost certainly contains the information you are looking for.

- **High relevance:** This document probably contains the information you are looking for.

- **Medium relevance:** This document may contain the information you are looking for.

- **Low relevance:** This document, though it matched the query, probably does not contain the information you are looking for.

- **Very low relevance:** This document, though it matched the query, almost certainly does not contain the information you are looking for.

Several factors will affect the relevance rankings that Search calculates for a document. These factors depend on the type of search you are performing and the number of terms you are searching for. For instance:

- If you use only one search term, the more often the term appears in the document, the higher its relevance ranking

- If you use the **Proximity** search option, the closer the two search terms are to each other in a document, the higher the document's relevance ranking

- If you use an OR condition in your search, documents that contain both of the search terms will have a higher relevance ranking than documents that contain only one of the search terms.

The higher the proportion of search terms to other terms in the document, the higher the document's relevance ranking. For instance, a one-page article that has 20 occurrences of the search term will have a higher relevance ranking than a one-hundred-page article that has 20 occurrences of the search term.

Search Options

Search provides several search options that can make it easier to find just the text you are looking for. The **Word Stemming**, **Thesaurus**, and **Sounds Like** options broaden searches by including words that are related to your search text in the search; **Match Case** and **Proximity** narrow searches by imposing additional conditions on matches.

Selecting an Index to Search

You may have several indexed collections of PDF documents available to you. To maximize the efficiency of your searches, you can select which of the indexes Search will search for each query that you make. You may search one index, several indexes, or every available index.

To select an index to search:

1. Select the **Tools | Search | Indexes** command, or select the **Indexes** button when the Adobe Acrobat Search or Word Assistant dialog boxes are open. The Index Selection dialog box will appear.
2. Click on the check box to the left of the index you want to search, so that an "x" appears in the box. The index will then be selected to search.

You can only add one index at a time to the list of searched indexes. If you want to add more than one index to the list, repeat these steps for each index you want to add.

To remove an index from the list of indexes that will be searched:

1. Select the **Tools | Search | Indexes** command, or select the **Indexes** button when the Adobe Acrobat Search or Word Assistant dialog boxes are open. The Index Selection dialog box will appear.
2. Click on the check box to the left of the index you do not want to search, so that no "x" appears in the box. Search will not search the index until you select it again.

You can only remove one index at a time from the list of searched indexes. If you want to remove more than one index from the list, repeat these steps for each index you want to remove.

To close the Index Selection dialog box:

• Press the **OK** button.

When Search cannot find an index in your **Available Indexes** list, the index will be grayed out.

The most common reasons that Search cannot find an index are:

- The network connection to the system where the index is stored is not active

- The CD-ROM or other removable media that contains the index is not in the drive

- The index file has been moved or deleted.

Adding an Index to the Available Indexes List

To add an index to the **Available Indexes** list:

1. Press the **Add** button. The Add Index dialog box will appear.
2. Use the controls of the Add Index dialog box to select the file that contains the index you want to add.
3. Press the **OK** button. If you decide you don't want to add an index, press the **Cancel** button.

You can only add one index to the list at a time. If you want to add more than one index to the list, repeat these steps for each index you want to add.

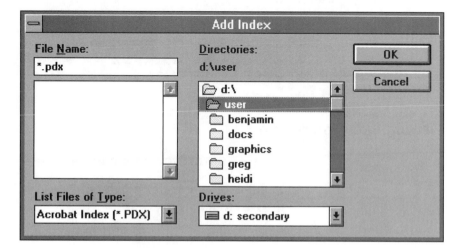

Removing an Index from the Available Indexes List

To remove an index from the **Available Indexes** list:

1. In the **Available Indexes** list box, highlight the name of the index you want to remove, using the mouse or the cursor control keys.
2. Press the **Remove** button. The index will be removed from the list.

You can only remove one index from the list at a time. If you want to remove more than one index from the list, repeat these steps for each index that you want to remove.

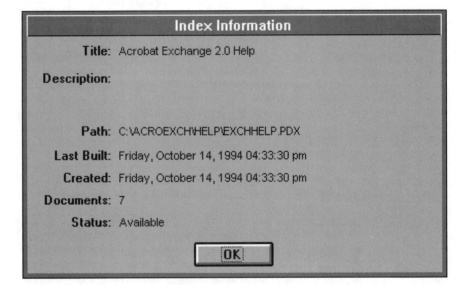

Viewing Index Information

To view information about an index:

1. Click on the index's name in the **Available Indexes** list box.

2. Press the **Info** button. Search will display the Index Information dialog box, which contains the following information about the index:

- The index's title

- A description of the index

- The path and filename of the index file

- The date and time when the index was last built

- The date and time when the index was first created

- The number of documents in the index

- The availability status of the index.

3. Press the **OK** button of the Index Information dialog box to return to the Index Selection dialog box.

Constructing Queries

Unlike the word-by-word search available with the **Tools | Find** command, which limits search terms to text strings, Search allows you to make queries using text from different fields, wildcards, and Boolean expressions.

Searching for a Single Word

Queries for single words or word fragments are the simplest type of query. To construct a query for a single word, type in the word. If the word you are searching for is a stopword or a Boolean operator, you must enclose the word in quotation marks.

Searching for Phrases

A phrase is simply a number of search terms arranged in order. To construct a query that contains a phrase, just type in the phrase. For instance, the query "I have a dream" will find all occurrences of the text "I have a dream" in the indexed documents. If a phrase contains Boolean operators, it must be enclosed in parentheses, as in (Give me liberty or give me death).

When it searches for phrases, Search ignores separator characters, which are the characters that Search and Catalog use to mark breaks between words. If you place any separator characters in the text of your phrase, Search will remove them before it executes the query. Search can generally find phrases that contain separator characters, however. For instance, if you search for a telephone number using the query 000-555-????: Search will match "415-555-1212," "(415)555-1212," and other combinations.

The **Thesaurus**, **Word Stemming**, and **Match Case** options are not available for phrase searches, but you can use the **Proximity** option to refine searches for two or more phrases, and you can refine searches for phrases with Document Info and Document Date queries.

Searching for Numbers

Numbers, in the context of searches, are any sequences of one or more digits. Numbers can also include the following characters:

- A preceding dash [-]: For instance, -65535

- Separators, which can be commas [,] or periods [.]: For instance, 65,535 or 4.294.967.296

- A decimal point, which can be a comma [,] or a period[.]: For instance, 3.14159 or 3,14159.

The publisher of an index has the option to exclude numbers from the index. If numbers are excluded from an index, sequences of digits that contain one or more letters will be treated as search terms, and they will be placed in the index. As an example, the sequence $1,000,000.00 would be treated as a number and excluded from the index; the sequence 500Mb would be treated as a search term, and included.

Search Options

Several search options are built into the Search Plug-In module. These options allow you to broaden or narrow the scope of a search easily. They are:

- Word Stemming
- Thesaurus
- Sounds Like
- Match Case
- Proximity

Creators of indexes may decide not to support the **Match Case**, **Sounds Like**, or **Word Stemming** options. If the index does not support the **Match Case** option, Search will ignore the option. If the index does not support the **Word Stemming** or **Sounds Like** options, Search can still use the options, but you will not be able to use the Word Assistant to see what alternate search terms the options would generate.

Word Stemming

The **Word Stemming** option broadens searches by automatically searching for words that have the same word stem as the word you are searching for. For instance, if you search for the word "develop" with the **Word Stemming** option activated, Search will also look for: develop, developed, development, developer's, developers, developing, development, developments, develops. Word stemming does not find words that end in "er" or words with prefixes before the stem.

To include words with similar stems in a search:

- Click on the **Word Stemming** check box.

Word stemming cannot be used if the search term contains wildcards or if the **Match Case** option is activated. You can use the Word Assistant to look up words in the active indexes that have the same stem as the word you are searching for. For more information on the Word Assistant, see the "Using the Word Assistant to Refine a Query" section.

When you set the **Word Stemming** option, it remains set for subsequent searches until you clear it by clicking on the **Word Stemming** check box again.

Thesaurus

The **Thesaurus** option broadens searches to include words that have meanings similar to that of the search word.

To include words with similar meanings in a search:

- Click on the **Thesaurus** check box.

You cannot use the Thesaurus with search phrases, wildcards, or with either the **Match Case** or the **Proximity** options. You can use the Word Assistant to look up words in the Thesaurus that match the word you are searching for. It is a particularly good idea to use the Word Assistant for Thesaurus queries; a word may have dozens of Thesaurus entries which will slow down the search and yield many irrelevant matches. For instance, a Thesaurus search on the word "authentic" yielded 15 words! The word "unusual" has 29 entries! For more information on the Word Assistant, see the "Using the Word Assistant to Refine a Query" section.

When you set the **Thesaurus** option, it remains set for subsequent searches until you clear it by clicking on the **Thesaurus** check box again.

Sounds Like

The **Sounds Like** option broadens searches to include words that sound like the search word and start with the same letter. For instance, if you search for the word "listen" with the **Sounds Like** option activated, Search will also look for: listing, locating, location, locations.

To include sound-alike words in a search:

- Click on the **Sounds Like** check box.

The **Sounds Like** option cannot be used if the search term contains wildcards or if the **Match Case** option is activated.

The **Sounds Like** option is designed to work best with proper names. If you use it with other words, you may find that many of the words it matches bear only a slight resemblance to the word you entered. To refine your search, you can use the Word Assistant to look up words in the active indexes that sound like the word you are searching for. For more information on the Word Assistant, see the "Using the Word Assistant to Refine a Query" section.

When you set the **Sounds Like** option, it remains set for subsequent searches until you clear it by clicking on the **Sounds Like** check box again.

Match Case

The **Match Case** option narrows searches by stipulating that the search term and the document text must match in case as well as letters for a match to be reported.

The **Match Case** option narrows searches by stipulating that all matches must have the same capitalization as the search term. For instance, if you search for the word "PostScript" with the **Match Case** option activated, Search will report a match if it finds "Post-Script," but not if it finds "POSTSCRIPT" or "post-script."

To specify a case-sensitive search:

• Click on the **Match Case** check box.

When you set the **Match Case** option, it remains set for subsequent searches until you clear it by clicking on the **Match Case** check box again.

Proximity

The **Proximity** option narrows searches that use the AND Boolean expression (see the "Using Boolean Expressions in Searches section") by stipulating that the two search terms be found within two or three pages of each other. When the **Proximity** option is activated, the relevance ranking for the document is based on how close the two search terms are to each other in the document.

To specify a proximity search:

- Click on the **Proximity** check box.

When you set the **Proximity** option, it remains set for subsequent searches until you clear it by clicking on the **Proximity** check box again.

Searches Using Simple Boolean Expressions

You can use the following Boolean expressions to construct more complex queries:

- **AND:** Will only return a match if both searchterm1 and searchterm2 are found in a document. You can also use the @ character as the AND operator. Syntax is searchterm1 AND searchterm2.

- **OR:** Will return a match if either searchterm1 or searchterm2 are found in a document. You can also use the comma [,] or the vertical bar [|] characters as the OR operator. Syntax is searchterm1 OR searchterm2.

- **NOT:** Will return a match if searchterm is not found in a document. You can also use the [!] character as the NOT operator; be sure to place a space between the [!] and the searchterm. Syntax has two forms: searchterm1 AND NOT searchterm2; NOT searchterm.

Tech Note

The Search Plug-In does not take case into account when looking for Boolean expressions in queries, even when the **Match Case** option is on; you can use and, AND, or aNd as a Boolean expression.

If you want to search for a phrase that contains "or," "and," or "not," you must enclose the phrase in quotation marks; if you do not, Search will try to interpret "and," "or," or "not" as Boolean expressions. For instance, to find Shakespeare's famous phrase, you would enter the query "To be or not to be," not To be or not to be.

PART 5

The query not searchterm will return every document in the index that does not contain searchterm. Acrobat cannot highlight a word that does not exist in a document, so it simply displays the first page of the document. If you use the **Search | Next**, **Search | Next Document**, **Search | Previous**, and **Search | Previous Document** commands after this type of query, Acrobat will display the previous or the next document that does not contain the term.

Boolean expressions can be used in the **Document Info** fields as well as in the search text. For instance, in the **Author** field, you can use the expression Shakespeare or Carroll to find all the documents in an index written by William Shakespeare and Lewis Carroll.

When you perform an OR search, documents that contain both search terms have a higher relevance ranking than documents that contain only one of the search terms.

Complex Boolean Expressions

You can create complex Boolean expressions by combining simple expressions. For instance, the expression searchterm1 and searchterm2 and searchterm3 will match all documents that contain searchterm1, searchterm2, and searchterm3. The expression searchterm1 and searchterm2 or searchterm3 will match all documents: that contain both searchterm1 and searchterm2; that contain searchterm1, searchterm2, and searchterm3; or that contain searchterm3 only.

If your expression contains either the AND or the OR operators exclusively, you can make complex expressions without using parentheses. For example:

- Mozart and Beethoven and Chopin and Brahms

- Clinton or Bush or Reagan or Carter or Ford

are valid complex Boolean expressions.

To use more than one Boolean operator in a complex Boolean expression, you will have to take into account the order in which Search interprets operators. For more information, see the "Order of Execution in Complex Boolean Expressions" section.

Order of Execution in Complex Boolean Expressions

When Search interprets a complex Boolean expression, it looks for each Boolean operator according to its precedence and associates search terms with the operator according to its syntax.

The precedence of the Boolean operators, from highest to lowest, is:

- NOT

- AND

- OR.

Here's an example of how precedence affects the results of a search. When Search examines the query "piloting AND airplanes OR helicopters," it finds one AND operator and one OR operator. Since the AND operator has the higher precedence, Search interprets it first. The AND operator requires two values, one to its left and one to its right, so Search associates the values piloting and airplanes with it, forming one simple Boolean expression. Next, Search interprets the OR operator. The OR operator also requires a value to its left and a value to its right. Since Search has already associated the value airplanes to the AND operator, Search associates the entire first expression (piloting and airplanes) to the OR operator as the value on the left, and the value helicopters with it as the value on the right. This query will record as a match any document that contains:

- The word piloting and the word airplanes

- The word piloting, the word airplanes, and the word helicopters

- The word helicopters.

The precedence of operators can be overridden by placing parentheses around the expression you want Search to interpret first. If we change our original query to piloting and (airplanes or helicopters), Search will associate the value airplanes and the value helicopters with the OR operator, and then associate the value piloting and the expression (airplanes or helicopters) with the AND operator.

This new query will record as a match any document that contains:

- The word piloting and the word airplanes

- The word piloting and the word helicopters

- The word piloting, the word airplanes, and the word helicopters.

Queries Using Document Info Fields

Document Info fields are a new feature of Acrobat 2.0. **Document Info** fields contain information about a document, but they are separate from the document's text and graphics. You can construct queries that look for information only in the **Document Info** fields, or you can combine **Document Info** fields with search terms you enter in the **Find Results Containing Text** edit box to make more complex queries. You can use Boolean expressions and wildcards with **Document Info** fields.

The searchable **Document Info** fields are:

- Title

- Subject

- Author

- Keywords.

Displaying the Document Info Edit Boxes

To display the **Document Info** edit fields of the Adobe Acrobat Search dialog box:

1. Select the **Edit | Preferences | Search** command. Exchange will display the Acrobat Search Preferences dialog box.
2. Click on the **Show Fields** option to set the option.
3. Press the **OK** button.

Entering a Document Info Query

To enter a query that searches for information in the **Document Info** fields:

1. Enter the Document Info text you would like to search for in the **Title, Author**, **Subject**, or **Keyword** edit fields of the Adobe Acrobat Search dialog box.
2. Press the **Search** button.

To clear the **With Document Info** edit boxes:

• Press the **Clear** button.

Wildcards and Doc Info Queries

You can use wildcards in **Document Info** field search text, just as you can for search terms in the **Find Results Containing Text** edit box. For instance, if you enter *son in the **Author** edit box, Search will find documents written by Ralph Waldo Emerson, Robert Louis Stevenson, and others.

Boolean Expressions and Document Info Queries

Boolean Expressions in a Single Document Info Field

You can use the AND, OR, and NOT Boolean operators in **Document Info** field search text, just as you can for search terms in the **Find Results Containing Text** edit box. For instance, if you enter King or Prince in the **Title** edit box, Search will find documents that have King or Prince in their title.

Boolean Expressions in Multiple Document Info Fields

When you place search terms in two different **Document Info** fields, you create an implicit AND operator. For instance, if you enter "King" in the **Title** field and Shakespeare in the **Author** field, Search will find all works by Shakespeare with the word "King" in their title.

You can create a combination of the AND and NOT operators by entering a term in one field and entering a term with the NOT operator in another field. For instance, if you enter Shakespeare in the **Author** field and not comedy in the **Keywords** field, Search will find all of Shakespeare's works that are not comedies.

Combining Doc Info Queries with Document Text Search Terms

You can use the **Document Info** fields in the **Find Results Containing Text** edit box by giving the name of the field, the tilde [~] character, and the search term. For example, Author ~ Hemingway will find all documents written by Hemingway. This allows you to construct complex Boolean expressions that combine document text with **Document Info** fields, and allows you to use the OR operator between two different **Document Info** fields. For example, the query (Author ~ Shakespeare) or (Title ~ King) will find every one of Shakespeare's works and every work that contains King in the title.

If you enter search text with **Document Info** fields in the **Find Results Containing Text** edit box and place search text for one of those fields in the **Document Info** edit boxes, the condition in the **Document Info** field will override the one in the **Find Results Containing Text** edit box. For instance, if you enter the query (Author ~ Shakespeare) or (Keywords ~ Comedy), but the query Shakespeare is in the

Author Document Info field, Search will only return documents written by Shakespeare.

Queries Using Document Creation and Modification Date Info

You can search for documents based only on their creation or modification dates, or you can use creation and modification dates to refine queries on document text and **Document Info** fields. This can be helpful if you have a large archive of information, or information that changes quickly, and you only want to look at the latest information. You can use any combination of the following four date criteria to search for a document. They are:

1. Match any document that was **Created Before** a certain date.
2. Match any document that was **Created After** a certain date.

3. Match any document that was **Modified Before** a certain date.
4. Match any document that was **Modified After** a certain date.

If you combine the **Created Before** and **Created After** criteria, or the **Modified Before** and **Modified After** criteria, Search will match documents that were created or modified during a certain time period. Note that, if you use both the **Created After** and **Created Before** conditions or the **Modified After** and **Modified Before** conditions, the after date must be earlier than the before date. When you search with more than one date condition, you are using an implicit AND condition.

Since date matches are based on before/after comparisons, you cannot use wildcards or search options with dates.

Displaying the Document Date Edit Fields

To display the **Document Date** edit fields of the Adobe Acrobat Search dialog box:

1. Select the **Edit | Preferences | Search** command. Exchange will display the Acrobat Search Preferences dialog box.
2. Click on the **Show Dates** option to set the option.
3. Press the **OK** button.

Entering a Document Date Query

Each edit box in the **With Date Info** frame has three fields corresponding to month, day, and year, going from left to right.

To enter a query that searches for documents by date:

1. Enter the month, day, or year with which you would like to refine your search in the appropriate field: **Created After**, **Created Before**, **Modified After**, or **Modified Before**. When you enter a number in any one of the month, day, or year fields, Exchange will automatically put the numbers corresponding to today's date in the other fields. You can move the date forward by one month, day, or year by clicking on the scroll arrows when the cursor is in the field you want to change, or you can use the keyboard to enter the number.

2. Enter numbers in the other two fields in the edit box.

3. Repeat the process for any other date criteria you want to use.

4. Press the **Search** button.

To clear the **With Date Info** edit boxes:

- Press the **Clear** button.

Refining Queries Using the Word Assistant

Often, the **Word Stemming**, **Thesaurus**, and **Sounds Like** search options will generate a large number of alternate search terms, many of which will not be relevant to the query you want to make. Acrobat Search's Word Assistant allows you to see the alternate search terms that the search options will generate, so you can pick the ones that will be most helpful.

You can use the Word Assistant to look up words that are related to the word that you are looking for in the following ways:

- They have the same word stem (the **Word Stemming** option)

- They have similar meanings (the **Thesaurus** option)

- They sound the same (the **Sounds Like** option).

Word Assistant will search the available indexes for words that match your search term, and display the words that match.

Creators of indexes may decide not to support the **Sounds Like** or **Word Stemming** options. If the index does not support the **Word Stemming** or **Sounds Like** options, you will not be able to use the Word Assistant to see what alternate search terms the options would generate, but Search can still use the options.

```
┌─────────────────────────────────────────────────────┐
│ ▬        Word Assistant                               │
├─────────────────────────────────────────────────────┤
│                                                       │
│  Word: ┌──────────────────────────┐   ┌──────────┐  │
│        │                          │   │  Lookup  │  │
│        └──────────────────────────┘   └──────────┘  │
│                                                       │
│  Assist: ┌──────────────────────┬─┐   ┌──────────┐  │
│          │ Sounds Like          │▼│   │  Close   │  │
│          └──────────────────────┴─┘   └──────────┘  │
│                                                       │
│        ┌──────────────────────────┐   ┌──────────┐  │
│        │                          │   │ Indexes..│  │
│        │                          │   └──────────┘  │
│        │                          │                 │
│        │                          │                 │
│        │                          │                 │
│        │                          │                 │
│        │                          │                 │
│        └──────────────────────────┘                 │
│  ┌─────────────────────────────────────────────┐   │
│  │ Searching in the Acrobat Exchange 2.0 Help index.│ │
│  └─────────────────────────────────────────────┘   │
└─────────────────────────────────────────────────────┘
```

Looking Up Alternate Terms with the Word Assistant

To look up alternate terms with the Word Assistant:

1. Select the **Tools | Search | Word Assistant** command. The Word Assistant dialog box will appear.
2. Enter the word in the **Word:** edit box.
3. Click on the **Assist:** drop-down list box. A list of search options will appear.
4. Click on the search option you want to use.
5. Press the **Lookup** button.

Search will display a list of search terms related to your original search term in the **Word Assistant** list box.

To close the Word Assistant dialog box:

- Press the **Close** button.

The status bar at the bottom of the Word Assistant dialog box shows:

- The name of the index, if only one index is selected
- The number of indexes that will be searched, if more than one index is selected.

Pasting Word Assistant Results into a Query

To paste Word Assistant Results into a query:

1. Look up alternate words in the Word Assistant (for more information, see the "Looking Up Alternate Terms with the Word Assistant" section).
2. Double click on a word you want to paste into the query. The word will appear in the **Word:** edit box.
3. Copy the word to the Clipboard.
4. If the Adobe Acrobat Search dialog box is not open, open it using the **Tools | Search | Query** command or the **Search Query** toolbar button.
5. Place the cursor at the appropriate place in the **Find Results Containing Text** edit box.
6. Paste the word into the edit box from the Clipboard.

If you want to paste more than one word into the query, repeat steps 1–6 above, and use the OR operator to link the words.

Entering a Query

Setting Query Preferences

In Exchange, you can customize how the search feature works by specifying **Query Preferences**.

To view or edit the **Query Preferences**:

- Select the **Preferences** | **Search** command.

With the options in the **Query** frame, you can modify the appearance of the Adobe Acrobat Search dialog box (displayed with the **Tools** | **Search** | **Query** command). You can specify whether or not the dialog box is hidden when you perform a search, and you can switch the display of the following sections of the dialog box on and off:

- **Document Info** fields (**Title**, **Author**, **Subject**, **Keywords**)

- Creation and Modification dates

- Search Options.

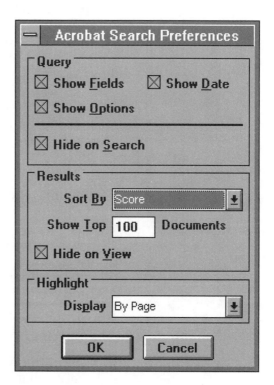

When these sections of the Adobe Acrobat Search dialog box are turned off, you cannot specify the options in these sections when performing a search.

To turn the display of **Document Info** fields on and off:

- Click on the **Show Fields** check box.

To turn the display of Creation and Modification dates on and off:

- Click on the **Show Dates** check box.

To turn the display of Search Options on and off:

- Click on the **Search Options** check box.

To turn the display of the Adobe Acrobat Search dialog box on and off while searches are performed:

- Click on the **Hide on Search** check box.

If the **Hide on Search** option in the Acrobat Search Preferences dialog box has been turned on, the Adobe Acrobat Search dialog box will close when you press the **Search** button. If the **Hide on Search** option has been turned off, you will have to close the dialog box yourself.

To close the Adobe Acrobat Search dialog box:

- Click on the dialog box's **Control Menu** button and select the **Close** command from the menu that appears

Or

- Double click on the **Control Menu** button

Or

- Press the **<Escape>** key.

The status bar at the bottom of the Adobe Acrobat Search dialog box shows:

- The name of the index, if only one index is selected

- The number of indexes that will be searched, if more than one index is selected.

Entering a Query

To enter a query:

1. Select the **Tools | Search | Query** command, or press the **Search Query** toolbar button.

   Acrobat will display the Adobe Acrobat Search dialog box.
2. Select the indexes you want to search by pressing the **Indexes** button. The Index Selection dialog box will appear; use the controls of the Index Selection dialog box to select the indexes (see the "Selecting an Index to Search" section). This is optional.
3. Enter the query text in the **Find Results Containing Text** edit box.
4. If the **With Document Info** frame is displayed, enter the **Document Info** text you would like to search for in the **Title**, **Author**, **Subject**, and **Keyword** edit fields. This is optional.
5. If the **With Date Info** frame is displayed, enter the earliest and most recent creation and modification dates in the **Created After**, **Created Before**, **Modified After**, and **Modified Before** edit fields. This is optional.
6. If the **Options** frame is displayed, select the search options you would like to use for the search from the **Options** frame. This is optional.
7. Press the **Search** button.

To clear the **Find Results Containing Text** edit box:

- Press the **Clear** button.

Viewing Search Results

When Search has completed a search, it displays the Search Results dialog box. The Search Results dialog box lists the title and relevance ranking of every document that matched the search.

You may display the results of the last search you performed at any time by reopening the Search Results dialog box. To reopen the Search Results dialog box:

- Select the **Tools** | **Search** | **Results** command, or press the **Search Results** toolbar button.

The Search Results dialog box is resizeable.

If the **Hide on View** option in the Acrobat Search Preferences dialog box has been turned on, the Search Results dialog box will close when you press the **View** button. If the **Hide on View** option has been turned off, you will have to close the dialog box yourself.

To close the Search Result dialog box:

- Click on the dialog box's **Control Menu** button and select the **Close** command from the menu that appears

Or

- Double click on the **Control Menu** button.

Or

- Press the **<Escape>** key.

Viewing a Document that Matches the Search

To view a document that matches the search:

- Double click on the document's title

Or

1. Highlight the title of the document you want to view using the mouse or the cursor control keys.
2. Press the **View** button. Acrobat will display the document.

Setting Results Preferences

With the options in the **Results** frame, you can modify how results are displayed in the Search Results dialog box (displayed after a search, or with the **Tools | Search | Results** command). You can specify the criterion used to sort the results, the maximum number of documents that are displayed in the dialog box, and whether or not the dialog box is hidden when you view a document that contains a match.

To change the criterion used to sort the results:

1. Click on the **Sort By** drop-down list box. A list of sorting criteria will appear.
2. Click on the sorting criterion you want to use. You can choose from:

   - **Author:** The author, listed in the Document Info

   - **Created:** The create date, listed in the Document Info

   - **Creator:** The program used to create the document, listed in the Document Info

   - **Keywords:** The keywords, listed in the Document Info

   - **Modified:** The modification date, listed in the Document Info

   - **Producer:** The Acrobat program used to create the PDF file, listed in the Document Info

   - **Score:** The relevance ranking, computed by Search

   - **Subject:** The subject, listed in the Document Info

   - **Title:** The title, listed in the Document Info.

To change the maximum number of documents Search will report matches in:

- Enter the new number in the **Show Top Documents** edit box.

To turn the display of the Search Results dialog box on and off while you view documents that contain matches:

- Click on the **Hide on View** check box.

If the **Hide on View** option is turned off, the dialog box will remain in view until you close it; if the option is turned on, the dialog box will close automatically when you press the **View** button.

Moving to the Next Match

To move to the next match:

- Select the **Tools | Search | Next** command, or press the **Search Next** toolbar button.

This command has different effects depending on the highlighting option you have selected in the **Search Preferences Box**.

Setting Highlight Preferences

Acrobat Search allows you to highlight every match on a page at once or each match individually; you can also disable match highlighting.

To change the type of highlighting Search uses:

1. Click on the **Display** drop-down list box. A list of highlighting options will appear.

2. Click on the highlighting options you want to use. You can choose from:

- **By Page:** Every match on a page is highlighted at once, and the **Tools | Search | Previous** and **Tools | Search | Next** commands move forward and backward by pages

- **By Word:** Each match is highlighted individually, and the **Tools | Search | Previous** and **Tools | Search | Next** commands move forward and backward by matches

- **No Highlighting:** The matches are not highlighted, and the **Tools | Search | Previous** and **Tools | Search | Next** commands move forward and backward by pages.

Moving to the Next Document

To move to the first match in the next document in the document list:

- Select the **Tools | Search | Next Document** command, or press the **<Shift>** key and the **Search Next** toolbar button simultaneously.

Acrobat will close the active search document automatically when you select the **Tools | Search | Next Document** command.

The **Tools | Search | Next Document** command moves to documents in the order of their appearance in the Search Results dialog box.

Moving to the Previous Occurrence

To move to the previous match:

- Select the **Tools | Search | Previous** command, or press the **Search Previous** toolbar button.

This command has different effects depending on the highlighting option you have selected.

Moving to the Previous Document

To move to the first match in the previous document in the document list:

- Select the **Tools | Search | Previous Document** command, or press the **<Shift>** key and the **Search Previous** toolbar button simultaneously.

Acrobat will close the active search document automatically when you select the **Tools | Search | Previous Document** command.

The **Tools | Search | Previous Document** command moves to documents in the order of their appearance in the Search Results dialog box.

The status bar at the bottom of the Search Results dialog box shows:

- The filename and location of the highlighted document, if you are not viewing the document.

Or, if the results are either highlighted by page or not highlighted at all:

- The location of the document within the document list

- The location of the active page in the list of pages that contain the search text.

Or, if the results are highlighted by word:

- The location of the document within the document list

- The location of the highlighted match in the list of matches for the active document.

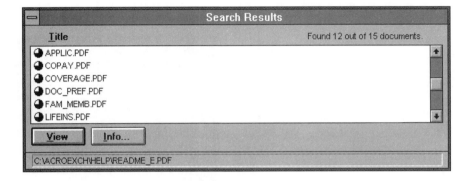

Viewing Document Info

To view information about a document:

1. Click on the document's name in the **Title** list box.
2. Press the **Info** button. Search will display the Document Info dialog box which contains the following information about the document:

    - The document's path and filename

    - The document's title

    - The document's subject

    - The document's author

    - The document's keywords

    - The date and time when the document was first created

- The date and time when the document was last modified

- The relevance score of the document

- The index the document was found in.

3. Press the **OK** button of the Document Info dialog box to return to the Search Results dialog box.

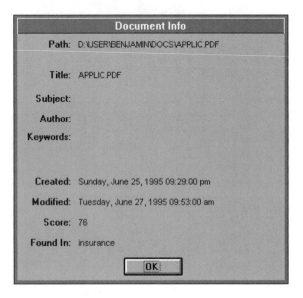

Tips For More Efficient Searches

There are two types of problem queries:

1. Queries that are too broad; the results they return are either too numerous or too irrelevant to be useful.
2. Queries that are too narrow; they return either no useful results or no results at all.

If a query is too broad, you can do the following things to refine it:

- Instruct Search to list results by their relevance ranking, and only view those documents that have the highest relevance ranking. Relevance ranking is a measure of how closely, overall, a document matches your query.

- If you used wildcards to construct the query, use more specific terms. For instance, if you were to use the* as a search term, when you were looking for "theatre," you might inadvertently match many documents because the* matches the word "the."

- Use the AND Boolean operator to add more terms to the search. For instance, the search term automobile might result in many matches; automobile AND transmission AND repair will match far fewer.

- Use the **Proximity** option to further refine a query that already contains an AND operator. The **Proximity** option restricts matches using AND operators to those documents where the two terms are within a few pages of each other. For instance, the query troubleshooting AND printer may turn up matches for "troubleshooting" and matches for "printer" in separate sections of many documents; the **Proximity** option would help filter out those documents.

- Use the **Match Case** option to restrict matches to text that has the same capitalization as the search term.

- Use the **Refine Search** feature to search only those documents that matched the previous search.

- Enter search terms for **Document Info** fields to restrict matches to those documents whose **Document Info** fields match the search terms.

- Enter date ranges to restrict matches to those documents whose creation and / or modification dates fall within the specified ranges.

If your query is too narrow, you might try these tips:

- Use the **Word Stemming** option to search for words that have the same stem as the search term

- Use the **Thesaurus** option to search for words that have similar meanings to that of the search term

- Use the **Sounds Like** option to search for words that sound like the search term

- Use the OR Boolean operator to search for several related search terms at once

- Use wildcards to search for prefixes.

CHAPTER

23
Catalog

Creating Indexes with Adobe Catalog

Acrobat Catalog creates full-text indexes of one or more PDF documents. In the index, Catalog stores a list of every word used in the collection of documents, the documents that contain the word, and the location of the word in each document. Acrobat Search can search through the indexes Catalog creates for PDF documents that contain certain words, phrases, or document information, or for documents whose creation and modification dates fall within certain ranges. Catalog is currently available only for Windows.

Indexed searches have several advantages over the built-in word-by-word searches Reader and Exchange use. They are faster because the Catalog program has already done the time-consuming work of reading every word in the file. They also allow you to search many PDF documents in one operation, unlike Find, where you must open each file that you want to search, and then search each file individually. With Catalog, you can build indexes of the thousands of documents on a CD-ROM or network file server, and Search users can search through all of the documents in seconds.

In this chapter, you learn how to:

- Use the catalog interface
- Prepare PDF files for indexing
- Create indexes
- Edit indexes
- Build indexes and schedule automatic builds

- Select index options
- Optimize indexes
- Update indexes
- Move indexes
- Delete indexes
- Use the ACROCAT.INI file.

The Catalog Interface

The catalog interface consists of one fixed-size window. It has a title bar, minimize button, Control menu button, menu bar, and a client area where Catalog displays its activities and status. The client area contains the following areas:

- **Status field**: The messages in this field tell you if Catalog is busy processing an index, or if Catalog is available to start a new task

- **Index field**: This is where Catalog displays the name of the index it is currently processing

- **File field**: This is where Catalog displays the name of the file it is adding to the index

- **Page field**: This is where Catalog displays the page number of the file it is currently reading for search terms

- **File count field**: This is where Catalog displays the number of files it has processed in the current index group

- **Progress indicator**: This is where Catalog displays the percentage of the total number of files that have been processed

- **Messages list box**: This is where Catalog displays a detailed account of its activities.

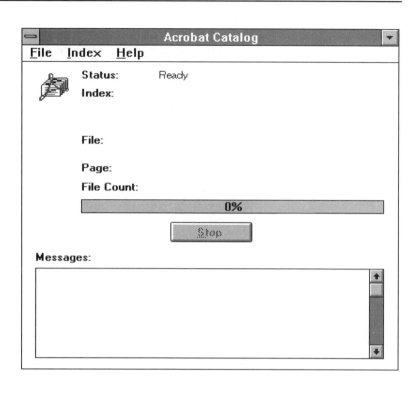

Preparing PDF Files to be Indexed

Before you create an index of a collection of documents, there are several steps you should take to ensure that the index is available to users with different types of computers, and that it is as informative as possible.

1. Enter Document Info fields for the indexed documents.

When a user receives results from a search, the documents that match the search criteria are identified by their **Title Document Info** field, and the user can display the **Document Info** fields. By entering descriptive information in the **Document Info** fields, you make it easier for a user to discover if a document contains the information he/she is looking for without opening the document.

2. Change the names of PDF files and folders / directories on Macintosh and UNIX servers to conform to the DOS filenaming conventions.

Catalog is a Windows program, and it uses the DOS file naming conventions when it stores the paths and filenames of indexed PDF files. If you are using Catalog to index files that are stored on Macintosh or UNIX computers, and the files or directories you are using do not have DOS-compliant filenames, your network software is *mapping* those file and directory names to names that are DOS-compliant. The mapped names may not be the same for other users in your network. The names may even be mapped *dynamically* with certain types of networking software, such as PC-NFS; if this is so, the file and directory names will be mapped to different DOS-compliant names every time a computer is connected to the server.

To overcome mapping problems such as those described previously, Acrobat 2.0 files contain unique *document identifiers*. Catalog stores these document identifiers in its index, and Search uses these identifiers to find files that match search criteria, even if the filename or path is different than what is recorded in the index. Document identifiers are powerful; I changed the extensions of all the PDF files in a directory from .pdf to .pdq, and Search was able to find them and open them. I also moved a group of PDF files from one directory to another; Search could find them then as well. Document identifiers will not always work, however, especially if the top-level directory names in the path are long, or if the file is stored in a deeply nested subdirectory. Searches that rely on document identifiers are slower as well. You can add document identifiers to version 1.0 PDF files by selecting the **Add Ids to 1.0 PDF files** option in the Index options dialog box.

To minimize potential problems, PDF documents and the directories in which they are stored should have DOS-compliant file names. DOS files and directories have an eight-letter name and an optional three-letter extension separated by a period; you should use only letters, numbers, and the underscore character [_] in the filename. All PDF documents should have the .pdf extension.

3. **Place all of the documents that you want to index on the same disk drive or volume.**

An index and the PDF files to which it refers must be stored on the same disk drive or volume.

4. **Remove File Open passwords from password-protected PDF files.**

Catalog must open files to index them, and it cannot open a password-protected file. If the document contains information that necessitates password protection, replace the password after the file has been indexed.

Creating a New Index

All of the data pertaining to the creation of an index, including its title, its description, the directories it refers to, the search options it supports, and its stop-word list, are stored in an *index description file*. Index description files are the files that Search users look for when they add indexes to the list of available indexes; they have a .pdx extension. When you build an index, you enter all of the information that is stored in the index description file, then you tell Catalog to build the index of all of the PDF files in the directories you specified.

To create a new index:

1. Select the **Index | New** command. The New Index Definition dialog box will appear.
2. Enter the new index's title in the **Index Title:** edit box.
3. Enter a description of the index in the **Index Description** edit box.
4. Specify the directories you want to include in the index: using the controls in the **Include Directories** frame.
5. Specify the directories you want to exclude from the index: using the controls in the **Exclude Directories** frame.

6. Select options for the index, by pressing the **Options** button and using the controls of the dialog box that appears. The options include:

- The stopwords you want excluded from the index

- The search options you want the index to support

- The index options you want to use.

7. Press the the **Build** button to build the index. Alternately, you can press the **Save As** button to save the index description file without building the index; you will have to build it later.

Specifying Directories to Include

When you include a directory in an index, Catalog indexes all of the PDF files stored in the directory and any of its subdirectories.

To specify a directory whose contents you want to index:

1. Press the **Add** button in the **Include Directories** frame of the New Index Definition dialog box. Catalog will display the Select Directory dialog box.
2. Select the drive or volume where the directory is stored, by:

   - Clicking on the **Drives** drop-down list box. A list of the available drives and volumes will appear

   - Clicking on the name of the drive you want to use.

3. Select the directory whose contents you want to index from the **Directories** list box. To move up and down the directory tree, double click on directory names.
4. Press the **OK** button of the Select Directory dialog box. Catalog will place the directory you specified in the **Include Directories** list box. If you decide not to include the directory, press the **Cancel** button.

You can only add one directory to the **Include Directories** list at a time. If you want to add more than one directory, repeat these steps for each directory that you want to add.

To remove a directory from the **Include Directories** list:

1. In the **Include Directories** list box, highlight the name of the directory you want to remove using the mouse or the cursor control keys.
2. Press the **Remove** button. The directory will be removed from the list.

You can only remove one directory from the **Include Directories** list at a time. If you want to remove more than one directory, repeat these steps for each directory that you want to remove.

Specifying Directories to Exclude

When you specify that a directory's contents are to be included in an index, Catalog will index PDF files that are stored in that directory and any of its subdirectories. If you do not want to include a subdirectory of an included directory in an index, you must exclude it from the index.

To specify a directory whose contents you want to exclude from an index:

1. Press the **Add** button in the **Exclude Directories** frame of the New Index Definition dialog box. Catalog will display the Select Directory dialog box.
2. Select the drive or volume where the directory is stored, by:

   • Clicking on the **Drives** drop-down list box. A list of the available drives and volumes will appear.

   • Clicking on the name of the drive you want to use.

3. Select the directory whose contents you want to exclude from the **Directories** list box. To move up and down the directory tree, double click on directory names.
4. Press the **OK** button of the Select Directory dialog box. Catalog will place the directory you specified in the **Exclude Directories** list box. If you decide not to exclude the directory, press the **Cancel** button.

You can only add one directory to the **Exclude Directories** list at a time. If you want to add more than one directory, repeat these steps for each directory that you want to add.

To remove a directory from the **Exclude Directories** list:

1. In the **Exclude Directories** list box, highlight the name of the directory you want to remove using the mouse or the cursor control keys.
2. Press the **Remove** button. The directory will be removed from the list.

You can only remove one directory from the **Exclude Directories** list at a time. If you want to remove more than one directory, repeat these steps for each directory that you want to remove.

Editing an Index Definition File

You can edit any of the data in an index definition file, including its title, its description, the directories it refers to, the search options it supports, and its stopword list.

To open an index file for editing:

1. Select the **Index | Open** command. Catalog will display the Select Index File Definition to Edit dialog box.
2. Use the controls of the Select Index File Definition to Edit dialog box to to select the index definition file that you want to edit.
3. Press the **OK** button; the Edit Index Definition dialog box will appear. If you decide you don't want to edit an index, press the **Cancel** button.

The Edit Index Definition dialog box has the same controls as the New Index Definition dialog box. For more information about the controls of these dialog boxes, see the "Creating a New Index" section. For more information about modifying index options, see the "Selecting Index Options" section.

When you edit an index definition file, you must rebuild the index for the changes to take effect. Some changes to the index definition file, however, require that the index be purged and rebuilt before they take effect. These changes include modifications of the stopword list and modifications to the search options that the index supports. For more information, see the "Purging an Index" section.

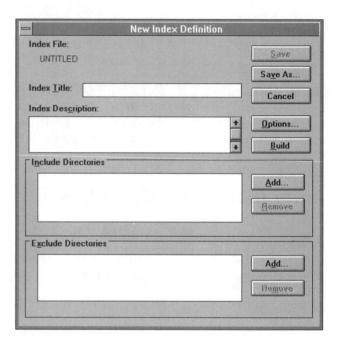

Building Indexes

There are several reasons you may want to build or rebuild an index. These are:

- You created an index definition file, but you did not build the index for it

- You want to update an index that you previously built

- You modified an index definition file, and you want the modifications to take effect in the index.

To build or update an index:

1. Select the **Index** | **Build** command. Catalog will display the Select Index File to Build dialog box.
2. Use the controls of the Select Index File to Build dialog box to select the index definition file that corresponds to the index you want to build or update.
3. Press the **OK** button. If you decide you don't want to build an index, press the **Cancel** button.

When you press the **OK** button, Catalog starts to build the index, displaying its status and progress messages in its window.

If the index already exists, Catalog will perform an incremental update of the index.

Stopping a Build

To stop a build that is in progress:

• Press the **Stop** button.

Catalog will stop building the index. To finish building the index, select the **Index** | **Build** command.

If the build you stopped was a scheduled build, you must restart scheduled builds.

To restart scheduled builds:

1. Select the **Index** | **Schedule** command. The Schedule Builds dialog box will appear.
2. Press the **Start** button. Catalog will start any builds that are waiting to run.

Purging an Index

To purge an index is to remove all entries from it. When an index has been purged, the index cannot be searched. You must purge and rebuild an index in the following situations:

1. When you change the stopword list.
2. When you change the Search options the index supports.

When you rebuild an index that has been purged, Catalog builds the index as if it were new, rather than performing an incremental update, as it does for an existing index. It is a good idea to periodically purge and rebuild indexes that are updated frequently, because incremental updates of indexes take up more disk space than an index that has been purged and rebuilt. Indexes that are updated more frequently, or that are modified extensively with each update, should be purged and rebuilt more frequently.

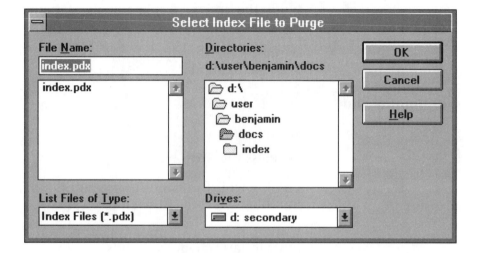

To purge an index:

1. Select the **Index | Purge** command. Catalog will display the Select Index File to Purge dialog box.
2. Use the controls of the Select Index File to Purge dialog box to to select the index you want to purge.
3. Press the **OK** button. If you decide you don't want to purge the index, press the **Cancel** button.

4. If you press the **OK** button, Catalog will ask you to confirm your decision to purge the index. To confirm the purge, press the **Yes** button. If you decide you don't want to purge the index, press the **No** button.

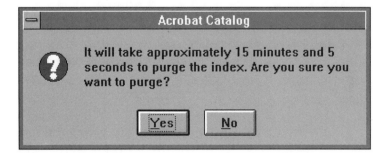

When Catalog purges the index, it prevents any new searches of the index, but it allows all currently running searches to complete before it removes the index entries.

Scheduling Automatic Builds of Indexes

Catalog can automatically build and update indexes once, periodically, or continuously. This can make it much easier to keep fast-changing indexes up to date.

If Catalog is waiting to process scheduled builds, and perhaps if it is building an index, a dialog box will appear, asking if you want Catalog to stop what it is doing.

To schedule an automatic build:

1. Select the **Index | Schedule** command. The Schedule Builds dialog box will appear.
2. Use the controls of the Schedule Builds dialog box to select the files that will be built automatically, and to specify how and when the builds should be scheduled.

3. To save the list of indexes and scheduled build options, press the **Save** button. Catalog will save the information in the ACROCAT.INI file.

4. To start the scheduled builds, press the **Start** button.

Adding Indexes to the Schedule Builds List

To add an index to the schedule builds list:

1. Press the **Add** button. Catalog will display the Select Index File to Add to Schedule dialog box.

2. Use the controls of the Select Index File to Add to Schedule dialog box to select the index you want to purge.

3. Press the **OK** button. If you decide you don't want to add an index to the schedule, press the **Cancel** button.

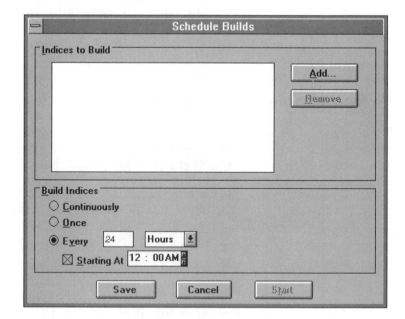

Removing Indexes from the Scheduled Build List

To remove an index from the **Indices to Build** list:

1. In the **Indices to Build** list box, highlight the name of the index you want to remove using the mouse or the cursor control keys.
2. Press the **Remove** button. The index will be removed from the list.

You can only remove one index from the list at a time. If you want to remove more than one index, repeat these steps for each index that you want to remove.

Building Indexes Once

With a one-time scheduled build, you can create a list of the indexes you want to build or update, and then tell Catalog to build the indexes at any time. You can, for instance, add several indexes to the **Indices to Build** list over the course of a day, and then build them at the end of the day when you are not using your computer. This can be useful if you want to create several new indexes, or you must update several indexes that are not updated on a regular basis, and it would be too time-consuming to build them individually.

To build indexes once:

1. Add the indexes you want to build to the **Indices to Build** list.
2. Click on the **Once** radio button in the **Build Indices** frame.
3. When you want Catalog to start building the indices, press the **Start** button.
4. If you want to close the Schedule Builds dialog box before you start the builds, press the **Save** button. Catalog will store the list of indexes in the ACROBAT.INI file and close the Scheduled Builds dialog box.

Building Indexes Periodically

If you need to update certain indexes on a regular basis, you may want to schedule the updates periodically. Catalog can build indexes at intervals of minutes, days, or weeks, starting at a prescribed time.

To build indexes periodically:

1. Add the indexes you want to build to the **Indices to Build** list.
2. Click on the **Every** radio button in the **Build Indices** frame.
3. Select the interval you want to use (minutes, days, or weeks) by clicking on the **Every** drop-down list box, and then clicking on the interval.
4. Enter the multiple of the interval you want to use (for instance, every 3 days) in the **Enter** edit box.
5. If you want to start the periodic builds at a certain time, click the **Starting At** check box so an "x" appears in the box. Use the keyboard or the scroll buttons to set the hour, minute, and AM/PM setting at which you want the builds to start.
6. Press the **Start** button.

When you press the **Start** button, Catalog will close the Schedule Builds dialog box. If you have specified a time for the builds to start, Catalog will also:

• Display the message "Waiting for scheduled build" in the **Status:** field.

• Display the title of the first index to be built in the **Title:** field, and the message "1 out of 'x' scheduled" in the **Index:** field.

If you have not specified for the builds to start, Catalog will start building the indexes immediately.

Tech Note

For the builds to take place, Catalog must be running at the time you prescribed. If you stop Catalog, you will have to restart the scheduled builds.

Updating Indexes Continuously

If the information in a collection of documents is time-sensitive, you may want to update the index continuously, so the index of the documents is always accurate. When you specify continuous updates of indexes, Catalog will update the indexes in a loop, starting at the top of the list, updating each list in turn, and then returning to the top of the list.

To update indexes continuously:

1. Click on the **Continuously** radio button in the **Build Indices** frame.
2. Press the **Start** button. If you do not want to start the continuous updates right away, press the **Save** button; Catalog will store the schedule information, and you can start the updates later.

Indexes that are updated continuously can become very large; make sure to purge the indexes periodically to avoid wasting disk space.

Restarting Scheduled Builds after Stopping a Scheduled Build

If you stopped builds in progress by pressing the **Stop** button on Catalog's main window, or if you stopped Catalog while it was waiting to process periodic builds, you will need to restart scheduled builds.

To restart scheduled builds:

1. Select the **Index | Schedule** command to display the Schedule Builds dialog box.
2. Press the **Start** button.

Selecting Index Options

You can choose from several options when you create an index, including:

- The stopwords to exclude from the index
- Whether or not to include numbers in the index
- Whether or not to support the **Word Stemming**, **Sounds Like**, or **Match Case** search options

- Whether or not to optimize the index for storage on a CD-ROM

- Whether or not to add document identifiers to PDF files created with version 1.0 of Acrobat.

You select these options using the controls of the **Options** dialog box. You open the **Options** dialog box by pressing the **Options** button on the New Index Definition or the Edit Index Definition dialog boxes; these dialog boxes appear when you create a new index with the **Index | New** command or edit an existing index with the **Index | Open** command, respectively.

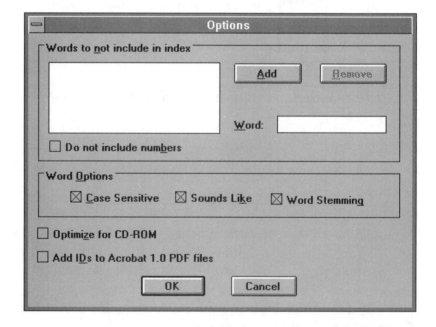

Creating the Stopword List

Stopwords are common words that do not give evidence of a document's topic or that are excluded from an index to reduce its size.

The most common stopwords are:

- Articles, like "the," "a," and "an"
- Conjunctions, like "and" and "but"
- Prepositions, like "for," "to," and "at"

For each index, you maintain a Stopword list that contains all of the words that you want to exclude from an index. The list may be any number of words from zero (no words excluded from the index) to 500; the maximum length of a stopword is 24 characters. Stopwords are case sensitive; if you want to exclude "The" and "the" from an index, for example, you will need to add two stopwords to the list.

To add a stopword to the Stopword list:

1. Type the word in the **Word** edit box.
2. Press the **Add** button. The word will appear in the **Words to Not Include in Index** list box.

To remove a word from the Stopword list:

1. In the **Words to Not Include in Index** list box, highlight the stopword you want to remove, using the mouse or the cursor control keys.
2. Press the **Remove** button. The Stopword will be removed from the list.

When you change the stopword list, you must purge and rebuild the index for the changes to take effect. For more information about purging and rebuilding indexes, see the "Purging an Index" and "Building an Index" sections of this chapter.

While excluding stopwords from an index reduces the size of the index, it also prevents search from finding phrases that contain stopwords. For more information about the advantages and disadvantages of Stopwords, see the "Constructing Queries" section of Chapter 16.

Including Numbers in an Index

By default, Catalog includes numbers as search terms in indexes, so you could, for instance, search for a telephone number in an index. To reduce the size of the indexes you create, you can exclude numbers from indexes. Catalog's rules for what are and are not numbers can be found in the "Constructing Queries" section of Chapter 16.

To remove numbers from or add numbers to an index:

- Click on the **Do Not Include Numbers** check box. When an "x" appears in the box, numbers will be excluded from the index; when the box is clear, numbers will be included in the index.

Enabling and Disabling Search Options

If the index is built to support them, users of indexes may select the following search options:

- **Sounds Like:** Search will search for terms that sound like the search term and have the same first letter

- **Match Case:** Search will only find terms that have the exact capitalization of the search term

- **Word Stemming:** Search will search for terms that have the same word stem as the search term. Note that users of indexes can use the **Word Stemming** search option even if the index does not support it, but they will be unable to use the Word Assistant to see what terms match the search term.

Tech Note

By default, all of these options are supported, but you can disable support for any of them to reduce the size of the index.

To enable or disable support for search options:

- Click on the appropriate check box in the **Word Options** frame. When an "x" appears in the box, the index will support the option; when the box is clear, the index will not support the option.

Optimizing Indexes for CD-ROM

To compensate for the slower access times of CD-ROM drives, Catalog will increase the number of files that are grouped together in an index, making searches of the index faster.

To enable or disable the CD-ROM optimization:

- Click on the **Optimize for CD-ROM** check box. When an "x" appears in the box, Catalog will increase the number of files that are grouped together in an index; when the box is clear, Catalog will group the files in smaller numbers.

You can specify the number of files that Catalog groups together when the **Optimize for CD-ROM** option is enabled by modifying the ACROCAT.INI file; for more information, refer to the section titled "The ACROCAT.INI File."

Adding Document IDs to Acrobat 1.0 Files

Acrobat version 2.0 adds unique document IDs to PDF files to make it easier for Search to find the files on systems that do not use the DOS filename conventions. Catalog can add document IDs to PDF files created with version 1.0 of Acrobat as it indexes the files.

To add document IDs to Acrobat 1.0 files:

- Click on the **Add IDs to Acrobat 1.0 PDF files** check box. When an "x" appears in the box, Catalog will add IDs to the files; when the box is clear, Catalog will not add the IDs.

Optimizing Indexes

Depending on how your indexes are used, certain characteristics may be more important. For instance, in an environment where disk space is limited, small indexes may be important; up-to-the-minute information may be crucial, and so on. Catalog's options allow you to tailor the performance of the index to match the characteristics that are most important for your application.

Some of the optimizations listed require you to change the settings in the ACROCAT.INI file; for more information about changing settings in this file, see the "The ACROCAT.INI File" section.

Optimizing Indexes for Minimum Size

To optimize indexes for minimum size:

- Exclude stopwords and numbers from the index. This reduces the number of search terms in the index, and thus the size of the index.

- Disable the **Word Stemming**, **Sounds Like**, and **Match Case** search options.

- Increase the build-group size setting in the ACROCAT.INI file. The larger the number of files that are indexed in a group, the smaller the size of the index.

- Increase the maximum document section size setting in the ACROCAT.INI file. If a file is larger than this setting, Catalog will break the index for the document into two sections, which increases the size of the index.

- If the index already exists, purge and rebuild it instead of updating it. This prevents obsolete entries from appearing in the index.

Optimizing for Fastest Query Execution Speed

To optimize indexes for fastest query execution speed:

- Exclude stopwords and numbers from the index. Queries execute faster when there are fewer search terms in the index.

- Disable the **Word Stemming**, **Sounds Like**, and **Match Case** search options.

- Increase the build-group size setting in the ACROCAT.INI file. If you are distributing the index and documents on CD-ROM select the **Optimize for CD-ROM** option; this increases the build-group size setting. The build-group size setting for CD-ROM can also be found in the ACROCAT.INI file. The larger the number of files that are indexed in a group, the faster a query will execute.

- Increase the maximum document section size setting in the ACROCAT.INI file. If a file is larger than this setting, Catalog will break the index for the document into two sections, which increases the size of the index.

- If the index already exists, purge and rebuild it instead of updating it. By removing obsolete entries from the index, its structure is improved, increasing search speed.

In addition to these index optimizations, you can increase the speed at which queries execute by placing the index and documents on a faster file server or by making local copies of the index and documents.

Optimizing for Frequent Updates

To optimize indexes for frequent updates:

- Update the index continuously

- Decrease the build-group size setting in the ACROCAT.INI file to 100 or less. While this increases the time it takes to update the index, it decreases the number of files that Catalog processes at one time, making updated portions of the index available more quickly.

- Increase the maximum document section size setting in the ACROCAT.INI file.

In addition to these index optimizations, you can increase the speed at which indexes are updated by placing the index and documents on a faster computer, or by dedicating a server to the task of updating the indexes.

Optimizing to Minimize Impact on Server Performance

To minimize an index's impact on server performance:

- Do not update indexes continuously; this creates a constant drain on the server's resources. Instead, schedule updates for those times when the server is least heavily used.

- Exclude stopwords and numbers from the index. Queries execute faster when there are fewer search terms in the index.

- Disable the **Word Stemming**, **Sounds Like**, and **Match Case** search options.

In addition to these index optimizations, avoid building or updating indexes when the server is performing a backup.

Optimizing Indexes for CD-ROM

Enable the **Optimize for CD-ROM** option, and increase the size of the CD-ROM build-group size setting. The build-group size setting for CD-ROM can be found in the ACROCAT.INI file.

Updating Indexes

As time passes, you may need to update your indexes so that they correspond to the data contained in the indexed documents. You need to update an index when:

- The indexed documents change

- Documents are added to or removed from the index.

- The directory structure of the indexed directories changes

- The indexed documents are moved to a new disk drive or volume with a different name

- You modify the index definition file. When you modify index options, such as Stopword lists and the search options an index supports, you must purge and rebuild the index instead of updating it.

- A new custom document data field is defined for the documents, and data is added to the field.

Update Methods

To update an index, all you need to do is build it again. Catalog has commands to manually build single indexes and can build one or more indexes automatically. If you are editing a single index, and want your modifications to take effect, it is usually easier to build the index manually; for more information about manual builds, see the "Building an Index" section. Automatic builds are especially useful when:

- You have many indexes to update

- The indexes are large

- You update the indexes frequently

- Your server's performance suffers considerably from the build process

- It is easier to schedule the updates for a convenient time.

For more information about scheduled builds, see the "Scheduling Automatic Builds of Indexes" section of this chapter.

How Incremental Updates Work

Rather than recreating the entire index, Catalog performs incremental updates of indexes. Catalog does this by marking the index entries for deleted and changed documents as invalid and adding new index information to the end of the index. Incremental updates take less time to create, but they also increase the size of indexes and reduce the speed at which queries execute.

You can search an index while Catalog updates it. As is the case when it builds an index, Catalog processes a certain number of files at a time when performing an update. This number, known as the build-group size, is specified in the ACROCAT.INI file. Once Catalog has finished processing the files in a group, it updates the index information for those files, making that portion of the update accessible to people using the index. If you want to make sure that the people using the index see the most current information, you should set the build-group size to a small number, for example, 100 or less. Since Catalog processes the index in smaller "chunks" when the build-group size is small, the time between the start of the update and the availability of the first update results is reduced. Note, however, that small build-group sizes increase the time it takes Catalog to complete an update.

Moving Indexed Collections of Documents

If the relative path between the index description file and the indexed documents remains the same, you can move indexed collections of documents to other directories or volumes without rebuilding the index. If the relative path changes, however, the index must be rebuilt. If you want to use the same Stopword list and index options settings after you move the files, change the lists of included and excluded directories in the original index description file, then rebuild the index.

Deleting an Index

If you want to delete an index without disrupting queries that are currently executing, purge the index before you delete it. Purging the index allows currently executing queries to finish, but does not allow any new queries of the index to be made.

Once the index is purged, you can delete it. To delete an index:

1. Delete the index's index definition (PDX) file.
2. Delete the subdirectory with the same name as the index definition file, and all of its subdirectories. This subdirectory is stored in the same directory as the index definition file. For instance, if you are deleting the REPTINDX.PDX index definition file, delete the REPTINDX subdirectory, all of its subdirectories, and all the files they contain.

The ACROCAT.INI File

The ACROCAT.INI file is an ASCII file, found in your Windows directory, that contains configuration information for Catalog.

Structure of the ACROCAT.INI File

The ACROCAT. INI file is divided into three sections: Options, Schedule, and Fields. The structure of the ACROCAT.INI file follows the conventions for Windows initialization (.INI) files. Each section has a section heading, which is a line with the section name in square brackets, for instance, [Options]. The sections are:

- **Options**: The Options section is where the Catalog's options settings are stored

- **Schedule**: The Schedule section is where Catalog stores information about scheduled builds

- **Fields**: The Fields section is where Catalog stores custom **Document Info** field definitions.

Each piece of configuration information in the file is written in the form:

```
SettingName=Value
```

Note that there are no spaces on either side of the equals sign. You can place comments in the ACROCAT.INI file. Comment lines start with the semicolon character [;]:

```
;Catalog will ignore this line
```

Explanations of each line of the ACROCAT.INI file can be found in the following sections.

The Options Section

The Options section of the ACROCAT.INI file contains settings for Catalog's indexing and user interface options.

```
DocumentWordSectionsSelection=1
```

The DocumentWordSectionsSelection setting specifies which of the DocumentWordSectionsSize settings Catalog will use to obtain the maximum number of search terms an index of a document can contain. A table of DocumentWordSectionsSelection settings and their corresponding DocumentWordSectionsSize settings is givenhere:

DocumentWordSectionSelectionSetting	DocumentWordSectionSize
0	Small
1	Medium
2	Large

If the number of search terms in the document exceeds the number in the DocumentWordSectionsSize setting, the index is split into multiple indexes.

```
IndexAvailableGroupSize=512
```

The IndexAvailableGroupSize setting specifies the build-group size Catalog will use when building or updating indexes. Catalog processes PDF files in batches when it builds or updates indexes, and then makes the results from each batch available for indexing. The build-group size is the number of PDF documents in the batch. Specifying a larger build-group size decreases the time it takes for a query to execute and decreases the disk space the index requires; specifying a smaller build-group size makes partial updates to the index available more quickly. The minimum value for IndexAvailableGroupSize is 16; the maximum value is 4000.

If you select the **Optimize for CD-ROM** option (see the "Selecting Index Options" section), Catalog will find the build-group size from the GroupSize-ForCDROM setting instead of the IndexAvailable-GroupSize setting.

```
SearchEngineMessages=Yes
```

The SearchEngineMessages setting specifies whether or not search engine error messages are displayed in Catalog's **Messages** list box and recorded in message log files. If the SearchEngineMessages value is Yes, the messages are displayed and recorded; if the value is No, they are not.

```
WindowsOnlyFilenames=No
```

The WindowsOnlyFilenames setting specifies whether or not. Do not set this option to **Yes** unless [the document server and] every computer that can search the index is running Windows, and each of those computers uses the same drive letter to refer to the drive where the index and documents are stored.

```
PurgeTime=905
```

The PurgeTime setting is the time, in seconds, that Catalog waits for queries to execute before it begins to purge an index. The default PurgeTime setting is 905 seconds, or 15 minutes and 5 seconds. You can set the PurgeTime to as low as 1 second, but you should set it to at least several minutes to allow even the most time-consuming of queries to execute before the index is purged.

```
MemoryPercent=20
```

The MemoryPercent setting specifies the minimum amount of memory that must be available to Catalog for it to continue a build, expressed as a percentage of the memory available when the build was started. For instance, if 8Mb of memory are available when Catalog starts a build, and MemoryPercent is set to 25, Catalog will stop the build if the available memory falls below 2Mb. If your system does not have much memory, you can lower this setting to allow Catalog to build larger indexes, but you increase the risk that Catalog will fail.

```
DocumentWordSectionsSmall=200000
DocumentWordSectionsMedium=400000
DocumentWordSectionsLarge=800000
```

The DocumentWordSectionsSize settings specify the maximum number of search terms an index of a document can contain. The DocumentWordSectionsSelection setting specifies which of the DocumentWordSectionsSize settings Catalog will use. For instance, if the value of the DocumentWordSectionsSelection setting is 2, and the value of the DocumentWordSectionsLarge setting is 800000, the maximum number of search terms Catalog will be able to store in an index is eight hundred thousand.

If the number of search terms in the document will exceed the number in the DocumentWordSectionsSize setting, the index is split into multiple indexes. Query matches in separate sections of the index will each have their own listing in the Search Results dialog box. The listings in the Search Results dialog box would look like this:

Oxford English Dictionary: Pages 1 to 1050
Oxford English Dictionary: Pages 1051 to 2213
Oxford English Dictionary: Pages 2214 to 2975

Catalog adds the page numbers to each section of the index automatically when it splits the index. Splitting the index into multiple indexes slows query execution speed and increases the disk space required to index the document.

To calculate the amount of memory in bytes required to build an index section, multiply the DocumentWordSectionsSize settings by 10. For instance, if the DocumentWordSectionsMedium setting has a value of 400000, Catalog will require 4Mb of memory. If less than 4Mb of memory is available, and Catalog attempts to build an index of maximum size, it will report an error. If this happens and you are using the DocumentWordSectionsMedium or DocumentWord-SectionsLarge setting, you can change Document-WordSectionsSelection to point to a smaller DocumentWordSectionsSize setting. If you are using the DocumentWordSectionsSmall setting, you can reduce the value of the setting.

If your computer has a very small or a very large amount of memory, you can scale all of the settings to a size that reflects your computer's resources. For instance, if your computer has 32Mb of memory, you may want to quadruple all of the settings.

```
MaxLogFileSize=500000
```

The MemoryPercent setting specifies the maximum size, in bytes, that a log file can become; the maximum number you can assign to this setting is 1000000. When a log file grows to the size in the MaxLogFileSize setting, Catalog empties the file and resumes writing messages into it. All information stored in the file when it is emptied is lost.

```
GroupSizeForCDROM=4000
```

The GroupSizeForCDROM setting specifies the build-group size Catalog will use when building or updating indexes when the Optimize for CD-ROM option is selected (see the Selecting Index Options section). If the Optimize for CD-ROM option is not selected, Catalog uses the build-group size specified in the Index-AvailableGroupSize setting. A large build-group size is used for CD-ROM distribution to increase the speed at which a query executes and to minimize the disk space required to store the index. Since indexes disctributed on CD-ROM cannot be updated, it is not useful to for this setting to have a small value.

There is no direct limit to the GroupSizeForCDROM setting, but this setting can affect the size of index data files, which have a 64 Mb limit. If you set the GroupSizeForCDROM setting to a high enough value that index entries for a group of files to be indexed require more than 64Mb of disk space, Catalog will be unable to build the index.

```
DisplayAboutDialog=1
```

The DisplayAboutDialog setting controls whether or not Catalog displays its splash screen when the program is launched. The splash screen contains version and copyright information; it can also be viewed by selecting the **Help | About Acrobat Catalog** command. To display the splash screen when Catalog launches, set **DisplayAboutDialog** to 1; to suppress the display of the splash screen, set **DisplayAbout-Dialog** to 0.

The Schedule Section

The Schedule section of the ACROCAT.INI is where Catalog stores scheduled build data. Catalog stores the data when you select the **Save** button of the Scheduled Builds dialog box; see the "Scheduling Automatic Builds of Indexes" section of this chapter for more information on entering and saving scheduled build information.

```
i0=c:\data\acrobook\acrinact.pdx
i1=c:\data\kaiser\kaiser.pdx
i2=
```

The inumber settings contain the names of indexes that are in the **Scheduled Build** list. These indexes will be built automatically by Catalog when the scheduled build takes place.

```
nTimeInterval=24
```

The nTimeInterval setting specifies the number of time units between scheduled builds, which is entered in the **Every** edit box in the Scheduled Builds dialog box. The time units are specified by the nTimeUnits setting.

```
nTimeUnits=1
```

The nTimeUnits setting specifies the time unit to be used when scheduling builds, which is entered in the **Every** edit box in the Scheduled Builds dialog box. Valid values for the nTimeUnits setting are:

nTimeUnits	nTimeInterval
0	Minutes
1	Hours
2	Days

Catalog uses the nTimeUnits setting and the nTimeInterval setting to determine the interval between scheduled builds. For instance, if nTime-Interval is set to 7 and nTimeUnits is set to 2, Catalog will build the listed indexes every 7 days.

```
nTimeHour=12
```

The nTimeHour setting specifies the hour of the day when builds will take place, if the **Starting at** option is set in the Scheduled Builds dialog box or in the bStartingAtSetting. The setting corresponds to the number that appears in the hour and the **AM/PM** fields of the **Starting at** edit box. The range of valid values for the nTimeHour setting is from 0 (12 midnight) to 23 (11PM). Catalog uses the nTimeHour setting and the nTimeMinute setting to determine the exact time of day when builds will take place. For instance, if nTimeHour is set to 0 and nTimeMinute is set to 15, Catalog will build the listed indexes at 12:15AM.

```
nTimeMinute=0
```

The nTimeMinute setting specifies the number of minutes past the hour the builds will take place. The hour is specified in the nTimeHour setting and the Starting at option must be set in the Scheduled Builds dialog box. The setting corresponds to the number that appears in the minutes field of the **Starting at** edit box. The range of valid values for the nTimeM-inute setting is from 0 (on the hour) to 59 (59 minutes past the hour).

```
nBuildWhichWay=1
```

The nBuildWhichWay setting specifies whether Catalog will build the indexes listed in the Scheduled Builds dialog box continuously, once, or at specified intervals. The valid values for nBuildWhichWay are:

nBuildWhichWay	Build Frequency Setting
0	Continuously
1	Once
2	At specified intervals

If nBuildWhichWay is set to 2, Catalog uses the nTimeInterval and nTimeUnits settings to determine how long the interval between builds is, and uses the bStartingAt, nTimeHour, and nTimeMinute settings to determine whether or not to build the indexes at a specified time and what the specified time is.

```
bStartingAt=0
```

The bStartingAt setting specifies whether or not to start scheduled builds at the time specified in the nTimeHour and nTimeMinute settings. The two valid values for this setting are 0, which corresponds to disabling the **Starting at** option in the Scheduled Builds dialog box, and 1, which corresponds to enabling it. If this setting is set to zero, builds will start as soon as you press the **Start** button of the Scheduled Builds dialog box; if it is set to 1, when you press the **Start** button, Catalog will wait until the specified time to build the indexes.

The Fields Section

The Fields section of the ACROCAT.INI file is where you add custom **Document Info** field definitions for Catalog to use when creating indexes. To edit and search custom **Document Info** fields, you will need to have either a customized copy of Exchange or familiarity with the PDF file format; see the *Portable Document Format Reference Manual* for more details.

```
[Fields]
;You can add custom field definitions here
;Examples:
```

```
;Field0=FieldInt,int (integer field)
;Field0=FieldDate,date (date field)
;Field0=FieldStr,str (character string field)
```

The syntax for a custom **Document Info** field definition is:

- FieldNumber = FieldName,int|date|str

- Number is a unique number. Do not skip field numbers

- FieldName is a name you select to describe the field, up to 64 characters long

- int, date, and str are the field data type identifiers, corresponding to integer, date, and character string data, respectively.

A custom field may have only one field data type. For more information about the allowed date formats in custom fields; see the *Portable Document Format Reference Manual*.

How Catalog Creates an Index

When Catalog creates an index, it uses white space and separator characters to separate each search term in a PDF file from the rest of the file. It makes an alphabetized list of all the search terms in the document, and then eliminates any stopwords from the list.

For example, when Catalog indexes a document that contains the text: "Ask not what your country can do for you, but what you can do for your country."

Catalog produces this list of search terms:

- Ask
- But
- Can
- Country
- Do
- For

- Not
- What
- You
- Your.

Next, Catalog checks the search terms it has found against the **Stopword** list you have entered, and elminates any terms that are in the list. If you use the typical **Stopword** list found in Appendix A, the "for" term would be eliminated. The final search term list becomes:

- Ask
- But
- Can
- Country
- Do
- Not
- What
- You
- Your.

Often, text is not placed in PDF files on a line-by-line basis, but on a word-by-word basis. In other words, the text "Ask not what your country can do for you, but what you can do for your country" is not placed on the page in one group. Instead, each word in the text ("Ask," "not," "what," ...) is placed on the page individually. In such cases, the words are not separated by space characters, and Catalog must determine the order of the words by examining their placement on the page.

Log Files

As Catalog builds an index, the status and error messages it displays in its **Messages** list box are also stored in a file. These files are ASCII log files which are viewable using text editors and word processing applications making them easy for you to inspect later. Catalog maintains a master log file, ACRO-CAT.LOG, where it stores messages from every index it processes. Catalog also creates a log file for each index. In these individual log files, Catalog stores messages pertaining to an individual index only. The log files for individual indexes are named after the index description filename, with the extension .LOG added; they are stored in the directory where the index description file is stored.

Catalog places a limit on the size of log files; when a log file reaches the limit, Catalog deletes the existing messages in the file and begins writing new messages at the beginning of the file. All information stored in the log file is lost when Acrobat deletes it. The size limit for log files, in bytes, is determined by the MaxLogFileSetting in the ACROCAT.INI file; you can increase the size limit up to 1Mb.

The following is an example of a log file:

```
03/16/95 12:22:12: Starting build.
03/16/95 12:22:13: Connecting to index.
03/16/95 12:22:20: Searching: C:\DATA\ACROBOOK
03/16/95 12:22:21: Indexing 13 documents.
03/16/95 12:22:31: Extracting from c:\ch1.pdf
03/16/95 12:22:35: Extracting from c:\ch2.pdf.
03/16/95 12:22:36: Extracting from c:\ch3.pdf.
03/16/95 12:22:38: Extracting from c:\ch4.pdf.
03/16/95 12:22:39: Extracting from c:\ch5.pdf.
03/16/95 12:22:40: Extracting from c:\ch6.pdf.
03/16/95 12:22:41: Extracting from c:\ch7.pdf.
03/16/95 12:22:43: Extracting from c:\ch8.pdf.
03/16/95 12:22:44: Extracting from c:\ch9.pdf.
03/16/95 12:23:01: Removing index entries for
changed or deleted documents.
03/16/95 12:23:06: Waiting for about 20 sec-
onds to perform routine index update.
03/16/95 12:23:29: Acrobat In Action! - Index
Build Successful.
03/16/95 12:23:29:   Total Acrobat files in
all directories: 13
03/16/95 12:23:29:   Total new files: 9
03/16/95 12:23:29:   Total pages indexed: 82
```

```
03/16/95 12:23:29:    Total number of files
skipped: 0
03/16/95 12:23:29:    Total deleted files: 0
03/16/95 12:23:30: Index Build Successful.
```

Custom Document Info Data Fields

You can add custom **Document Info** fields to the ones supplied by Acrobat by using Catalog to include them in indexes and search for them. To enter and edit the fields, you will need to be familiar with customizing Acrobat Exchange with the Adobe Acrobat Software Development Kit (SDK), and you will need to be familiar with the Portable Document Format. You will also need to use the SDK to provide a user interface for searching the custom fields.

Custom **Document Info** data fields must be defined in the ACROCAT.INI file for Catalog to index them. For more information about defining custom data fields, see the The ACROCAT.INI File section.

Displaying On-line Help

Catalog's on-line help is in PDF format, naturally. To view it, select the **Help | Using Acrobat Catalog** command. Your Acrobat viewer will launch, and the help file will be displayed.

Distiller

Converting PostScript to PDF

Distiller is a program that converts PostScript files to PDF files; version 2.0 is available for the Windows and Macintosh platforms, and version 1.0 is available for SunOS / Solaris. Distiller is designed to complement PDFWriter in several important ways:

- It allows you to create PDF files directly from existing PostScript files. If your documents are already in PostScript format, you can convert them to PDF format with Distiller much more quickly than you could using PDFWriter.

- There may be times when you have a document in PostScript format, but not in a format that you can process with PDFWriter. This may be the case with legacy documents, documents that were not produced on Macintosh or Windows systems, or documents you download from the Internet. You can convert these documents to PDF with Distiller.

- Certain PostScript features , such as custom halftone functions, are not available in Windows GDI or Apple's QuickDraw. Distiller can include these features in PDF documents, but PDFWriter cannot.

- It offers more sophisticated data compression and graphics options than the PDFWriter program.

- Distiller allows you to embed some or all of the characters in a PostScript Type 1 font in a PDF document. PDFWriter can only write the font descriptor to the PDF file. When the full Type 1 font is present in the PDF document, Reader and Exchange can recreate the look of the font exactly. When only the file descriptor is present, Reader and Exchange use the Adobe Multiple Master fonts to simulate the look of the font, giving an approximation of the original font.

- Distiller is designed to work in a networked environment; you can direct Distiller to monitor, or *watch*, several directories on a network, and create PDF files from any PostScript files that are placed in those directories. This capability, in effect, allows several people using a network to "share" Distiller, even though it is running on only one of the computers on the network.

- To reduce the size of the PDF file it produces, Distiller can *downsample* (reduce the resolution of) graphics images that are embedded in PostScript file; PDFWriter cannot.

- Distiller supports the PostScript *pdfmark* operator, which allows other applications to insert PDF objects such as links and bookmarks in a PostScript file. Distiller places the objects in the PDF file when it interprets the PostScript file.

- Many documents are posted on the Internet in PostScript format because of its widespread use and platform independence. Using Distiller, you can create PDF versions of these documents and view them electronically, rather than printing them to a PostScript printer. Once the documents are in the PDF format, you can index them with Catalog or annotate them with Exchange, advantages that a static paper copy of the document cannot provide.

When to Use Distiller

Although both PDFWriter and Distiller create PDF files, you should use Distiller:

- When you want to embed PostScript Type 1 fonts in your PDF document

- When your document includes EPS (Encapsulated PostScript) images

- When you want to set separate compression options for color and grayscale images

- When you want to downsample graphics images

- When the PostScript version of a document is the only version available

- When it is more convenient to create the PDF version of a document from the PostScript version than from the original version

- When you can create PostScript output, but do not have access to PDFWriter. Usually, in such cases, you will gain access to Distiller through a *watched directory* on a network; for more information about watched directories, see the "*Watched Directories*" section in this chapter.

- When you want to create one PDF file from several source files in the most efficient way possible. Distiller can combine font information in multiple source files, making the resulting PDF document smaller than the one processed with PDFWriter and concatenated with Exchange.

- When your document includes PostScript-specific features, such as image control features.

Creating PostScript Files for Distiller

Distiller can create a PDF file from any valid PostScript file. You can check the validity of a PostScript file by printing it on a PostScript printer; if the file prints correctly, it is valid, and Distiller will have no problem converting the file to PDF.

Creating a PostScript File - Windows

To create a PostScript file, you will need to have a PostScript printer driver installed, and you will need to be able to send the PostScript output to a file. You can use any PostScript driver to create the PostScript file.

Different Windows applications have different ways of selecting the printer driver to use for a print job and for setting print options such as printing to a file. As an example, here is the procedure you would use in Microsoft Word 6.0 to create a PostScript file using the Windows generic PostScript driver:

1. Select the **File | Print** command. Word will display the Print dialog box.
2. Press the **Printer** button. Word will display the Print Setup dialog box.
3. Double-click on the **PostScript Printer on Port:** driver in the **Printers** list box, where **Port** may be a parallel printer port (LPT1-LPT3) or a file (FILE).
4. Press the **Close** button to close the Print Setup dialog box. Word will display PostScript Printer on **Port:** in the Printer text field of the Print dialog box.
5. Click on the **Print to File** check box so an "x" appears in the box.
6. Select the page range that you want to print to the PostScript file.
7. Press the **OK** button. Word will display the Print to File dialog box.
8. Use the controls of the Print to File dialog box to specify the name of the PostScript file and the directory where it will be stored. You should give the file a ".ps" extension to identify it as a Post-Script file.
9. Press the **OK** button. Word will generate the Post-Script output and store it in the file you specified.

The process of creating a PostScript file is similar for other applications, but the process for specifying the PostScript printer driver may differ. Many applications use the **File | Print Setup** command for this purpose.

Most applications give you the option of directing printer output to a file; this is usually done with a control on the Print dialog box, which appears when you select the **File | Print** command. If your application does not have this option, you can create a new printer entry in the Windows **printer driver** list that will enable you to print to a file. To do this:

1. Launch the **Windows Control Panel** application. Control Panel is found in the Program Manager's Main program group.
2. Double click the **Printers** icon. The Printers dialog box will appear.
3. Press the **Add** button to add a new printer driver. The **List of Printers:** list box and the **Install** button will be added to the bottom of the Printers dialog box.
4. From the **List of Printers:** list box, select the Adobe PostScript driver version 2.1.2, the generic Windows PostScript driver, or the PostScript driver that matches your printer. If you select a printer driver other than the generic Windows printer driver, make sure you have the disks that contain the driver available.
5. Press the **Install** button. The printer driver will appear in the **Installed Printers:** list box.
6. Press the **Connect** button. The Connect dialog box will appear.
7. Select the **File** port from the **Ports**: list box.
8. Press the **OK** button. The Connect dialog box will close, and the **Installed Printers:** list box of the Printers dialog box will show **DriverName on FILE:**, where **DriverName** is the name of the printer driver you selected.
9. Press the **Close** button.
10. Close the Control Panel.

If you are using version 2.0 of Distiller, set your printer driver to convert TrueType fonts to Adobe Type 1 fonts. The converted fonts are known as synthetic Type 1 fonts. You can use your application's **Print Setup** command to configure the printer driver, or you can use the Control Panel. To configure the generic Windows PostScript driver:

1. Launch the Windows Control Panel application. Control Panel is found in the Program Manager's Main program group.

2. Double click the **Printers** icon. The Printers dialog box will appear.
3. Select the PostScript driver from the **Installed Printers:** list box.
4. Press the **Setup** button. The Options dialog box will appear.
5. Press the **Advanced** button. The Advanced Options dialog box will appear.
6. Click on the **Send to Printer as:** drop-down list box. A list of conversion options will appear.
7. Click on **Adobe Type 1**.
8. Press the **OK** button.
9. Press the Options dialog box's **OK** button.
10. Press the Printers dialog box's **Close** button.
11. Close the Control Panel.

Tech Note

Version 1.0 of Distiller will not work correctly with synthetic Type 1 fonts. If you are using version 1.0, set your printer driver to substitute Type 1 or Type 3 fonts for TrueType fonts, rather than converting them.

Creating a PostScript File - Macintosh

To create a PostScript file on a Macintosh:

1. Select the **Chooser** from the Apple menu. The Chooser dialog box will appear.
2. Select the **LaserWriter**.
3. Click the close box to close the Chooser.
4. Open the document for which you want PostScript output.
5. Select the **File | Print** command. The Print dialog box will appear.
6. Click on the **Destination:** PostScript® File radio button. The **Print** button will become the **Save** button. If your document is in color, or contains grayscale images, click on the **Print: Color/ Grayscale** button.
7. Press the **Save** button. The Save dialog box will appear.

8. Use the controls of the Save dialog box to select a drive, folder, and filename. By convention, Post-Script files have the .ps extension. Using this extension will make it easier for you and others to identify the file as a PostScript file.

9. Press the **Save** button.

Tips for Creating PDF Files

For Distiller to create high-quality, efficient PDF files, it must receive high-quality, efficient PostScript files as input. Acceptable quality for a PDF file is a function of what devices you use to view and print it. If you are preparing PDF files that will be used only on 96dpi VGA screens, PDF files of that resolution will be of acceptable quality; if you use the same PDF files for 2400dpi typesetting, however, the quality will not be acceptable! In most cases, the smallest PostScript file that produces the output you want will create the smallest and the fastest-displaying PDF file.

General Tips

Make sure you are using the correct PostScript driver, and that your PostScript printer driver options are properly set.

When using the generic Windows PostScript driver, which doesn't support color, all the colors in the chart will be translated to black.

There are two limitations to Distiller that you should know about when you are creating PostScript files:

1. *Distiller replaces certain fill patterns in certain applications with gray.* Sometimes, two fill patterns will be replaced by the same shade of gray, making it difficult or impossible to distinguish between the two coded areas in the PDF document, even though they were distinguishable in the source document. Also, some applications create fill patterns by printing Type 3 characters in the fill area. Fill patterns that use Type 3 characters result in

large PDF files that display slowly. You can avoid these difficulties by using color or solid gray fills.

2. *Second, Distiller does not take custom halftone functions into account.* If Distiller encounters a custom halftone function, it substitutes a standard halftone function. Usually, this substitution will be acceptable, but the appearance of the PDF output may not match the appearance of a printed copy of the original document.

Creating High-quality PostScript Files

To ensure that the PostScript files that you send to Distiller are of the highest possible quality, check the following things:

- Make sure you are using the latest version of the PostScript printer driver for your application or operating system

- Use Level 2 PostScript, if your printer driver supports it

- If you are producing PostScript files on a Macintosh, do not use the **Graphics Smoothing** option. When smooth graphics are used, many small images will be placed inside the PostScript file. These images will remain in the PDF file, greatly increasing the file's size and slowing the display of the document.

- If your document is in color, use a color PostScript printer driver to create the PostScript file. Some applications will not create color PostScript output unless a color PostScript printer driver is used.

- If you want your documents to have custom page sizes, use a PostScript printer driver that supports custom page sizes. You should make sure to select the page size you want in the printer driver's options, as well as in the page setup options of the application with which you are creating the document. Some applications will not produce custom page size output if you do not specify it in the printer driver's options.

Distilling Custom-sized EPS (Encapsulated PostScript) Files

Encapsulated PostScript is a subset of the PostScript language that is designed for transferring PostScript code between applications. It is most often used by graphics applications such as Adobe Illustrator to create graphics images that will be "pasted" into pages created by another application. Unlike PostScript, EPS does not contain page size information. Distiller can distill EPS files, but the output will appear on 8.5" x 11" pages, even if you used a different size when you created the artwork.

To produce artwork of the correct size:

1. Import the EPS graphic into another application.
2. Set the page size using the application's page setup options.
3. Print the page to a PostScript file using the same custom page size in the printer driver's options as you used in the application's page setup options.

Using Distiller

Starting Distiller - Windows

To start Distiller under Windows

- Double click its program icon in the Program Manager

Or

- Use the Program Manager's **File | Run** command. The Run dialog box will appear. If you know the name of the directory where the Distiller program, ACRODIST.EXE, is stored, you can enter the full path and filename of the Distiller program. If you are not sure where Distiller is stored, press the **Browse** button, and locate the ACRODIST.EXE file with the controls of the Browse dialog box. If you wish, you can specify command line options and PostScript files to be distilled on the command line.

Or

- Double-click on the ACRODIST.EXE file in the File Manager.

Starting Distiller - Macintosh

To start Distiller under Macintosh:

- Double click on the Distiller's name or file folder icon located in the Finder

Or,

- Double click its program icon if the icon is on the desktop

Or

- Drag a PostScript file to the Distiller icon if the icon is on the desktop.

How Distiller Names PDF Files

Distiller gives the output PDF file the same name as the input PostScript file, replacing the PostScript file's extension with the .pdf extension. If a file with that name already exists, Distiller will overwrite that file with the new file.

Distiller, as a Windows program, uses the DOS file naming convention even if it is writing to directories on other types of systems. If an input PostScript file has a filename that does not conform to the DOS file naming conventions, Distiller will truncate it so that the output file is a DOS filename. For instance, if Distiller processes a Macintosh PostScript file named March status report.ps, it may truncate the output filename to march_st.pdf or to a similar mapping. Also, PDF files that Distiller writes to Macintosh directories will not be opened automatically by your Acrobat Viewer; to open the files, you will need to drag the file to the viewer's icon, or use the viewer's **File | Open** command.

Distilling a File on a Local System

If Distiller is running on your local computer, you can have Distiller distill files automatically using its watched directory feature (see the "Watched Directories" section), or you can tell Distiller to distill a specific file.

To distill a specific file:

1. Select the **File | Open** command. Distiller will display the Open PostScript File dialog box.
2. Use the controls of the "Open PostScript File" dialog box to select the file you want to distill.
3. Press the **OK** button. Distiller will display the Specify PDF File Name dialog box.
4. Use the controls of the Specify PDF File Name dialog box to specify the name you want the output PDF file stored under. The default name is the input PostScript filename, with the .ps extension replaced by the .pdf extension. The default directory is the directory where the input PostScript file is stored.
5. Press the **OK** button. If you decide not to distill the file, press the **Cancel** button.
6. If a PDF file with the filename you specified already exists, Distiller will ask you if you want to overwrite the file. If you want to overwrite the file, press the **Yes** button; if you do not, press the **No** button.

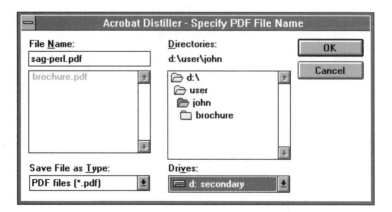

You can also distill a file by dragging and dropping it onto Distiller's window or icon. When you distill a file by dragging and dropping it, Distiller will not prompt for the name of the output PDF file, but will use the name of the PostScript file, replacing the .ps extension with the .pdf extension. If you do not want Distiller to name the file automatically, press the **<Shift>** key (Windows) or the **<Command>** key (Macintosh) while dragging and dropping the file. In Windows, you can also distill a file by double clicking on its icon in the File Manager.

The Distiller Window

When Distiller processes a PostScript file, it displays information about its progress in the Distiller window. If you are running Distiller on your computer, you can keep track of what Distiller is doing by looking at the window. You can also interrupt Distiller's processing temporarily or cancel a job with Distiller window commands.

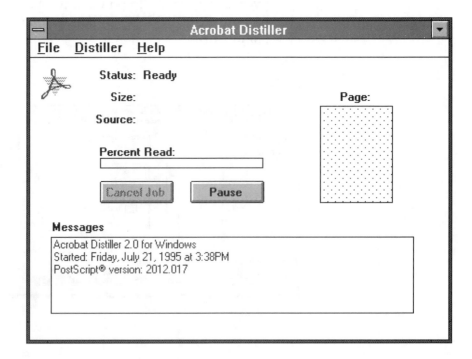

Status Text Field

In the **Status** text field, Distiller displays a brief description of what it is doing. When Distiller is not busy, it displays "Ready" in this field. For a description of each of the messages Distiller displays in the **Status** text field, see the "Distiller Status Messages" section.

Size Text Field

In the **Size** text field, Distiller displays the size in kilobytes of the file it is processing. When Distiller is not processing a file, the **Size** text field is blank.

Source Text Field

In the **Source** text field, Distiller displays the method by which the current job was started. If the job was started using the **File | Open** command, Distiller displays "User selection" in the field. If the job was started from a watched directory, Distiller displays "Watched directory" in the field. When Distiller is not processing a file, the **Source** text field is blank.

Percent Read Text Field

In the **Percent Read** text field, Distiller displays the percentage of the PostScript file it has read so far. When Distiller is not processing a file, the **Percent Read** text field is blank.

Percent Read Progress Bar

The **Percent Read** progress bar is a graphical representation of Distiller's progress in reading the input PostScript file. As Distiller reads the file, it fills in the progress bar with color.

Cancel Job Button

The **Cancel Job** button stops the current job and starts processing the next available PostScript file. All work done on the cancelled file is discarded.

When you press the **Cancel Job** button, Distiller displays this message in the **Messages** list box:

```
"User requested job termination...
%%[ Error: interrupt; OffendingCommand: inter-
rupt ]%% "
```

The message is also written in the MESSAGES.LOG file and the log file of the job that was interrupted.

Pause / Resume Button

The **Pause** button stops Distiller temporarily once it has finished processing the current file. When you press the **Pause** button, it is replaced by the **Resume** button. The **Resume** button restarts Distiller; when you press it, Distiller will begin processing the next available PostScript file.

When Distiller starts, it will initialize, then it will begin processing PostScript files in watched directories. If you want to change Distiller's settings at startup, press the **Pause** button while it is initializing. Distiller will pause before processing files in watched directories, giving you the opportunity to change its settings. The **Pause** and **Resume** buttons are also convenient when you need to change job options or alter the **Watched Directory** list when Distiller is busy processing files.

Messages Box

When Distiller processes a PostScript file, it displays information about the processing in the **Messages** box. This information includes:

- The name of the PostScript that is being distilled
- The name of the PDF file that is being created
- The time the job was started
- The total time it took to process the file.

Distiller also writes these messages to the MESSAGES.LOG file and to the job's log file.

Here is an example of the messages that are displayed in the **Messages** list box when a file is distilled:

```
Distilling: fildskt3.ps
Source: a:\watched\in\fildiskt3.ps
Destination: a:\watched\out\fildiskt.pdf
```

```
Start Time: Wednesday, March 29, 1995 at
8:46PM
Distill Time: 18 seconds (00:00:18)
**** End of Job ****
```

Page Box

Distiller displays the thumbnails it generates in the **Page** box.

When the **Generate Thumbnails** option is enabled, Distiller paints the **Page** field gray. As Distiller creates thumbnails, it displays them in the **Page** box, and displays the page number above the box. When the **Generate Thumbnails** option is disabled, Distiller displays a field of dots in the **Page** box.

Using Watched Directories

One of Distiller's most important strengths is its ability to automatically generate PDF files from any PostScript files that are moved to one of its watched directories. A watched directory is a directory that Distiller monitors for new or changed PostScript files. The watched monitors can be in any directory that Distiller has access to on DOS/Windows, Macintosh, or UNIX. You specify which directories Distiller watches and how often it checks them.

Tech Note

The UNIX watched directories daemon, distilld, cannot watch non-UNIX directories.

When you designate a directory as a watched directory, Distiller will create two subdirectories in the directory, In and Out. When Distiller finds a PostScript file in the In directory, Distiller distills it and places the PDF file in the Out directory. Depending on the option you specify, Distiller will delete the input PostScript file or move it to the Out directory once it is distilled.

PART 5

Tech Note

If a PDF file with the same name as the current file exists in an Out directory, Distiller overwrites the file without warning.

You use the controls of the Watched Directories Options dialog box to specify the directories that Distiller will monitor, how often Distiller will monitor them, and how often Distiller will manage the files it processes.

To display this dialog box:

- Select the **Distiller | Watched Directories** command.

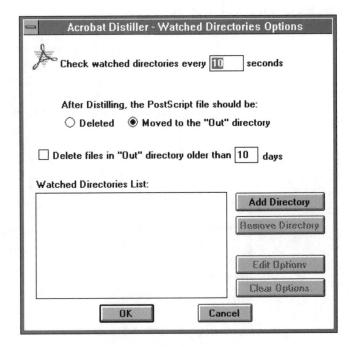

Adding a Watched Directory

To add a directory to the **Watched Directory** list:

1. Press the **Add Directory** button. The Add Directory dialog box will appear.
2. Use the controls of the Add Directory dialog box to select the drive and directory you want Distiller to watch. Distiller must have read, write, create, and delete access for this directory.
3. Press the **OK** button. Distiller will close the **Add Directory** list and display the directory you selected in the **Watched Directories** list. If you decide you don't want to add a directory, press the **Cancel** button.

You can only add one directory to the list at a time. If you want to add more than one directory to the list, repeat these steps for each directory you want to add.

Distiller can watch up to 100 directories at at time. Monitoring directories is a resource-consuming task, however, and you should generally watch 10 or fewer directories at one time.

You can specify different Job Options for each directory that Distiller watches. This can be a convenient way of customizing how different categories of documents are distilled. By designating a different watched directory for each category of document, you can give people that use Distiller on a network the ability to "control" how it processes their documents, even though it is not running on their computer.

Removing a Watched Directory

To remove a directory from the **Watched Directories** list:

1. In the **Watched Directories List** list box, highlight the name of the directory you no longer want Distiller to watch, using the mouse or the cursor control keys.
2. Press the **Remove** button. The directory will be removed from the list.

You can only remove one directory from the list at a time. If you want to remove more than one directory from the list, repeat these steps for each directory that you want to remove.

Specifying How Often Watched Directories Are Checked

When Distiller is not busy distilling files, it will check all of the directories in the **Watched Directories** list periodically. You can specify how often Distiller checks watched directories by entering a number of seconds in the **Check watched directories every... seconds** edit box. Distiller can check watched directories at intervals from 1 to 10,000 seconds.

Managing Files in Watched Directories

When several users are actively using watched directories, a large number of PostScript and PDF files can accumulate in the directories, potentially causing file management problems. Distiller has several file management options that can help alleviate this problem. Distiller can delete PostScript files after it processes them, it can move PostScript files it processes into the Out directory, and it can delete all files in Out directories that are older than a specified age.

To choose between deleting PostScript files and moving them to the Out directory:

Browsing
  Interface
  Navigating
  Zoom
  Features
  Printing
  Clipboard
  Preferences
Creating
  PDFWriter
  PDF Files
Enhancing
  Pages
  Thumbnails
  Bookmarks
  Notes
  Links
  Articles
Web Publishing
  Introduction
  Getting On
  Reader
  Author
  Publisher
  Cool Sites
Advanced
  Search
  Catalog
  Distiller

- Click on the **Deleted** or the **Moved to the "Out" directory** radio button.

To delete all files in Out directories that are older than a specified age:

1. Click on the **Delete files in "Out" directory older than ... days** check box so that an "x" appears in the box.
2. Enter a number of days in the **Delete files in "Out" directory older than ... days** edit box.

How Distiller Schedules Distillation Jobs

Jobs started using the **File | Open** command or by dragging and dropping will be scheduled before files that appear in watched directories. If a file is currently being processed, the jobs will start after Distiller is finished with the file.

If there are files in more than one watched directory, Distiller will process one file from each directory in turn, according to the **Watched Directory** list. Within each directory, the order in which files are processed depends on the operating system. In DOS directories, files will be processed in the order that they are listed by the DOS `dir` command. In Macintosh folders, files will be processed in alphabetical order.

How to Tell if a File Has Been Distilled

If you are running Distiller on your own machine, you can monitor its progress by reading the status messages it displays in its window. But how can you tell if Distiller has processed your file when it is on a remote computer and you cannot see its window? In contrast to many PostScript drivers, Distiller does not write a PDF file to disk until it is completely generated. Therefore, when a file appears in the Out directory, you can be certain that Distiller has completely finished processing it.

How to Tell if Distiller Is Monitoring a Directory

When you are running Distiller on your own machine, you can use the **Distill | Watched Direc-**

tories command to see which directories it is monitoring, and how often it checks them. On a remote computer you cannot execute this command, so how can you determine if a directory is being watched? Distiller makes it possible by writing a file called DTIME.TXT in every watched directory approximately once per minute.

To find out if a directory is being monitored, check the modification date and time of the DTIME.TXT file.

To check the modification date and time:

On a DOS system:

- Use the **DIR** command.

On a Macintosh:

- Use the **Finder's File | Get Info** command, or press **<Command>** + **<I>**.

On a Sun:

- Use the **ls -l** command.

Remember, the system time on a remote system may not be the same as that of your system. If you are not sure that the system time on a remote system is correct, wait a little more than a minute, then re-check the modification date of the DTIME.TXT file to see if it has changed.

When a Watched Directory Is Full

When the disk or volume that contains a watched directory runs out of space, Distiller will attempt to write the following message in the MESSAGES.LOG file and in the log file of the job that was interrupted:

```
Error 12 relocating files.
```

Distiller will stop watching a directory if the disk or volume containing it is full. To resume watching the directory, open and close the Watched Directory dialog box.

Avoiding File Access Conflicts

Complex PostScript files can take a long time to create. If an application is generating a complex PostScript file in a watched directory, Distiller may attempt to process it before the application is finished generating it. In Windows, you can prevent this by running share.exe, a DOS program that prevents two applications from opening a file at the same time. You can start share.exe from the config.sys file, using the INSTALL command, or you can run it from the DOS command line. For more information, see your DOS reference manual.

Job Options

To optimize the PDF files you generate for size, speed, and transmission across computer systems, you can choose from several PDF file generation options. With these options, you can specify:

- Whether and when Distiller uses compression

- What types of compression Distiller uses for images

- Image resolution

- The character set used to encode the PDF file

- Whether or not Distiller generates thumbnails

- Whether or not Distiller embeds all the characters of a font or a subset of them.

You change Distiller's job options using the controls of the Job Options dialog box or by inserting a special PostScript operator, *setdistillerparams*, into the PostScript you want to distill.

General Options

General options are those options that apply to the entire document, rather than to images. General options control:

- Whether Distiller compresses text and graphics data

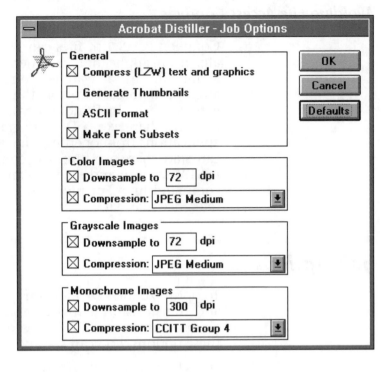

- The character set used to encode the PDF file

- Whether or not Distiller generates thumbnails

- Whether or not Distiller embeds all the characters of a font or a subset of them.

To compress text and graphics with the LZW method:

- Click on the **Compress (LZW) text and graphics** check box so that an "x" appears in the box.

This option only affects text and vector-based graphics, such as line drawings; text and graphics cannot be compressed with a method that discards data. The LZW compression method, which typically gives 2:1 compression ratios, does not discard any information. The compression settings for images, which are based on bitmaps, are specified separately.

To generate thumbnails as a file is distilled:

- Click on the **Generate Thumbnails** check box so that an "x" appears in the box.

Tech Note

If a document consists mainly of text, thumbnails will be of little help as navigation aids; the thumbnails will be nearly identical! Since automatic thumbnail generation increases the time it takes Distiller to process a file, and increases the amount of disk space that the resulting PDF file requires, it would be wasteful to use it for such a document. You should only use this option when you are sure that thumbnails will make the document easier to use.

To write PDF files using only the printable ASCII characters:

• Click on the **ASCII Format** check box so that an "x" appears in the box.

When this option is off, Distiller writes files in binary format which uses characters other than the printable ASCII characters.

Some file transfer methods will damage binary files. Writing a file using only the printable ASCII characters ensures that it can be transferred without damage, but increases the size of the file by 20%. If you are certain that your file transfer mechanism can handle binary files, you can leave this option off to save disk space.

Distiller has the ability to embed subsets of Type 1 fonts in PDF documents. When Distiller embeds a subset of a font, it does not store all of the font information in the PDF file; it only stores the information pertaining to the characters that appear in the document.

To embed subsets of Type 1 fonts:

• Click on the **Make Font Subsets** check box so that an "x" appears in the box.

When this option is off, Distiller places every character in the font in the PDF file.

A full Type 1 font description takes about 40K to store; typical subsets take about 25K to store; and the most extreme case, where only one character of a font is used, takes only about 12K to store. Since unused font characters waste so much space, it's a good idea to keep the **Make Font Subsets** option on.

As more extensive PDF editing capability becomes available, you may want to consider whether or not a file is likely to be edited before embedding font subsets. If a change to the file requires characters that were not embedded in the file, a substitute font will have to be used for those characters, possibly degrading the appearance of the document.

Image Options

Image options apply only to bitmap-based images. They control:

- Whether and when Distiller uses compression
- What types of compression Distiller uses
- Image resolution.

Each image type has its own image options. Color image options, found in the **Color Images** frame, apply to full-color bitmaps. Grayscale image options, found in the **Grayscale Images** frame, apply to grayscale bitmaps; pixels in grayscale bitmaps can be black, white, or one or more shades of gray. Monochrome image options, found in the **Monochrome Images** frame, apply to monochrome bitmaps; pixels in monochrome bitmaps can be either black or white.

Downsampling Images

To downsample an image is to reduce its resolution. When Distiller downsamples an image, it reduces the storage space required by the image.

To downsample an image:

1. In the appropriate frame, click on the **Downsample to ...** dpi check box so that an "x" appears in the box.
2. Enter a resolution in the **Downsample to ...** dpi edit box.

Compressing Images

To compress an image is to rewrite the image's data in a more compact format, decreasing the space needed to store an image. Distiller provides two types of compression, or compression schemes, LZW and JPEG, with different options for each type.

To compress color images:

1. In the appropriate frame, click on the **Compression:** check box so that an "x" appears in the box.
2. Click on the **Compression:** drop-down list box. A list of compression methods appears.
3. Click on the compression method you want to use.

The following compression methods are available for color and grayscale images:

- JPEG High
- JPEG Medium-High
- JPEG Medium
- JPEG Medium-Low
- JPEG Low
- LZW (4 bit)
- LZW.

These compression methods can be used on monochrome images:

- CCITT Group 3
- CCITT Group 4
- LZW
- Run-Length.

Specifying the Current Job Options

Distiller's current job options are the job options it will use for:·

- Files processsed with the **File | Open** command
- Watched directories whose job options have not been specified.

If you change job options while a file is being distilled, the changes to the job options will take effect after Distiller is finished processing the file.

To change the current job options:

1. Select the **Distiller | Job Options** command. Distiller will display the Acrobat Distiller - Job Options dialog box.
2. Use the controls of the Job Options dialog box to specify the current job options, or press the **Defaults** button to use the job options Distiller used when it was first installed.
3. Press the **OK** button. If you decide you don't want to change the current job options, press the **Cancel** button.

Specifying Job Options for a Watched Directory

You can specify different sets of job options for each directory Distiller watches, or you can use Distiller's current job options.

To specify job options for a watched directory:

1. Select the **Distiller | Watched Directories** command. Distiller will display the Watched Directories Options dialog box.
2. Using the cursor control keys or the mouse, select the directory whose job options you want to specify in the **Watched Directories List:** list box.
3. Press the **Edit Options** button. Distiller will display the Job Options dialog box.
4. Use the controls of the Job Options dialog box to specify the job options.
5. Press the **OK** button to close the Job Options dialog box. If you decide you don't want to change the directory's job options, press the **Cancel** button.
6. If you want to change the job options of more than one directory, repeat steps 2–5.
7. Press the **OK** button of the Watched Directories Options dialog box to set the new job options. If

you decide not to set the new job options, press the **Cancel** button.

```
┌─────────────────────────────────────────────────────────┐
│ ▬     Acrobat Distiller - Watched Directories Options     │
├─────────────────────────────────────────────────────────┤
│                                                           │
│  ✂   Check watched directories every  [10]   seconds      │
│                                                           │
│       After Distilling, the PostScript file should be:    │
│        ○ Deleted    ● Moved to the "Out" directory        │
│                                                           │
│     ☐ Delete files in "Out" directory older than [10] days│
│                                                           │
│   Watched Directories List:                               │
│   ┌──────────────────────────┐   ┌──────────────────┐     │
│   │                          │   │  Add Directory    │     │
│   │                          │   └──────────────────┘     │
│   │                          │   ┌──────────────────┐     │
│   │                          │   │ Remove Directory  │     │
│   │                          │   └──────────────────┘     │
│   │                          │   ┌──────────────────┐     │
│   │                          │   │   Edit Options    │     │
│   │                          │   └──────────────────┘     │
│   │                          │   ┌──────────────────┐     │
│   └──────────────────────────┘   │   Clear Options   │     │
│                                   └──────────────────┘     │
│         ┌──────────┐        ┌──────────┐                  │
│         │    OK    │        │  Cancel  │                  │
│         └──────────┘        └──────────┘                  │
└─────────────────────────────────────────────────────────┘
```

When you change the job options of a watched directory, Distiller places a º mark before the directory's name in the **Watched Directories List:** list box. The job options of directories that have this mark will not change when you change the **Distiller | Job Options** command. They will only change if you explicitly change them again using the procedure described in this section or if you reset the watched directory to use Distiller's current job options.

To reset, or clear, a directory's job options to the current job options:

1. Select the **Distiller | Watched Directories** command. Distiller will display the Watched Directories Options dialog box.

2. Using the cursor control keys or the mouse, select the directory whose job options you want to reset in the **Watched Directories List:** list box.
3. Press the **Clear Options** button.
4. If you want to change the job options of more than one directory, repeat steps 2 and 3.
5. Press the **OK** button of the Watched Directories Options dialog box to reset the job options. If you decide not to reset the job options, press the **Cancel** button.

The job options of directories that have the » mark in front of their names are changed with the **Distiller I Job Options** command. When you add a new directory to the **Watched Directory** list, it will be marked with the » mark, and it will use the current job options.

Specifying Job Options Using PostScript Operators

If you are familiar with PostScript language programming, you can use two Distiller-specific PostScript operators to control Distiller's job options. The currentdistillerparams operator returns Distiller's current settings, and the setdistillerparams operator changes them. These operators give you a greater degree of control over the creation of a PDF file than any other method; you can, for instance, use them to set different compression and downsampling options for each image in a PostScript file. They do, however, require familiarity with the PostScript programming language and the structure of PDF files. For more information about how to use PostScript operators to control the generation of PDF files, see the "Using PostScript Programs To Control Distiller" section.

How to Tell What Job Options Distiller Is Using - The DTIME.TXT File

The DTIME.TXT file is a plain ASCII file that Distiller writes in the Out directory of each directory it is watching. Besides indicating if Distiller is monitoring a directory, the DTIME.TXT file lists:

• How often the directory is checked

• The file management options for the directory

- The Job options used when processing files from the directory.

Here is an example of the contents of the DTIME.TXT file:

```
Acrobat Distiller 2.0 for Windows
Wednesday, July 26, 1995 at 10:29AM

================================================
========
Watched Directory Frequency = 10 seconds
After Distilling, PostScript Files = Moved
Text and Graphics LZW Compression = ON
Thumbnail Generation = OFF
Text and Graphics ASCII85 Filter = OFF
Make Subsets of Embedded Fonts = ON
Color Image Downsampling = ON
Color Image Downsampling Resolution = 72
Color Image Compression = ON
Color Image Compression Using = JPEG Medium
Grayscale Image Downsampling = ON
Grayscale Image Downsampling Resolution = 72
Grayscale Image Compression = ON
Grayscale Image Compression Using = JPEG
Medium
Monochrome Image Downsampling = ON
Monochrome Image Downsampling Resolution = 300
Monochrome Image Compression = ON
Monochrome Image Compression Using = CCITT
Group 4

================================================
========
```

Distiller and Fonts

To distill a document, Distiller must have access to all the fonts that were used in the document. The fonts can come from two sources:

- Embedded in the PostScript file itself
- Directories on local and remote computer systems that are in Distiller's **Font Locations** list.

In Windows, Distiller automatically adds ATM's font directory and its own font directory to the **Font Locations** list when you install it. On the Macintosh, Distiller automatically adds the System folder, the System:Extensions and Fonts folder, and Distiller's font folder to the **Font Locations** list when you install it. If you have Adobe Type 1 fonts in a Font Folio or Type on Call CD-ROM, Macintosh Distiller will also add those folders to the **Font Locations** list. Macintosh Distiller will search open suitcases for fonts as well, if Suitcase or another program of its type is installed on the system.

Font Embedding

Distiller can include three levels of font information in a PDF document:

1. **The font name only.** When the font name is the only available information about the font, Reader and Exchange will not be able to display the font or to create a reasonable substitute for it. Distiller will include the font name only in those cases where the font is certain to be found on the system where it is viewed (see "When Distiller Includes Font Names").

2. **The font descriptor.** The font descriptor is used to substitute a multiple master font for the described font. It includes information such as:

   - Characteristics of the font, such as whether it is Serif or Sans Serif, if it is an all-capitals or small-capitals font, if it is a symbolic or script font, or if it is italic.

   - The italic angle of the font

   - The maximum height of a character

   - The height of capital letters

   - The depth of descenders.

   Font descriptors are typically 1-2K.

3. **The entire font.** In this case, the entire font is embedded in the PDF file, and the document can be viewed exactly as it was created, even if the font does not exist on the system. Depending on

Distiller's settings, it may embed the entire font, or just the characters that are actually in the document (a font subset). Type 1 fonts are typically 40K. Type 1 font subsets are generally 25K, but in the case of a single character, can be as small as 12K.

Tech Note

You may need permission to distribute some copyrighted fonts as embedded fonts in PDF files. You do not need permission to embed and distribute any of the fonts in the Adobe Type Library.

When Distiller Includes Font Names

Since a font name does not give any description about the look of a font, Distiller must be certain that the font can be found on the system where the document is viewed. This is the case with the Adobe Base 14 fonts.

These fonts and the Adobe Type Manager (ATM) are installed with version 2.0 of the Acrobat viewers, and must be installed for the version 1.0 viewers to work. Distiller assumes they will be present on any viewing system, and thus only includes their names in PDF files.

The Base 14 fonts are:

Courier	Helvetica-BoldOblique
Courier-Bold	Symbol
Courier-Oblique	Times-Roman
Courier-BoldOblique	Times-Bold
Helvetica	Times-Italic
Helvetica-Bold	Times-BoldItalic
Helvetica-Oblique	ZapfDingbats

When Distiller Includes Font Descriptors

Distiller will write a font descriptor in the PDF file for every non-base 14 font if either of the following two conditions is true:

- A Multiple Master font can be substituted for the font, and the font is not the the **Always Embed** list

- The font is in the **Never Embed** list.

Acrobat can substitute a multiple master font for every Type 1 font that uses the ISO Latin 1 character set.

Acrobat also includes font descriptors for the following types of fonts:

- Multiple Master fonts that use the ISO Latin 1 character set

- Multiple Master fonts that use the Expert character set.

When Distiller Embeds Fonts

Distiller embeds a font if either of the following two conditions is true:

- The font is not a standard Type 1 font, and thus cannot be simulated with Acrobat's Multiple Master fonts

- The font is in the **Always Embed** list.

Acrobat cannot substitute Multiple Master fonts for the following kinds of Type 1 fonts, and so embeds them:

- Expert fonts

- Symbolic - except for Symbol and Zapf Chancery, which are part of the Base 14 font set

- Small Caps and Old Style Fonts (SC + OSF)

- Cyrillic fonts - note that Windows does not support the Cyrillic character set and will substitute Courier for Cyrillic fonts.

Distiller always embeds Type 3 outline and bitmap fonts.

Embedding TrueType Fonts

You cannot embed TrueType fonts directly with Distiller, but you can embed them indirectly as synthetic Type 1 fonts. To do this set your PostScript driver to convert the TrueType font to a synthetic Type 1 font, then embed the synthetic Type 1 font in the PDF file. Since the synthetic Type 1 font will not be found in any of Distiller's font locations, you must place the name of the synthetic font in the **Always Embed** list; the synthetic font's name is the name of the True-Type font. For more information on embedding fonts by name, see the "Embedding Options For Fonts That Are Not In Font Lists" section.

The Macintosh PostScript driver will embed the actual TrueType font data and a TrueType font rasterizer in the PostScript files it creates, as well as embedding the synthetic Type 1 font, but Distiller only uses the synthetic Type 1 data. If you want to embed the actual TrueType font data in the PDF file, use the PDFWriter to create the file.

Distiller and PCL Fonts

The Windows PostScript driver substitutes TrueType fonts for PCL bitmap and outline fonts. Distiller handles the substituted TrueType fonts like any other TrueType fonts.

Distiller and Windows Bitmap Fonts

The Windows bitmap fonts are:

- Courier
- MS Serif, also known as Tms Rmn
- MS Sans Serif, also known as Helv
- Symbol
- Fixed Sys (not in Win.INI)
- Terminal (not in WIN.INI)
- System (not in WIN.INI)
- Small fonts.

The Windows PostScript driver substitutes Courier for Windows bitmap fonts and includes the Courier font descriptor in the PostScript file.

Distiller and Windows Vector Fonts

The Windows vector fonts are:

- Modern

- Roman

- Script.

Tech Note

The Windows PostScript driver uses graphics to draw each individual character that is in a Windows vector font. This is an extremely wasteful way to generate characters. Avoid using these fonts. A 3600-word document created using the Windows Script font resulted in a PostScript file that was 2.8Mb. The same document created using Courier resulted in a 48Kb PostScript file.

The Font Locations Dialog Box

You use the controls of the Font Locations dialog box to add directories to or delete directories from the **Font Locations** list.

To display the Font Locations dialog box:

- Select the **Distiller | Font Locations** command.

Adding a Directory to the Font Locations List

To add a directory to the **Font Locations** list:

1. Press the **Add Directory** button. Distiller will display the Add Directory dialog box.
2. Select the drive or volume where the directory is stored, by:
   - Clicking on the **Drives:** drop-down list box. A list of the available drives and volumes will appear.

- Clicking on the name of the drive you want to use.

3. Select the directory that contains the fonts from the **Directories** list box. To move up and down the directory tree, double click on directory names.
4. Press the **OK** button. Distiller will close the Add Directory dialog box, and the name of the directory will appear in the Font Directories List dialog box. If you decide not to include the directory, press the **Cancel** button.
5. If you want to add other directories to the **Font Locations** list, repeat steps 1–3 for each directory that you want to add.
6. Press **OK** to add the new directories to the **Font Locations** list. If you decide not to add any directories to the list, press the **Cancel** button.

Removing a Directory from the Font Locations List

To remove a directory from the **Font Locations** list:

1. Use the mouse or the cursor control keys to highlight the name of the directory you want to remove in the **Font Directories** List.
2. Press the **Remove** button.
3. If you want to remove other directories from the **Font Locations** list, repeat steps 1–2 for each directory that you want to remove.
4. Press **OK** to remove the directories from the **Font Locations** list. If you decide not to remove any directories from the list, press the **Cancel** button.

Availability of Directories in the Font Directories List

When Distiller is able to connect to a font directory, it places a ">>" (Windows) or a "•" (Macintosh) before the directory's name in the **Font Directories** list. If Distiller is unable to connect to a font directory, it leaves the space before the directory name blank. The most common reason that Distiller cannot connect to a font directory is a broken connection to a networked computer.

Font Directories Lists: Cross-platform Issues

Type 1 fonts created for one type of computer cannot be used on another. Therefore, you cannot place a directory on the other type of machine in the **Font Locations** list. When a font is included in a PostScript file, however, it is compatible with the Distiller programs on both platforms, no matter where the PostScript file originated. You can embed the font in a PDF file by placing the font in the **Always Embed** list by name; for more information see the "Embedding Options For Fonts That Are Not In Font Lists" section.

Embedding Fonts - The Font Embedding Dialog Box

You use the controls of the Font Embedding dialog box to determine which Type 1 fonts Distiller will always embed in a document and which ones it will never embed. You do this by selecting a list of fonts, then adding fonts from the list to either of two lists, the **Always Embed** list and the **Never Embed** list.

You can override the **Always Embed** and **Never Embed** list by selecting the **Embed All Fonts** option.

To display the Font Embedding dialog box:

- Select the **Distiller | Font Embedding** command.

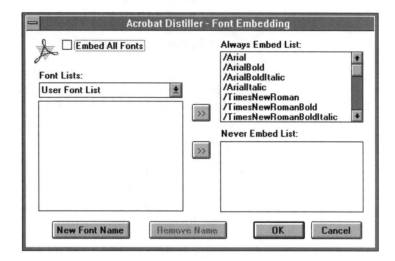

Embedding All Fonts

To embed all the Type 1 fonts referenced in PostScript files:

- Click on the **Embed All Fonts** check box, so that an "x" appears in the box.

[The **Never Embed** list overrides the **Embed All Fonts** option. When you select the **Embed All Fonts** option, fonts in the **Never Embed** list will not be embedded.]

Choosing a Font List

Distiller keeps two types of font lists:

- **Font Location** font lists, which include all of the fonts in a particular directory

- The **User Font** List, which includes frequently-used fonts from different **Font Location** lists and fonts that are not found in **Font Location** lists. You select the fonts that are in this list.

To select a font list:

1. Click on the **Font Lists** drop-down list box. A list of font list names will appear.
2. Click on the name of the font list you want to use. The fonts in the list will be displayed in the **Font Lists** list box.

Adding Fonts to the Always Embed or Never Embed Lists

You add fonts to the **Always Embed** list or to the **Never Embed** list from a **Font Location** list or **User Font** list. To add fonts to one of these lists:

1. Select a font list using the **Font Lists** drop-down list box.
2. Highlight a font name in the **Font Lists** list box.
3. Press the **Transfer** button that is next to the list box to which you are transferring the font. The font will appear in the list.

You cannot place a font in both the **Always Embed** and the **Never Embed** lists at the same time. If you have already placed a font in one of the lists, and you try to add it to another of the lists, Distiller will display a dialog box asking you where the font should be placed.

The **Never Embed** list overrides the **Embed All Fonts** option. When you select the **Embed All Fonts** option, fonts in the **Never Embed** list will not be embedded.

Adding Fonts to the User Font List

When you install Distiller, there will be no fonts in the **User Font** list. You cannot add fonts to the **User Font** list until you have added fonts from one or more **Font Location** lists to the **Always Embed** list or the **Never Embed** list. To add fonts to the **User Font** list:

1. Select the **User Font List** using the **Font Lists** drop-down list box.
2. Highlight a font name in the **Always Embed** list or the **Never Embed List** list box.
3. Press the **Transfer** button that is next to the list box from which you are transferring the font. The font will appear in the list.

Embedding Options for Fonts That Are Not in Font Lists

As discussed in the "Font Directories Lists: Cross-platform Issues" section, the Type 1 font file formats on different computer types are incompatible. This incompatibility makes it impossible, for instance, for a Windows Distiller to connect to a font directory on a Macintosh and use the fonts it contains. Distiller can read the font information if it is embedded in the PostScript file, however.

You can embed these fonts in your PDF document but you must specify them by name instead of selecting the name from a list.

To add an individual font to the **Always Embed** or the **Never Embed** list:

1. Press the **New Font Name** button. Distiller will display the Add Font Name dialog box.
2. Enter the name of the font in the **Add the Font** edit box.
3. Click on the **Always Embed** list radio button to add the font to the **Always Embed** list, or click on the **Never Embed** list radio button to add the font to the **Never Embed** list.

4. Press the **Add** button. The font will appear in the list you selected.
5. If you want to add other fonts to the lists, repeat steps 1–4. When you are done adding fonts to the list, press the **Done** button.

Once you have included a font in the **Always Embed** or **Never Embed** lists, you can transfer the font to the **User Font** List.

To make sure that Type 1 fonts are available to Distiller across the Windows and Macintosh platforms, make sure that the PostScript printer drivers on each plaform are set to automatically include Type 1 fonts in PostScript files. For information about how to do this, see the "Creating PostScript Files For Distiller" section.

Distiller Troubleshooting

Distiller does not embed some Type 1 Symbolic, Expert, or non-Latin fonts in the PDF file.

Some fonts that do not use the ISO Latin1 character set, such as symbolic, expert, and non-Latin character set fonts, may appear to Distiller to be ISO Latin 1 fonts because of programming errors. To correct this problem, place the font in Distiller's **Always Embed** list.

Distiller displays a findfont message and cancels the distillation job.

In order to embed a font in a PDF file or to place the font's descriptor in the file, Distiller must have access to the font. If Distiller cannot find the font in any of the directories in its **Font Locations** list, it will do one of two things:·

- Substitute Courier for the missing font

- Display a findfont error message and cancel the distillation job without producing a PDF file.

To correct this problem, find the directory where the font is stored and add it to the **Font Locations** list.

Distiller substitutes Courier for a font.

In order to embed a font in a PDF file or to place the font's descriptor in the file, Distiller must have access to the font. If Distiller cannot find the font in any of the directories in its **Font Locations** list, it will do one of two things:

- Substitute Courier for the missing font

Or

- Display a findfont error message and cancel the distillation job without producing a PDF file.

To correct this problem, find the directory where the font is stored and add it to the **Font Locations** list.

Pages printed in landscape mode have their long sides to the left instead of at the bottom.

When you print a page in landscape mode on a typical printer, the paper travels through the printer in the direction of its long axis, the same way it does for portrait mode pages. To create the landscape page, the PostScript driver rotates the page markings 90 degrees to the left, so that the page markings are placed within the boundaries of the paper as it travels through the printer. When you remove the landscape page from the printer, you turn it back 90 degrees to the right to see the page as you expect to. When you "print" PostScript output to Distiller, it interprets the rotated PostScript page markings the same way a printer does. You cannot physically turn the page of a PDF file when you remove it from the printer, however, so the top edge of the paper appears on the left edge of the screen.

You can correct this in two ways:

1. Rotate the pages 90 degrees to the right with Exchange's **Edit | Pages | Rotate** command.
2. Use a PostScript driver that supports 11" x 8.5" inch paper size, rather than 8.5" x 11", and set the page layout of your document to that size as well. Set the page orientation of the driver to Portrait so it does not rotate the output.

Some applications will automatically set Distiller's paper size to the paper size you are using within the application. To produce landscape output from these applications, just set the paper size to 11" x 8.5".

You cannot produce landscape pages with the Windows PostScript driver. To produce landscape pages, you must have a PostScript driver that supports custom page sizes.

Distiller and Images

Distiller allows you to balance image fidelity and file size by giving you a range of compression and downsampling options that can be independently set for color, grayscale, and monochrome images. You can also use PostScript operators to individually set Distiller's image compression and downsampling options for each image.

Downsampling Images

To downsample an image is to decrease its resolution. Downsampling provides two benefits: it decreases the space needed to store an image and speeds up the display of the image. If you are creating documents that will be viewed on the screen and not printed, or if you are working with unusually high-resolution images, downsampled images can provide these benefits with little or no loss in readability. This is because typical computer monitors have fairly low resolution compared to typical printers; the resolution of most monitors is less than 100dpi (IBM PC VGA is 96dpi), while the resolution of popular laser printers is 300 or 600dpi.

Distiller downsamples images by integer amounts, making the integer reduction that comes closest to the desired resolution without going below it. For instance, if you distill a 300dpi image when the downsampling resolution is set to 72dpi, distiller will reduce the resolution by 4, to 75dpi. Some graphics applications, such as Adobe Photoshop, can downsample images by arbitrary factors, allowing you to use exactly the resolution you want.

Downsampling Color Images

As an example, a .pcx format 24-bit color image was chosen, with 300dpi resolution in the x direction and 200dpi resolution in the y direction, and placed in a MS Word for Windows document. Then a PostScript file of the document was created with Distiller Assistant. The image was distilled three times, once without downsampling, once with downsampling set to 144dpi, and once with downsampling set to 72dpi. Compression was set to JPEG medium. The PDF file of the image that was not downsampled was 16512 bytes. The PDF file of the image that was downsampled to 144dpi was 7097 bytes, a 57% reduction in file size. The PDF file that was downsampled to 72dpi was 3725 bytes, a 77% reduction in file size.

Here is the PDF file with the original image, displayed at 100% and 600% magnification:

Here is the PDF file with the image downsampled to 144dpi, displayed at 100% and 600% magnification:

Here is the PDF file with the image downsampled to 72dpi, displayed at 100% and 600% magnification:

When viewed on the screen (Super VGA, about 100dpi) at 100% magnification, the 300 and 144dpi images are practically indistinguishable, even at 300% magnification; some loss of detail can be seen in the 72dpi image.

What Distiller Does When It Encounters an Image

When Distiller encounters an image:

1. It determines whether the image is color, gray-scale, or monochrome.
2. It recalls the appropriate downsampling setting for the image type.
3. It recalls the appropriate bit depth setting for the image type.
4. It downsamples the image, changing the bit depth as appropriate. If the output image type is different from the input image type, Distiller will use the compression settings you specified for the output image type.

Lossy and Lossless Compression

The LZW compression method is a lossless compression method, which means that all of the image information is retained in the compressed version. The advantage of lossless compression methods is that they do not reduce the fidelity of the image; the disadvantage of these methods is that their compression ratios are relatively small, about 2:1 on average.

The JPEG compression method is a lossy compression method, which means that it discards some of the image data when it compresses it. The advantage of lossy compression methods is their relatively high compression ratios, often reaching 10:1; the disadvantage of these methods is that they reduce image fidelity.

Each compression method works best on a particular type of image.

Lossless compression is best for images that have a small number of colors and that contain large areas of distinct colors, such as screen shots, or simple bitmap art. There are two reasons for this:

1. Images of this type will show distortion from lossy compression very clearly.
2. The JPEG lossy compression scheme achieves higher compression ratios on images of this type than the LZW lossless compression scheme.

A direct comparison of the output images and PDF file sizes for a typical screen shot demonstrates the superiority of LZW compression for images of this type.

Displayed at 200% magnification:

Acrobat
Distiller 2.0

No compression, 22210 bytes

Acrobat
Distiller 2.0

LZW compression, 2065 bytes, 91% compression

4-bit LZW compression, 1970 bytes, 91% compression

Note: 4-bit LZW compression reduces the bit depth of the image to 4 bits (16 colors)

JPEG low compression, 6184 bytes, 72% compression

JPEG Medium-Low compression, 5136 bytes, 77% compression

JPEG Medium compression, 4082 bytes, 82% compression

JPEG Medium-High compression, 3606 bytes, 84% compression

JPEG High compression, 3379 bytes, 85% compression

- Lossy compression is best for continuous-tone images, such as scanned photographs, or bitmap art with complex blends. There are two reasons for this:

  1. Images of this type do not show distortion from lossy compression very clearly.

  2. JPEG compression achieves very high compression ratios on images of this type, while LZW gives lower compression ratios.

A direct comparison of the PDF file sizes for a scanned photograph demonstrate the superiority of JPEG compression for images of this type. The images were downsampled to 144dpi, with screen captures made at 300% magnification, except where noted.

No compression, 49290 bytes

LZW compression, 46660 bytes, 5% compression

4-bit LZW compression, 14817 bytes, 70% compression

Note: LZW (4 bit) compression reduces the bit depth of the image to 4 bits (16 colors)

JPEG Low compression, 15763 bytes, 68% compression (at 800% magnification)

JPEG Medium-Low compression, 10663 bytes, 78% compression

JPEG Medium compression, 7097 bytes, 86% compression

JPEG Medium-High compression, 5581 bytes, 89% compression

JPEG High compression, 4818 bytes, 90% compression (at 800% magnification)

Distiller Preferences

You can change the way Distiller reacts to the following conditions with the **Distiller | Preferences** command:

- PostScript fatal errors

- Unable to find a watched directory

- Lack of free space in the volume where Distiller is stored.

When you select the **Distiller | Preferences** command, Distiller displays the Preferences dialog box; you use the controls of this dialog box to specify how Distiller should react.

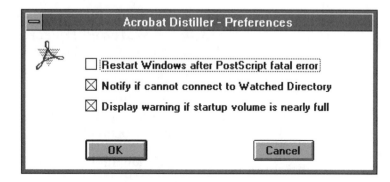

If a file that Distiller processes causes a PostScript fatal error, Distiller may not be able to recover fully from the error, leaving your system unstable. This problem can be serious if you have dedicated a server to watch several directories on a network. For instance, Distiller may falsely mark subsequent PostScript files as invalid if the unstable system prevents it from processing them properly. Also, the error may effectively make the system unable to watch directories; if the server is running unattended, the system may be down an unacceptably long time. To avoid these problems, you can set Distiller to restart the system when a Post-Script fatal error occurs. When you set this option, Distiller will:

- Move the problem PostScript file to the watched directory's out subdirectory, as it does whenever it encounters an error

- Place the following message in the MESSAGES.LOG file:
  ```
  Attempting to restart Distiller
  ```

- Restart the system to ensure that subsequent files are processed properly.

To set Distiller to restart the system after a PostScript fatal error:

- Click on the **Restart Windows after PostScript fatal error** check box, so that an "x" appears in the box.

This option is off by default when Distiller is installed.

When Distiller starts, it attempts to find every directory in the **Watched Directories** list. A directory in this list may not be available for two reasons:

1. The directory is on a network volume, and the network connection is not active.
2. The directory has been moved or deleted, or its name has been changed.

You can set Distiller to notify you if it cannot find a watched directory. To set this option:

- Click on the **Notify if cannot connect to Watched Directory** check box, so that an "x" appears in the box.

This option is on when Distiller is installed.

If the **Notify if cannot connect to a Watched Directory** option is on, and Distiller cannot find a watched directory, it will:

- Display the Watched Directory Alert dialog box
- Write the message Warning: Some watched directories were not found to both the **Messages** list box and the MESSAGES.LOG file.

The Watched Directory Alert dialog box contains two buttons, **Open List** and **OK**.

When you press the **Open List** button, Distiller displays the Watched Directories Options dialog box. You can use the controls of this dialog box to add or remove directories from the **Watched Directories** list or to specify a watched directory's job options; for more information about the Watched Directories Options dialog box, see the "Watched Directories" section of this chapter.

When you press the **OK** button, Distiller starts watching the directories that it can find.

Distiller can be set to display a warning if the volume it is stored on has less than 1Mb of free space at startup. To display this warning:

- Click on the **Display warning if startup directory is nearly full** check box, so that an "x" appears in the box.

This option is on by default when Distiller is installed.

Using PostScript Programs to Control Distiller

Distiller is a Level 2 PostScript interpreter. Like all PostScript interpreters, you can write PostScript programs to change its behavior when processing a specific file or every file in a session. Specifically, you can combine separate PostScript files into one PDF file, change Distiller's job options, or insert PDF objects such as bookmarks and links into a file.

This section assumes that you are familiar with Post-Script programming concepts such as stacks, operators, procedures, and dictionaries. If you want to learn more about the PostScript programming language, there are several books available on the subject. Adobe has published three books that are valuable references: *PostScript Language: Tutorial and Cookbook*, *PostScript Language: Program Design*, and *PostScript Language Reference Manual (Second Edition)*.

The Startup Directory

The PostScript files in the startup directory will run as *unencapsulated jobs*, which means that their effects will persist after the PostScript program is finished. For instance, if you use a PostScript program in the startup directory to change the compression method for color images, all subsequent PostScript files will be processed with that option, unless it is expressly changed. By contrast, if you were to make the same changes with a PostScript program that was not in the startup directory, the changes would only affect the images in that program.

While you can write PostScript programs that do a variety of things, here are some of the most common things you can do with programs in the startup directory:

- Change the default page size
- Print messages to the **Messages** list box and to the MESSAGES.LOG file
- Display or change job options
- Alter JPEG compression settings
- Convert CMYK images to RGB images
- Add fonts to or remove fonts from the **Always Embed** and **Never Embed** lists
- Load fonts into Distiller's memory (this is the same as downloading fonts to a printer's memory).

The files you place in the startup directory may have any name or extension, as long as it is a text file. Here is a PostScript file that was created and named banner.txt.

```
%!
(Author's copy of) = flush
(ACROBAT DISTILLER) = flush
(is up and running!) = flush
%EOF
```

This program will display the following text in Distiller's Messages box when you start it:

```
"Author's copy of ACROBAT DISTILLER is up and
running!"
```

Combining PostScript Files to Make One PDF Document

Distiller has a built-in PostScript procedure called "RunFile" that allows you to combine several different PostScript files into one PDF file. When Distiller encounters the RunFile operator, it runs the PostScript code in the file that the operator points to. While you can combine PDF files together using Exchange, the RunFile operator has two advantages:

1. Once started, the PostScript program needs no further intervention, while you must open each source file and attach it with Exchange.

2. When working with font subsets, this method can produce a smaller PDF file than combining PDF files with Exchange.

To use the RunFile procedure you must write a PostScript program that will refer to the other PostScript files you want to combine into a PDF document.

Adobe includes a PostScript program, runfilex.ps, in the startup directory of Distiller 2.0 that adds certain desirable features to the RunFile operator.

Combining Named Files

Here is Adobe's example program for combining named files:

```
%!
/prun {/mysave save def dup = flush RunFile
clear cleardictstack mysave restore} def
(C:\\DATA\\ ACROBAT\\RUNFILEX\\FILE1.PS) prun
(C:\\DATA\\ ACROBAT\\RUNFILEX\\FILE2.PS) prun
(C:\\DATA\\ ACROBAT\\RUNFILEX\\FILE3.PS) prun
%EOF
```

The first line:

```
%!
```

identifies the file to Distiller as a PostScript program.

The second line is the definition of the `prun` procedure, which we will use to distill the individual PostScript files. The call to `prun` will be preceded by the name of the file that is its argument. The line has several components:

- The fragment `/prun` is the name of the procedure that contains the `RunFile` operator

- The fragment `"/mysave save def"` gives the name `mysave` to the save object placed on the stack by save. This named save object will be used later to make sure that Distiller is in exactly the same state at the end of the included PostScript program as it was at the beginning.

- The `dup` operator makes a copy of the filename that is the argument to `prun`.

- The fragment "= flush" sends the copy of the file name to the standard output device, in this case the **Messages** list box and the MESSAGES.LOG file. The "=" operator sends the file name to standard output, and the flush operator flushes the output buffer, ensuring it is written.

- The RunFile operator instructs Distiller to interpret the PostScript code in the file whose name we gave to the prun procedure as an argument.

- The fragment "clear cleardictstack" removes any objects from the operand stack and dictionaries from the dictionary stack, respectively.

- The fragment "mysave restore" places the save object associated with the name "mysave" on the stack; "restore" returns Distiller to the state specified by the save object. This sets Distiller's internal structure back to the state it was in before the PostScript program was run, removing any artifacts it may have left behind.

- The "def" operator at the end of the line associates everything within the curly braces {} with the procedure name prun.

The lines:

```
(C:\\DATA\\ ACROBAT\\RUNFILEX\\FILE1.PS) prun
(C:\\DATA\\ ACROBAT\\RUNFILEX\\FILE2.PS) prun
(C:\\DATA\\ ACROBAT\\RUNFILEX\\FILE3.PS) prun
```

are the calls to the prun procedure for each file; note the double slashes in the path name. For a Macintosh, use Macintosh-style filenames, such as:

```
(PowerMac HD:Output:PostScript:Chapter 1.ps)
prun
(PowerMac HD:Output:PostScript:Chapter 2.ps)
prun
(PowerMac HD:Output:PostScript:Chapter 3.ps)
prun
```

If you are running Distiller over a network, the filenames you use should be relative to the Distiller's location.

Browsing
  Interface
  Navigating
  Zoom
  Features
  Printing
  Clipboard
  Preferences
Creating
  PDFWriter
  PDF Files
Enhancing
  Pages
  Thumbnails
  Bookmarks
  Notes
  Links
  Articles
Web Publishing
  Introduction
  Getting On
  Reader
  Author
  Publisher
  Cool Sites
Advanced
  Search
  Catalog
  Distiller

The line:
```
%EOF
```

marks the end of the PostScript program.

When Distiller runs a program of this type, the " text field and progress bar only keeps track how much of the RunFile PostScript program it has read. If your PostScript files have differing sizes, this will not accurately reflect the amount of processing that has been done.

If this example program is run with Distiller's job settings set to JPEG compression for color images, the resulting PDF file was about 560Kb. However, if the job options are switched to LZW compression, the PDF file is 242,285 bytes. Further, the screen shots have better image quality. You should always keep the content of the document in mind when Distilling a PostScript file.

Combining All of the Files in a Directory

You can easily combine all of the PostScript files in a directory into one PDF file using the filenameforall operator and wildcards. Here is an example PostScript program from Distiller's on-line help that combines all the files in a directory:

```
%!
/PathName (c:\\\\myfiles\\\\*.ps) def
/RunDir {
{ /mysave save def dup = flush RunFile clear
cleardictstack mysave restore}
255 string filenameforall
} def
PathName RunDir
%EOF
```

The line
```
/PathName (c:\\\\myfiles\\\\*.ps) def
```

associates the literal string (c:\\\\myfiles*.ps) with the name PathName. The extra backslashes in the DOS path name are needed for the filenameforall operator to work correctly. You can use wildcards with the filenameforall operator; the wildcards are:

- * matches zero or more consecutive characters

- ? matches one character

The path name you give should be relative to the machine on which Distiller is running; if you are running Distiller on a Macintosh, for instance, you should use Macintosh-style path names, no matter where the files are stored.

The order in which the `filenameforall` operator returns filenames will depend on the system on which you are running Distiller. Typically, on DOS systems, `filenameforall` uses the same order as the DOS dir command; on Macintoshes, it returns files in alphabetical order. The order `filenameforall` uses is important, because Distiller combines the files in the same order. You should make sure that the names you give to the PostScript files that make up your document will result in their being assembled in the correct order.

Note: If the filename of the PostScript program matches the file specification given to the `filenameforall` operator, Distiller will try to run it again when the `filenameforall` operator returns it. You should make sure that the PostScript program filename does not match the file specification.

The following program will display the filenames in the order that `filenameforall` returns them; you can use it to check that Distiller will assemble your document in the proper order.

```
%!
/PathName (c:\\\\myfiles\\\\*.ps) def
/ShowDir {
{ /mysave save def = flush mysave restore}
255 string filenameforall
} def
PathName ShowDir
%EOF
```

When you run this program, Distiller will display the following warning:

```
%%[Warning: Empty job. No PDF file produced]
%%
```

This is normal.

Now, let's take a closer look at the example program. The lines:

```
/RunDir {
```

and

```
} def
```

define everything in the two intervening lines, namely

```
{ /mysave save def dup = flush RunFile clear
cleardictstack mysave restore}
255 string filenameforall
```

as the RunDir procedure.

Every fragment of the line

```
{ /mysave save def dup = flush RunFile clear
cleardictstack mysave restore}
```

is identical to that of the previous example. Explanations of the fragments can be found there.

The fragment

```
255 string
```

creates a string 255 characters in length. filename-forall will store the filenames it returns in this string.

The filenameforall operator runs the procedure

```
{ /mysave save def dup = flush RunFile clear
cleardictstack mysave restore}
```

for every file matching PathName that it stores in the string created by 255 string. The filenameforall operator will be invoked when the RunDir procedure is run.

The line

```
PathName RunDir
```

calls the RunDir procedure, using the string associated with PathName as an argument.

When you use the RunFile operator with Distiller's **Make Font Subsets** option on, Distiller will combine each file's subsets for a particular font into one subset. Exchange does not have this capability; it keeps a font subset for each PDF file that you combine, leading to larger file sizes.

As an example, a PDF file was created from three PostScript files in two ways. First, the `RunFile` procedure was used to make the PDF file in one step, and then three separate PDF files were created using Distiller and combined using Exchange. The three files used a total of two fonts: the first font was used in all three files, while the second was used in only two of them. The PDF file created with Distiller was 94199 bytes, while the PDF file created by Exchange was 11% larger, at 104486 bytes. The difference in file size between the two methods will vary, based on the number of fonts the files have in common and the other material in the source files, but the savings can be substantial.

Unfortunately, the file size savings of using `RunFile` are harder to realize if you are using TrueType fonts in your documents. When the PostScript creates a synthetic Type 1 font from a TrueType font, the name it uses to refer to the font is different for each file. Since the synthetic Type 1 fonts in each PostScript file have different names, Distiller considers them to be different fonts, and thus it does not attempt to combine their subsets.

As an example, the same documents were used as in the first example, but TrueType fonts were substituted for the Type 1 fonts used before. When the composite document was created with Distiller, it was 153493 bytes, as opposed to a size of 154431 when it was created with Exchange.

Here is an example of the different font names given to a synthetic TrueType font each time a PostScript file of a document is written:

- AADOIA+MSTT31c63d
- AAHNAA+MSTT31c5aa
- AALPGI+MSTT31c5aa

Specifying Compression Options and Other Distiller Parameters

Distiller has two built-in PostScript operators that allow you to read and set Distiller's parameters.

These procedures, setdistillerparams and currentdistillerparams, affect the following Distiller actions:

- Compression of text and line graphics
- Compression of color, grayscale, and monochrome images
- Downsampling of color, grayscale, and monochrome images
- Font embedding
- Thumbnail generation.

The currentdistillerparams operator returns a [PostScript] dictionary of Distiller parameter names and values. The setdistillerparams operator sets values in the dictionary.

Distiller Status Messages

To inform you of its activity, Distiller displays status messages in the Status text field of its window. An explanation of each of these messages is given below.

Starting: Distiller displays this message when it is initializing and when it is reading PostScript files in the startup directory.

Purging Out Folders / Directories: Distiller displays this message when it is deleting files from watched directories that are older than the limit set in the Delete files in **"Out" directory older than...** days option. For more information about this option, see the "Watched Directories" section.

Ready: Distiller displays this message when it is ready to process a PostScript file.

Paused: Distiller displays this message when you press the **Pause** button. For more information on the Pause button and the other Distiller window controls, see "The Distiller Window" section of this chapter.

Distilling filename.ps: Distiller displays this message when it is processing a PostScript file. Filename.ps is the name of the file it is currently processing.

Relocating files: Distiller displays this message when it is moving files from the In subdirectory of a watched directory to the Out subdirectory.

Building Font Table: Distiller displays this message when you add or remove a directory to the **Font Directories** list.

Changing default job parameters...: Distiller displays this message when you change its job options. For more information about job options, see the "Job Options" section of this chapter.

Distiller's On-line Help

Distiller's on-line help is in PDF format. To display it:

- Select the **Help | Acrobat Distiller Help** command. Distiller will launch your viewer and display the on-line help file.

Distiller Assistant (For Windows)

Distiller Assistant has two functions:

- It allows you to distill PostScript files from applications using the **File | Print** command
- It launches Distiller when a PostScript file is dropped onto its icon or moved to a watched directory.

Distiller Assistant is currently available for the Windows platform only.

Distiller Assistant adds the printer entry "Acrobat Distiller on \DISTASST.PS" to the list of available printers. When you "print" to that printer, Distiller Assistant:

1. Instructs the Windows generic PostScript printer driver to direct its output to a file named \DISTASST.PS.
2. Launches Distiller, if necessary, and instructs it to distill \DISTASST.PS.
3. Deletes the \DISTASST.PS file once Distiller has created the PDF file.

If Distiller Assistant's **Ask for PDF File Destination** option is on, Distiller will ask you for the path and filename where it will store the PDF file it generates. If this option is off, Distiller will extract the filename from the `%%Title` line of the PostScript file. If Distiller cannot extract the name, it will use the name DISTASST.PDF.

Distiller Assistant must be running for the "Acrobat Distiller on \DISTASST.PS" printer entry to launch Distiller. If the \DISTASST.PS file exists when Distiller Assistant starts, it will launch Distiller.

Distiller Assistant does not have a **File | Open** command. To distill files on a local computer with Distiller Assistant, you must drag them to the Distiller Assistant icon or move them to a watched directory.

When you start Distiller, it consumes system resources, and those resources are unavailable to other applications for the entire time that Distiller is running, even if it is not distilling files. Distiller Assistant needs far fewer system resources to run.

Consider an example system that has 22,231Kb of available memory and 57% of system resources are free. After Distiller is launched, 18,719Kb of memory are available and 55% of system resources are free.

If Distiller Assistant is launched instead of Distiller, there will be 21,963Kb of available memory and 57% of system resources free. By using Distiller Assistant instead of Distiller, 3Mb more of memory are freed up for other work (as long as files are not being distilled).

The trade-off of using Distiller Assistant is that you will have fewer system resources during the time that a file is being distilled than you would if you were only running Distiller. If you need to distill files at arbitrary times, but the number of files you distill is relatively small, Distiller Assistant will reduce the strain on your computer's resources. If Distiller is processing files continuously, Distiller Assistant will not reduce the average amount of resources the system uses to distill files.

By acting as a printer driver, Distiller Assistant reduces the number of steps required to produce a PDF file from a PostScript file from four to two. Without Distiller Assistant, the steps are:

1. Print the document to a PostScript file.
2. Launch Distiller or make it the active application.
3. Specify the name of the PostScript file you want to distill.
4. Specify the name of the output PDF file.

With Distiller Assistant, the steps are:

1. Print the document to Distiller Assistant.
2. Specify the name of the output PDF file.

Distiller Assistant's Controls

Distiller Assistant does not have a user interface. All of its functions are available through its Control menu, which appears when you click on its icon. Distiller Assistant has three controls: **View PDF File**, **Exit Distiller when Idle**, and **Ask for PDF File Destination**. To turn any of these controls on or off, click on them in the Control menu; when there is a check next to them, they are active.

View PDF File

When the **View PDF File** option is active, Distiller Assistant will display PDF files once they are generated, launching a PDF viewer if necessary. The PDF viewer that Distiller Assistant will launch is the one defined in the **File Manager's Associations** list. In most cases, this will be Reader or Exchange; their associations are defined automatically when they are installed.

Exit Distiller when Idle

When the **Exit Distiller when Idle** option is active, Distiller Assistant will close Distiller when there are no files to be distilled. When this option is

Browsing
  Interface
  Navigating
  Zoom
  Features
  Printing
  Clipboard
  Preferences
Creating
  PDFWriter
  PDF Files
Enhancing
  Pages
  Thumbnails
  Bookmarks
  Notes
  Links
  Articles
Web Publishing
  Introduction
  Getting On
  Reader
  Author
  Publisher
  Cool Sites
Advanced
  Search
  Catalog
  Distiller

inactive, Distiller will remain running once Distiller Assistant launches it.

Ask for PDF File Destination

When the **Ask for PDF File Destination** option is active, Distiller Assistant will instruct Distiller to display the Specify PDF File Name dialog box when you drag a file to the Distiller Assistant icon.

Distiller Assistant: Type 1 and Type 3 Font Generation

When you use Distiller Assistant to generate PostScript output, the PostScript driver will automatically convert TrueType fonts to Type 3 bitmap fonts if the fonts are smaller than a certain size. The size is defined in a unit known as *pixels per em*, which is the width of the em dash (—) character of the font in printer pixels; its default setting is 101 pixels per em. At this size or greater, the driver will use the conversion method for TrueType fonts that you specified in the printer driver's Advanced Options dialog box; the default setting is conversion to a synthetic Type 1 font.

As an example, the width of the em dash character in a 24 point font is 1/3rd of an inch. The Windows PostScript printer driver Distiller Assistant uses has a defined "resolution" of 144 dots per inch, so the em dash character will be 48 pixels wide. Since this width is below the default setting for conversion to a Type 1 font, the font is converted to a Type 3 font, which Distiller embeds in the PDF file.

While the conversion to a Type 3 font can increase the speed at which the resulting PDF file is displayed, the PDF file is of a fixed and relatively low resolution, giving it a poor appearance when magnified or printed to a high-resolution printer. To avoid this problem, you can lower the minimum size for generation of a Type 1 font in your WIN.INI file.

To lower the minimum size for a generation a Type 1 font:

1. Make a backup copy of the WIN.INI file.
2. Open the WIN.INI file with Windows Notepad or another text editor.

3. Look for this line:

   ```
   Acrobat Distiller, \DISTASST.PS
   ```

   This line is a section heading for the part of the WIN.INI file that controls the PostScript printer's output when used with Distiller Assistant. It may have several lines below it; a typical section looks like this:

   ```
   Acrobat Distiller, \DISTASST.PS
   feed1=3
   EpsFile=
   ```

4. Add the following line to the bottom of the section:

   ```
   minoutlineppem=size
   ```

   where *size* is the size in pixels per em at or above which a Type 1 font should be generated. If you want the driver to generate Type 1 fonts no matter what the size of the font is, set *size* to 1. The altered section should look something like this:

   ```
   Acrobat Distiller, \DISTASST.PS
   feed1=3
   EpsFile=
   minoutlineppem=1
   ```

5. Save the WIN.INI file.

6. Restart Windows.

Tech Note

Make sure the printer driver is set to convert TrueType fonts to Adobe Type 1 fonts. If the driver is set to convert TrueType fonts to Type 3 fonts, this setting will have no effect.

Conversion of "small" TrueType fonts to Type 3 fonts is an optimization used for printer output. The Type 3 font will print faster than a Type 1 font, and since the printer's resolution is fixed, magnification is not a concern. When printing PostScript output to a file, the resolution of the final output device is not known, so this optimization is not made. Since Distiller Assistant is "pretending" to be a printer, Windows uses this optimization, even though its output resolution is not fixed.

INDEX

SOFTWARE LICENSE FOR QUICKTIME

Please read this license carefully before using the software. By using the software, you are agreeing to be bound by the terms of this license. If you do not agree to the terms of this license, promptly return the unused software to the place where you obtained it and your money will be refunded.

1. License. The application, demonstration, system, and other software accompanying this License, whether on disk, in read-only memory, or on any other media (the "Software") the related documentation and fonts are licensed to you by John Wiley & Sons. You own the disk on which the Software and fonts are recorded but John Wiley & Sons and/or John Wiley & Sons's Licensor(s) retain title to the Software, related documentation and fonts. This License allows you to use the Software and fonts on a single Apple computer and make one copy of the Software and fonts in machine-readable form for backup purposes only. You must reproduce on such copy the John Wiley & Sons copyright notice and any other proprietary legends that were on the original copy of the Software and fonts. You may also transfer all your license rights in the Software and fonts, the backup copy of the Software and fonts, the related documentation and a copy of this License to another party, provided the other party reads and agrees to accept the terms and conditions of this License.

2. Restrictions. The Software contains copyrighted material, trade secrets and other proprietary material. In order to protect them, and except as permitted by applicable legislation, you may not decompile, reverse engineer, disassemble or otherwise reduce the Software to a human-perceivable form. You may not modify, network, rent, lease, loan, distribute, or create derivative works based upon the Software in whole or in part. You may not electronically transmit the Software from one computer to another or over a network.

3. Termination. This License is effective until terminated. You may terminate this License at any time by destroying the Software, related documentation and fonts, and all copies thereof. This License will terminate immediately without notice from John Wiley & Sons if you fail to comply with any provision of this License. Upon termination you must destroy the Software, related documentation and fonts, and all copies thereof.

4. Export Law Assurances. You agree and certify that neither the Software nor any other technical data received from John Wiley & Sons, nor the direct product thereof, will be exported outside the United States except as authorized and as permitted by the laws and regulations of the United States. If the Software has been rightfully obtained by you outside of the United States, you agree that you will not re-export the Software nor any other technical data received from John Wiley & Sons, nor the direct product thereof, except as permitted by the laws and regulations of the United States and the laws and regulations of the jurisdiction in which you obtained the Software.

5. Government End Users. If you are acquiring the Software and fonts on behalf of any unit or agency of the United States Government, the following provisions apply. The Government agrees: (i) if the Software and fonts are supplied to the Department of Defense (DoD), the Software and fonts are classified as "Commercial Computer Software" and the Government is acquiring only "restricted rights" in the Software, its documentation and fonts as that term is defined in Clause 252.227-7013(c)(1) of the DFARS; and (ii) if the Software and fonts are supplied to any unit or agency of the United States Government other than DoD, the Government's rights in the Software, its documentation and fonts will be as defined in Clause 52.227-19(c)(2) of the FAR or, in the case of NASA, in Clause 18-52.227-86(d) of the NASA Supplement to the FAR.

6. Limited Warranty on Media. John Wiley & Sons warrants the diskettes and/or compact disc on which the Software and fonts are recorded to be free from defects in materials and workmanship under normal use for a period of ninety (90) days from the date of purchase as evidenced by a copy of the receipt. John Wiley & Sons's entire liability and your exclusive remedy will be replacement of the diskettes and/or compact disc not meeting John Wiley & Sons's limited warranty and which is returned to John Wiley & Sons or a John Wiley &

Sons authorized representative with a copy of the receipt. John Wiley & Sons will have no responsibility to replace a disk/disc damaged by accident, abuse, or misapplication. Any implied warranties on the Diskettes and/or compact disc, including the implied warranties of merchantability and fitness for a particular purpose, are limited in duration to ninety (90) days from the date of delivery. This warranty gives you specific legal rights, and you may also have other rights which vary by jurisdiction.

7. Disclaimer of Warranty on Apple Software. You expressly acknowledge and agree that use of the Software and fonts is at your sole risk. The Software, related documentation and fonts are provided "AS IS" and without warranty of any kind and John Wiley & Sons and John Wiley & Sons's Licensor(s) (for the purposes of provisions 7 and 8, John Wiley & Sons and John Wiley & Sons's Licensor(s) shall be collectively referred to as "John Wiley & Sons") expressly disclaim all warranties, express or implied, including, but not limited to, the implied warranties of merchantability and fitness for a particular purpose. John Wiley & Sons does not warrant that the functions contained in the software will meet your requirements, or that the operation of the software will be uninterrupted or error-free, or that defects in the software and the fonts will be corrected. Furthermore, John Wiley & Sons does not warrant or make any representations regarding the use or the results of the use of the software and fonts or related documentation in terms of their correctness, accuracy, reliability, or otherwise. No oral or written information or advice given by John Wiley & Sons or a John Wiley & Sons authorized representative shall create a warranty or in any way increase the scope of this warranty. Should the software prove defective, you (and not John Wiley & Sons or a John Wiley & Sons authorized representative) assume the entire cost of all necessary servicing, repair or correction. Some jurisdictions do not allow the exclusion of implied warranties, so the above exclusion may not apply to you.

8. Limitation of Liability. Under no circumstances including negligence, shall John Wiley & Sons be liable for any incidental, special or consequential damages that result from the use or inability to use the software or related documentation, even if John Wiley & Sons or a John Wiley & Sons authorized representative has been advised of the possibility of such damages. Some jurisdictions do not allow the limitation or exclusion of liability for incidental or consequential damages so the above limitation or exclusion may not apply to you. In no event shall John Wiley & Sons's total liability to you for all damages, losses, and causes of action (whether in contract, tort [including negligence] or otherwise) exceed the amount paid by you for the Software and fonts.

9. Controlling Law and Severability. This License shall be governed by and construed in accordance with the laws of the United States and the State of California, as applied to agreements entered into and to be performed entirely within California between California residents. If for any reason a court of competent jurisdiction finds any provision of this License, or portion thereof, to be unenforceable, that provision of the License shall be enforced to the maximum extent permissible so as to effect the intent of the parties, and the remainder of this License shall continue in full force and effect.

10. Complete Agreement. This License constitutes the entire agreement between the parties with respect to the use of the Software, the related documentation and fonts, and supersedes all prior or contemporaneous understandings or agreements, written or oral, regarding such subject matter. No amendment to or modification of this License will be binding unless in writing and signed by a duly authorized representative of John Wiley & Sons.

WILEY